D1766602

WORKS ISSUED BY
THE HAKLUYT SOCIETY

THE TRAVELS OF IBN BAṬṬŪṬA

A.D. 1325 – 1354

VOL. IV

SECOND SERIES
NO. 178

Chinese conjurors and acrobats. From *Eduward Meltons . . . Zee- en Land-Reizen*, Amsterdam, 1681. See p. 904.
By courtesy of the British Library

THE TRAVELS OF IBN BAṬṬŪṬA

A.D. 1325 – 1354

Translated with revisions and notes from the Arabic text edited by C. DEFRÉMERY and B. R. SANGUINETTI

by

H. A. R. GIBB

VOL. IV

The translation completed with annotations by

C. F. BECKINGHAM

THE HAKLUYT SOCIETY
LONDON
1994

ISBN 0 904180 37 9
ISSN 0072 9396

Typeset by Waveney Typesetters, Norwich
Printed in Great Britain at
the University Press, Cambridge

SERIES EDITORS
W. F. RYAN and SARAH TYACKE

British Library Cataloguing-in-Publication Data
A catalogue record for this book is available from
the British Library

Published by the Hakluyt Society
c/o The Map Library
British Library, Great Russell Street
London WC1B 3DG

CONTENTS

LIST OF ILLUSTRATIONS

FOREWORD TO VOLUME FOUR

This volume completes the translation of Ibn Baṭṭūṭa's travels. A fifth volume will contain further editorial matter and the index to the entire work.

The translation of the narrative of Ibn Baṭṭūṭa's travels has taken more than twice as long as the travels themselves. It was in 1922 that H. A. R. Gibb, then Lecturer in Arabic at the School of Oriental Studies, University of London, proposed to the Hakluyt Society that he should prepare what would be the first, complete, annotated English translation of the book usually known as the *Riḥla*. His intention was to publish it in four volumes, corresponding to those of the edition and parallel French translation by C. Defrémery and B. R. Sanguinetti (1874–9), of which he thought highly. Gibb's life was busy and his career distinguished. He became Professor of Arabic at London, Oxford and Harvard in succession, and was knighted for his services in 1954. It is not surprising that it was not till 1958 that the first volume was published. Volume II followed in 1962, volume III in 1971, shortly after Gibb had died, after having suffered severe strokes which had caused him to resign from his chair. In the meantime he had decided that a fifth volume would be desirable, which would include an essay on the chronology of the journeys, additional notes incorporating comments by reviewers of the volumes already printed, and an index. He had also published a volume of selections with annotations in the *Broadway Travellers* series (1929).

When he returned to England from Harvard he was a very sick man, unable to utter more than a sentence or two without being exhausted. It is evidence of great courage and determination, as well as impressive scholarship, that he completed volume III under such difficulties. I gave him some help with reading the proofs and preparing the maps. About six months before he died he proposed that I should take over the project from him. I was naturally flattered, but at first felt obliged to refuse; I had many other commitments, among them an undertaking to annotate D. M. Lockhart's translation of the *Itinerário* of Jerónimo Lobo for this Society. Gibb, however, was pressing. I suggested that I should seek a collaborator. He was, I now think rightly, opposed to this; the scope for disagreement would have been too vast. Eventually, with much hesitation, I agreed to do as he wished, though not before I had warned him and the Council of the Society that it would be some years before I could give much attention to Ibn Baṭṭūṭa. I had not expected how many these years would be. Even after my retirement from the University of London I incurred further inescapable obligations. For the unconscionable delay in producing this volume I apologize to the members.

When he handed over his work to me in 1971 Gibb had done nothing to annotate the remaining portion of the narrative, but he had translated as far as p. 191 of the French edition. The earlier part of this, up to p. 61, he had revised and retyped. It would be an impertinence for me to revise his translation, but I have found that, no doubt as a consequence of his illness, he sometimes omitted a word or phrase, and occasionally a whole sentence. Also, and no doubt for the same reason, he might change the order of items in a list of, for instance, presents or commodities. Again, especially in the part of his translation which he had not retyped, he at times used different equivalents for the same word in the text when the meaning was obviously the same. These I have felt justified in rectifying. Otherwise I have tried to follow his practice in the volumes already published, both from respect for him and for the convenience of readers. I have continued to indicate the page numbers of the Arabic text in the margin of the translation, and have shown as precisely as is possible the division between the pages by a vertical line. I have used the same English phrases for stereotyped Arabic formulae and have conformed to Gibb's usage with regard to a few familiar place names, writing Alexandria, Cairo and Mecca, but Dihlī, which he preferred to Delhi.

The Hakluyt Society has published very few translations from oriental languages, though there is ample suitable material in Arabic, Turkish, Persian and Chinese, to mention no others. One difficulty is the scarcity of adequate critical editions of the original texts. Books written in the Arabic script also present problems with which editors of narratives in European languages are not confronted. It is well known that the script as usually written does not represent short vowels and represents long vowels and diphthongs ambiguously. This can make the identification of non-Islamic proper names problematical. Fortunately Ibn Baṭṭūṭa when using such toponyms usually spells out precisely which vowel is to be read with each consonant. Occasionally ambiguity results from the absence of upper case letters in this script. Thus, was his rosary one from Zailaʿ in Somalia, or one made of cowries (p. 802)? Again, were the horses drawn up outside the Sultan's palace in Sumatra relays (*nauba*), or Nubian (*nūba*) (p. 879)?

A translator may have to choose between the meaning of a word in standard classical Arabic and its meaning in the Moroccan dialect with which Ibn Baṭṭūṭa must have been familiar. For instance, the word *dhi'b* means a wolf in literary Arabic; in Morocco where, as in all Africa, there are no wolves, it means a jackal. When it occurs in a passage relating to a country like India where both animals are found, it may only be possible to guess which is meant, or to explain the ambiguity in a note. Zoological names sometimes give rise to a subtler difficulty, which readers should bear in mind. When a twentieth-century observer names an animal or bird the category to which he assigns it is genetic; he assumes that it is the offspring of two creatures of the same species, and that if it has offspring of its own, they too will be of that species. For Ibn Baṭṭūṭa and his contemporaries, in Europe as well as in Dar al-Islam, the category was not genetic but descriptive, descriptive above all of size, shape and colour. Phenomena like melanism and albinism could be regarded as the unusual but not inconceivable consequence of parents having borne offspring of a species other than their own.

Confusion can also arise from the loose use of titles and terms indicative of rank in Arabic writings. *Amir*, for example, basically someone in a position to give orders, may designate the ruler of an independent state, the commander of an army, the governor of a province, or a city, or even the foreman in charge of a body of artisans, as on p. 902. Some titles, like *sultan* and *malik*, may also be used as personal names.

Ibn Baṭṭūṭa was a compulsive name-dropper; in his Foreword to volume I Gibb explained why he tried to identify at least some of the persons mentioned. There are voluminous biographical dictionaries in Arabic in which they may be sought. However, they are generally listed under their *ism*, the equivalent of the baptismal name of a Christian, which an author may not record at all. It will be followed by a selection of the names of his paternal ancestors and various epithets derived from his birthplace, a town in which he lived or held an important appointment, or from some personal peculiarity. An editor's quarry may be very elusive.

It will be a long time before a definitive commentary on the *Riḥla* can be attempted. It must be remembered that a considerable number of Arabic books, written in or before his time, has still not been catalogued, let alone printed. Mosque libraries and private collections in Morocco are believed to contain rich collections of such works. Ibn Baṭṭūṭa and Ibn Juzayy may have seen some of them. When they become accessible we may be able to identify many more of the *qāḍīs*, preachers and jurists of whom he speaks. We may also find the sources from which he took information which he presents as the result of his own observation.

NOTE TO FOREWORD TO VOLUME IV

It is not surprising that Gibb's usage should have varied slightly during the long time that he was concerned with the work. In volumes I and II he used standard English forms for place-names like Tangier, Alexandria, Cairo, Beirut and Damascus; in volume III he eschewed even Delhi and Calicut for Dihlī and Qāliqūṭ. With regard to transliteration it may be noted that, although he wrote *qāḍī* consistently, he did not use macrons or subscript dots in words like *sultan*, *amir*, *sharif*, *dinar* and *mithqal*. He used both *vizier* and *wazīr*, though not in the same context. For the occasional quotations in Persian and Turkish Ibn Baṭṭūṭa's text employs only the letters of the Arabic alphabet, and not the additional consonants available for writing these languages, so that *b* is not distinguished from *p*, *j* from *ch*, or *k* from *g*. In such instances it was Gibb's practice to represent the Persian or Turkish spelling.

ABBREVIATIONS

(See Bibliography for full references)

Brunschvig	*La Berbérie orientale sous les Hafsides.*
Dibaj	Ibn Farḥūn, *Al-dībāj al-mudhdhahab.*
Dozy	Dozy, R., *Supplément aux dictionnaires arabes.*
Durar	Ibn Ḥajar alʿAsqalānī, *Al-durar al-kāmina.*
EI	*Encyclopedia of Islam*
Gibb, *Selections*	*Ibn Battuta. Travels in Asia and Africa.* Translated and edited by H. A. R. Gibb.
Hobson-Jobson	Yule, Henry, and Burnell, A. C., *Hobson-Jobson.* New edition edited by William Crooke.
Ihata	Ibn al-Khaṭīb, *Al-iḥāṭa fi akhbār Gharnāṭa.*
JRAS	*Journal of the Royal Asiatic Society.*
Lévi-Provençal	*Le Voyage d'Ibn Battuta dans le royaume de Granada.*
Mahdi Husain	*The Rise and Fall of Muhammad bin Tughluq.*
Mauny, *Textes*	*Textes et documents relatifs à l'histoire de l'Afrique.*
Mžik	*Die Reise des Arabers Ibn Batuta durch Indien und China.*
Nail al-ibtihāj	Aḥmad Bābā, *Nail al-ibtihāj fi taṭrīz al-dībāj.*
Yule, *Cathay*	*Cathay and the Way Thither.*

ACKNOWLEDGMENTS

I am grateful to the School of Oriental and African Studies, University of London, for granting me one term's leave of absence which, combined with two adjoining vacations, enabled me to visit briefly India, Sri Lanka and the Maldives. I received much hospitality and kindness in these countries. In particular I wish to record my gratitude to two friends who took great trouble to facilitate my travels in Kerala and in Sri Lanka respectively, Professor P. M. Jussay and Desubandu L. A. Adithiya, ARIBA.

In annotating such a wide-ranging travel narrative as this, I have naturally incurred obligations to numerous scholars, many of them former colleagues and personal friends. I am especially grateful to Dr James Bynon for advice on the meaning of Berber and Moroccan Arabic words, to Dr David V. Field, of the Royal Botanic Gardens, Kew, for information about aloes wood, to Professor Dr Herbert Franke for his prompt answers to questions about Yüan China, to Professor J. D. Latham for his comments on a Hispano-Arabic poem, and for replying to many queries about Al-Andalus, to Mr Robert Nicholl for his knowledge of Brunei and the adjoining countries and seas, to Professor H. T. Norris for his knowledge of the western Sahara, to Mr C. H. B. Reynolds for his identification of Sinhalese and especially of Maldivian terms, and to Professor G. Rex Smith for his command of the sources for the history of fourteenth-century Arabia. For guidance in choosing Islamic paintings to illustrate the narrative I am grateful to Mr B. W. Robinson.

I have drawn freely on the notes which Gibb provided in the volume of selections from the narrative which he published in 1929. Among other works which I have utilized two deserve special mention, H. von Mžik's annotated German translation of a large part of the contents of the present volume, a model of thorough and painstaking scholarship, and Ross Dunn's *The Adventures of Ibn Battuta*, an enlightening study which sets the travels in the context of contemporary events.

At a time when several important libraries are becoming more difficult to use it is a pleasure to acknowledge the competence, helpfulness and forbearance of the Librarian of the Royal Asiatic Society, Mr M. J. Pollock.

Lastly, I have to thank my daughter, Miss Carolyn Beckingham, for bringing to my attention a number of inconsistencies, obscurities and infelicities in my text.

CHAPTER XV

From Dihlī to Kinbāya

Account of the reason for the sending of the gift to China, of those who were sent with me and of the gift itself. The king of China had sent to the Sultan a hundred mamluks and slave girls, five hundred pieces of velvet cloth, including a hundred of those which are manufactured in the city of Zaitūn [Ch'üan-chou] and a hundred of those which are manufactured in Khansā [Hangchou], five *maunds* of musk, five robes adorned with jewels, five embroidered quivers, and five swords, with a request that the Sultan would permit him to rebuild the idol-temple which is near the aforesaid mountains
called Qarājīl [Himalaya].[1] It is in a place known as Samhal, | 2
to which the Chinese go on pilgrimage; the Muslim army in India had captured it, laid it in ruins and sacked it.[2] The Sultan, on receiving this gift, wrote to the king saying that the request could not be granted by Islamic law, as permission to build a temple in the territories of the Muslims was granted only to those who paid a poll-tax; to which he added 'If thou wilt pay the *jizya* we shall empower thee to build it. And peace be on those who follow the True Guidance'. He requited his present with an even richer one – a hundred thoroughbred horses saddled and bridled, a hundred male slaves, a hundred Hindu singing- and dancing-girls, a hundred pieces of *bairamī* cloth, which are made of cotton and are unequalled in beauty,

[1] No reference to this embassy has yet been traced in either the Chinese or the Indian records.

[2] Yule (*Cathay*, IV, p. 18) identified this as Sambhal in Rohilkhand. Al-Samhal has been mentioned by I. B. (III, p. 614) as the district which includes Badâûn. However, no Buddhist remains have been found there, and the religion was probably extinct in that part of India by the fourteenth century. Besides, Sultan Muḥammad already controlled the area and on his Himalayan campaign marched in another direction, towards Nagarkot. Sambhal can hardly be described as being near the Himalayas.

each piece being worth a hundred dinars[3] – a hundred lengths
3 of the silk fabrics called *juzz*, in which the silk material | of
each is dyed with four or five different colours [4] – four hundred
pieces of the fabrics known as *ṣalāḥī*,[5] a hundred pieces of
shīrīn-bāf,[6] a hundred pieces of *shān-bāf*,[7] five hundred pieces
of *mirʿiz* woollens,[8] one hundred of them black and a hundred each in white, red, green, and blue, a hundred lengths of
Greek linen, a hundred pieces of blanket-cloth, a *serācha*, six
pavilions,[9] four candelabra in gold and six in silver enamelled,
four golden basins with ewers to match, and six silver basins,
ten embroidered robes of honour from the Sultan's own ward-
robe and ten caps also worn by him, one of them encrusted
with pearls, ten embroidered quivers one of them encrusted
with pearls, ten swords one of them with a scabbard encrusted
with pearls, *dasht-bān*,[10] that is gloves, embroidered with
pearls, and fifteen eunuchs.

As my fellow-voyagers with this present the Sultan appoint-
4 ed | the amir Ẓahīr al-Dīn of Zanjān, one of the most eminent
men of learning,[11] and the eunuch Kāfūr, the cup-bearer, into
whose keeping the present was entrusted. He sent with us the
amir Muḥammad of Harāt[12] with a thousand horsemen to
escort us to the port of embarkation, and we were accompanied by the ambassadors of the king of China, fifteen in
number, the chief of whom was called Tursī, along with their
servants, about a hundred men. We set out therefore in a great
company with an imposing body of troops. The Sultan gave
instructions that we were to be supplied with provisions while

[3] A cotton fabric, whose exact composition is not known (*Hobson-Jobson*, s.v. Beiramee).

[4] Mžik (p. 248, n. 5) would read *khazz*, a heavy, plushy velvet fabric of iridescent floss silk.

[5] Mžik (p. 248, n. 6) suggests that a Ḥijāzī fabric may be meant, *ṣalāḥī* being an epithet of Mecca.

[6] A fine cotton fabric, whose precise character is not known (*Hobson-Jobson*, s.v. Shireenbaf).

[7] A fine white fabric, perhaps that also called *sinabaff* (*Hobson-Jobson*, s.v. Shambaff, Sinabaff).

[8] *Mirʿizz*, the soft down below the outer coarser hair of goats.

[9] I.e. one large tent and six small ones.

[10] A mistake for *dastbān*, a Persian word.

[11] See III, p. 618, where he is described as 'a personage of high dignity at the Sultan's court', but where n. 91 says that he is not mentioned elsewhere.

[12] See III, p. 606, where he is mentioned as the *kutwāl*, i.e. chief of police.

we were travelling through his dominions. Our journey began on the 17th of Ṣafar 43 [22 July 1342]. That was the day selected because they choose either the 2nd, 7th, 12th, 17th, 22nd, or 27th of the month as the day for setting out on a journey.

On the first day's journey we halted | at the post-station of 5
Tilbat, two and one-third farsakhs from Dihlī.[13] From there we travelled to the post-station of Awu, thence to the station of Hīlū and thence to the town of Bayāna, a large and well-built town with fine bazaars.[14] Its cathedral-mosque is a magnificent building, the walls and the roof of it being made of stone. The governor of the town is Muẓaffar ibn al-Dāya, his mother being the Sultan's nurse. The governor there before him was the malik Mujīr ibn Abī al-Rajā', one of the principal maliks, who has been mentioned previously.[15] He claimed descent from Quraish and was insolent in character and cruel and tyrannical in rule. He put to death a great number of the inhabitants of this town and mutilated many of them. I saw one of its people, a man of fine appearance, sitting in the portico of his house with both hands and both feet cut off.
The Sultan came on one occasion | to this town and the 6
citizens complained against this malik Mujīr. The Sultan gave orders to arrest him; a manacle was put upon his neck and he was kept sitting in the *dīwān* before the vizier, while the people of the town presented written complaints of his violence. The Sultan commanded him to give them satisfaction and he compensated them with sums of money, after which he was put to death. Among the chief citizens of this town was the learned imam ʿIzz al-Dīn al-Zubairī, a descendant of al-Zubair b. al-ʿAwwām (God be pleased with him), a notable and upright jurist. I met him at Gālyūr in the service of the malik ʿIzz al-Dīn al-Banatānī known by the title of Aʿẓam Malik.[16]

[13] Tilpat, already mentioned (III, p. 742) as 'seven miles from the capital'.

[14] Awu and Hilu have not been identified satisfactorily on the route from Delhi to Aligarh. Bayāna is some 38 km west of Aligarh. Mžik (p. 249, n. 11) notes that this implies that I. B. had hitherto been travelling on the west side of the Jumna.

[15] See III, p. 665, n. 37, and p. 710.

[16] The malik ʿIzz al-Dīn Yaḥyā Bandat was given the title of Aʿẓam Malik and the fief of Satgaon by the Sultan on his accession (Mahdi Husain, p. 89). This is confirmed by Badā'ūnī (tr. G. S. Ranking, 1898, I, p. 302). Satgaon was lost to Fakhr al-Dīn of Bengal and ʿIzz al-Dīn is mentioned below as supreme amir of Chanderi (p. 791), and ʿIzz al-Dīn al-Zubairī as being in his company.

We journeyed on from Bayāna and came to the town of
Kuwil [Koel], a pretty town with orchards, most of their trees
being mangoes.[17] We encamped on a wide plain outside the
town. We met there the pious shaikh and devotee Shams al-
7 Dīn, known as the Ibn Tāj al-ʿĀrifīn, who was blind | and
advanced in age. Sometime later the Sultan cast him into
prison and he died there – we have already related his story.[18]

Account of an expedition in which we took part at Kuwil. On
reaching the town of Kuwil we heard that certain Hindu
infidels had invested and surrounded the town of al-Jalālī.[19]
Now this town lies at a distance of seven miles from Kuwil, so
we made in that direction. Meanwhile the infidels were engaged in battle with its inhabitants and the latter were on the
verge of destruction. The infidels knew nothing of our
approach until we charged down upon them, though they
numbered about a thousand cavalry and three thousand foot,
and we killed them to the last man and took possession of
their horses and their weapons. Of our party twenty-three
horsemen and fifty-five foot-soldiers suffered martyrdom,
amongst them the eunuch Kāfūr, the cup-bearer, into whose
hands the present had been entrusted. We informed the Sul-
8 tan by letter | of his death and halted to await his reply.
During that time the infidels used to swoop down from an
inaccessible hill which is in those parts and raid the environs of
al-Jalālī, and our party used to ride out every day with the
commander of that district to assist him in driving them off.

*Account of my trial by captivity, and of my deliverance from it and
from hardship thereafter at the hand of one of the saints of God.* On
one of these occasions I rode out with several of my friends
and we went into a garden to take our siesta, for this was in the
hot season. Then we heard some shouting, so we mounted our
horses and overtook some infidels who had attacked one of the
villages of al-Jalālī. When we pursued them they broke up into
small parties; our troop in following them did the same, and I
was isolated with five others. At this point we were attacked
9 by a body of cavalry and foot-soldiers from | a thicket there-
abouts, and we fled from them because of their numbers.

[17] Aligarh, originally the name of the citadel, now applied to the whole town.
[18] See III, pp. 704–5.
[19] A small town about 17 km east of Aligarh.

About ten of them pursued me, but afterwards all but three of them gave up the chase. There was no track at all before me and the ground there was very stony. My horse's forefeet got caught between the stones, so I dismounted, freed its foot and mounted again. It is customary for a man in India to carry two swords, one called the stirrup-sword, attached to the saddle, and the other in his quiver. My stirrup-sword fell out of its scabbard, and as its ornaments were of gold I dismounted, picked it up, slung it on me and mounted, my pursuers chasing me all the while. After this I came to a deep nullah, so I dismounted and climbed down to the bottom of it, and that was the last I saw of them.

I came out of this into a valley amidst a patch of tangle-
wood, through which there was a track, | so I walked along it, 10
not knowing where it led to. At this juncture about forty of the infidels, carrying bows in their hands, came out upon me and surrounded me. I was afraid that they would all shoot at me at once if I fled from them, and I was wearing no armour so I threw myself to the ground and surrendered, as they do not kill those who do that. They seized me and stripped me of everything that I was carrying except a *jubba*,[20] shirt and trousers, then they took me into that patch of jungle, and finally brought me to the part of it where they were staying near a tank of water situated amongst those trees. They gave me bread made of *māsh*, that is peas,[21] and I ate some of it and drank some water. In their company there were two Muslims who spoke to me in Persian, and asked me all about myself. I told them part of my story, but concealed the fact that I had come from the Sultan. Then they said to me: 'You are sure to
be put to death either by these men or by others, but | this 11
man here (pointing to one of them) is their leader'. So I spoke to him, using the two Muslims as interpreters, and tried to conciliate him. He gave me in charge of three of the band, one of them an old man, with whom was his son, and the third an evil black fellow. These three spoke to me and I understood from them that they had received orders to kill me. In the evening of the same day they carried me off to a cave, but God

[20] A loose robe, open in front, with wide, short sleeves.

[21] A Hindu word, *Phaseolus radiatus*, Roxb.

sent an ague upon the black, so he put his feet upon me, and the old man and his son went to sleep. In the morning they talked among themselves and made signs to me to accompany them down to the tank. I realized that they were going to kill me, so I spoke to the old man and tried to gain his favour, and he took pity on me. I cut off the sleeves of my shirt and gave them to him so that the other members of the band should not blame him on my account if I escaped.

About noon we heard voices near the tank and they thought
that it was their comrades, so they made signs to me to go
down with them, but when we went down we found some
12 other people. | The newcomers advised my guards to accom-
pany them but they refused, and the three of them sat down
in front of me, keeping me facing them, and laid on the
ground a hempen rope which they had with them. I was
watching them all the time and saying to myself: 'It is with
this rope that they will bind me when they kill me.' I remained thus for a time, then three of their party, the party that
had captured me, came up and spoke to them and I understood that they said to them: 'Why have you not killed him?'
The old man pointed to the Black, as though he were excus-
ing himself on the ground of his illness. One of these three
was a pleasant-looking youth, and he said to me: 'Do you wish
me to set you at liberty?' I said 'Yes' and he answered 'Go.' So
I took the tunic which I was wearing and gave it to him and he
gave me a worn double-woven [or indigo-dyed] cloak which
he had, and showed me the way. I went off but I was afraid
lest they should change their minds and overtake me, so I
13 went into a reed thicket | and hid there till sunset.

Then I made my way out and followed the track which the youth had shown me. This led to a pool from which I drank. I went on till near midnight and came to a hill under which I slept. In the morning I continued along the track, and sometime before noon reached a high rocky hill on which there were sweet lote-trees and zizyphus bushes. I started to pull and eat the lotus berries so eagerly that the thorns left scars on my arms that remain there to this day. Coming down from that hill I entered a plain sown with cotton and containing castor-oil trees. Here there was a *bā'in*, which in their language means a very broad well with a stone casing and steps by

which you go down to reach the water. Some of them have
stone pavilions, arcades, and seats in the centre and on the
sides, and the kings and nobles of the country vie with one
another | in constructing them along the highroads where 14
there is no water.[22] We shall have occasion later on to describe
some of these that we have seen. When I reached the *bā'in* I
drank some water from it and I found on it some mustard
shoots which had been dropped by their owner when he
washed them. Some of these I ate and saved up the rest, then
I lay down under a castor-oil tree. While I was there about
forty mailed horsemen came to the *bā'in* to get water and some
of them entered the sown fields, then they went away, and
God sealed their eyes that they did not see me. After them
came about fifty others carrying arms and they too went down
into the *bā'in*. One of them came up to a tree opposite the one
I was under, yet he did not discover me. At this point I made
my way into the field of cotton and stayed there the rest of the
day, while they stayed at the *bā'in* washing their clothes and
whiling away the time. At night time their voices died away,
so I knew that they | had either passed on or fallen asleep. 15
Thereupon I emerged and followed the trail of the horses, for
the nights were moonlit, continuing till I came to another *bā'in*
with a dome over it. I went down to it, drank some water, ate
some of the mustard shoots which I had, and went into the
dome. I found it full of grasses collected by birds, so I went to
sleep in it. Now and again I felt the movement of an animal
amongst the grass; I suppose it was a snake, but I was too worn
out to pay any attention.

The next morning I went along a broad track, which led to
a ruined village. Then I took another track, but with the same
result as before. Several days passed in this manner. One day
I came to some tangled trees with a tank of water between
them. The space under the trees was like a room, and at the
sides of the tank were plants like dittany and others. I intended to stop there until God should send someone to bring
me | to inhabited country, but I recovered a little strength, so 16
I arose and walked along a track on which I found the traces of
cattle. I found a bull carrying a packsaddle and a sickle, but

[22] The word is Hindi and the definition correct.

after all this track led to the villages of the infidels. Then I followed up another track and this brought me to a ruined village. There I saw two naked Blacks, and in fear of them I remained under some trees there. At nightfall I entered the village and found a house in one of whose rooms there was something like a large jar of the sort they make to store grains in. At the bottom of it there was a hole large enough to admit a man, so I crept into it and found inside it bedding of chopped straw, and amongst this a stone on which I laid my head and went to sleep. On the top of the jar there was a bird which kept fluttering its wings most of the night – I suppose it was frightened, so we made a pair of frightened creatures. This went on for seven days from the day on which I was
17 taken prisoner, which was | a Saturday. On the seventh day I came to a village of the infidels which was inhabited and possessed a tank of water and plots of vegetables. I asked them for some food but they refused to give me any. However, in the neighbourhood of a well I found some radish leaves and ate them. I went into the village, and found a troop of infidels with sentries posted. The sentries challenged me but I did not answer them and sat down on the ground. One of them came over with a drawn sword and raised it to strike me, but I paid no attention to him, so utterly weary did I feel. Then he searched me but found nothing on me, so he took the shirt whose sleeves I had given to the old man who had had charge of me.

On the eighth day I was consumed with thirst and I had no water at all. I came to a ruined village but found no tank in it. They have a custom in those villages of making tanks in which the rain-water collects, and this supplies them with drinking
18 water | all the year round. Then I went along a track and this brought me to an uncased well over which was a rope of vegetable fibre, but there was no vessel on it to draw water with. I took a piece of cloth which I had on my head and tied it to the rope and sucked the water that soaked into it, but that did not slake my thirst. I tied on my shoe next and drew up water in it, but that did not satisfy me either, so I drew water with it a second time, but the rope broke and the shoe fell back into the well. I then tied on the other shoe and drank until my thirst was assuaged. After that I cut the shoe and tied

its uppers on my foot with the rope of the well and bits of cloth
which I found there. While I was tying this on and wondering
what to do, a person appeared before me. I looked at him, and
lo! it was a black-skinned man, carrying a jug and a staff in his
hand, and a wallet on his shoulder. He gave me [the Muslim]
greeting: 'Peace be upon you' | and I replied: 'Upon you be 19
peace and the mercy and blessings of God.' Then he asked
me in Persian *Chīkas*: 'Who are you?'[23] and I answered: 'A man
astray', and he said: 'So am I.' Thereupon he tied a jug to a
rope which he had with him and drew up some water. I
wished to drink but he saying: 'Have patience', opened his
wallet and brought out a handful of black chick-peas fried with
a little rice. After I had eaten some of this and drunk, he made
his ablutions and prayed two prostrations and I did the same.
Thereupon he asked my name. I answered: 'Muḥammad' and
asked him his, to which he replied: 'al-Qalb al-Fāriḥ' ['Joyous
Heart']. I took this as a good omen and rejoiced at it. After this
he said to me: 'In the name of God accompany me'. I said: 'Yes'
and walked on with him for a little, then I found my limbs
giving way, and as I was unable to stand up I sat down. He
said: 'What is the matter with you?' I answered: 'I was able to
walk before meeting you, | but now that I have met you, I 20
cannot'. Whereupon he said: 'Glory be to God! Mount on my
shoulder'. I said to him: 'You are weak, and have not strength
enough for that', but he replied: 'God will give me strength.
You must do so'. So I got up on his shoulders and he said to
me: 'Say many times "God is sufficient for us and excellent the
guardian".[24] I repeated this over and over again, but I could
not keep my eyes open, and regained consciousness only on
feeling myself falling to the ground. Then I woke up, but
found no trace of the man and lo! I was in an inhabited village.
I entered it and found it was of Hindu peasants with a Muslim
governor. They informed him about me and he came to meet
me. I asked him the name of this village and he replied: 'Tāj
Būra'.[25] The distance from there to Kuwil, where our party

[23] Persian, *chi kasī*.

[24] Qur'ān, sūra iii, 172.

[25] Tajpur, about five km north-west of Aligarh. It is marked on the map of important historical places in Jamal M. Siddiqi, *Aligarh: Snippets from the Past*, a pamphlet published in connection with the Indian History Congress, 1975.

was, is two farsakhs. The governor provided a horse to take me
21 to his house and gave me hot food, and I washed. | Then he said to me: 'I have here a garment and a turban which were left in my charge by a certain Arab from Egypt, one of the soldiers belonging to the camp at Kuwil.' I said to him 'Bring them; I shall wear them until I reach camp'. When he brought them I found that they were two of my own garments which I had given to that very Arab when we came to Kuwil. I was extremely astonished at this, then I thought of the man who had carried me on his shoulders and I remembered what the saint Abū ʿAbdallāh al-Murshidī[26] had told me, as I have related in the first journey, when he said to me: 'You will enter the land of India and meet there my brother Dilshād, who will deliver you from a misfortune which will befall you there'. I remembered too how he had said, when I asked him his name, 'Joyous Heart' which, translated into Persian, is Dilshād. So I knew that it was he whom the saint had foretold that I should meet, and that he
22 too was one of the saints, but I enjoyed no more | of his company than the short space which I have related.

The same night I wrote to my friends at Kuwil to inform them of my safety, and they came, bringing me a horse and clothes and rejoiced at my escape. I found that the Sultan's reply had reached them and that he had sent a eunuch named Sunbul the *jāmdār*[27] in place of the martyred Kāfūr, with orders to pursue our journey. I found too that they had written to the Sultan about what had happened to me, and that they regarded this journey as ill-omened on account of what had happened in the course of it to me and to Kāfūr, and were wanting to go back. But when I saw that the Sultan insisted upon the journey, I urged them on with great determination. They answered: 'Do you not see what has befallen us at the very outset of this mission? The Sultan will excuse you, so let us return to him or stay here until his reply reaches us'. But I said: 'We cannot stay,
23 and wherever we are | his reply will reach us'.

We left Kuwil therefore, and encamped at Burj Būra, where there is a fine hermitage[28] in which lives a beautiful and

[26] See I, pp. 28–32.

[27] I.e. the cup bearer. His name means spikenard. He is mentioned below (p. 814) as a *malik*.

[28] Burjpur, about 16 km from Mainpur.

virtuous shaikh called Muḥammad the Naked, because he wears nothing but a cloth from his navel to the ground, with the rest of his body uncovered. He was the disciple of the pious saint Muḥammad the Naked who inhabited al-Qarāfa in Cairo[29] – God profit us by him.

A story of this Shaikh. He was one of the saints of God living upon the footing of total renunciation and wearing only a *tannūra*, that is to say a cloth covering his body from the navel down. It is told of him that when he had prayed the last evening prayer he cleared out everything that remained in the hospice in the way of food, seasonings, and water, distributing these to the poor, and threw the wick from his lamp, so that he began the
day lacking everything. It was his custom to give | his disciples 24
at dawn a meal of bread and beans, and the bakers and bean-sellers would try to outdo one another in arriving first at his hospice, when he would take from them enough for the needs of the poor brethren and would say to the man from whom he took this 'Sit down', so that he should receive the first charity which was given to him on that day, whether little or much.

One of the stories told of him relates to the time when Qāzān, the king of the Tatars, advanced into Syria with his armies and seized Damascus with the exception of its citadel. Al-Malik al-Nāṣir went out to drive him off, and the battle took place at a distance of two days' journey from Damascus at a place called Qashḥab. Al-Malik al-Nāṣir at that time was still a young man and inexperienced in warfare. The Naked Shaikh, who was in his company, alighted, took a shackle and shackled with it al-Malik al-Nāṣir's horse so that he should not move from his place at the moment of battle because of his youth, and thus occasion
the defeat | of the Muslims. Consequently al-Malik al-Nāṣir 25
held his ground and the Tatars suffered a sweeping defeat in which many of them were killed and many were drowned in the waters which were loosed upon them. The Tatars after that never again made an attack on the lands of Islam.[30] The

[29] For I.B.'s description of this famous cemetery see I, pp. 45–8.

[30] The story relates to the battle of Marj al-Suffār in April 1303. Ghazan, the Mongol Ilkhan of Persia, had invaded Syria and temporarily occupied Damascus. The Mamluk Sultan of Egypt, al-Malik al-Nāṣir, defeated the Mongols commanded, not by the Ilkhan, but by Qutlugh Shah and Amir Choban. I.B.'s Qashḥab is perhaps a mistake for Kushāf, where Qutlugh rejoined the Ilkhan (J. A. Boyle,

aforesaid shaikh Muḥammad the Naked, the disciple of this shaikh, told me that he was present at this battle, being then a young man.

We set out from Burj Būra and encamped at the water known as Āb-i Siyāh,[31] and from there went on to the city of Qinauj.[32] It is a large, well-built and fortified city; prices there are cheap and sugar plentiful, being exported from there to Dihlī, and it is surrounded by a great wall. We have had occasion to mention it before. There was living in it the shaikh Muʿīn al-Dīn al-Bākharzī, who offered us hospitality there,
26 and its governor was Fīrūz | of Badakhshān, a descendant of Bahrām Jūr (Chūbīn), the companion of Kisrā.[33] Among its inhabitants are a company of pious and upright men celebrated for their qualities and known as the 'sons of Sharaf Jahān'. Their ancestor was the Grand Qāḍī in Dawlat Ābād, a man notable for his benevolence and his charities, who attained to the primacy in religious leadership in the whole land of India.

A story about him. It is related of Sharaf Jahān that he was at one time removed from his judgeship, and one of his enemies charged him before the qāḍī who replaced him in office with being in possession of 10,000 dinars belonging to him [the plaintiff]. He had no written evidence, and his object was to have the oath administered to Sharaf Jahān. When the qāḍī sent for him he said to his messenger: 'What is it he claims against me?' He replied: '10,000 dinars', whereupon he sent that sum to the qāḍī's tribunal and it was paid over to the
27 plantiff. This came to the knowledge | of Sultan ʿAlā' al-Dīn, who was convinced of the falsity of that claim and restored him to the judgeship, as well as giving him 10,000 dinars.

We stayed in this city for three nights and during this time received the Sultan's reply to the letter about me, to the effect that if no trace were found of so-and-so, the qāḍī of Dawlat

---

Cambridge History of Iran, V, p. 394). I.B.'s final remark is incorrect. Ghazan's successor Öljeitü made an unsuccessful attack on Syria in 1312.

[31] The Kalindi river. The name I.B. uses is a Persian translation of the Urdu *kala nadi*, 'black river'.

[32] Kanauj.

[33] I.B. has confused Bahrām Gūr, the fifth-century Sasanian ruler of Persia, with the general Bahrām Chobin who rebelled against Khusrau Parvīz.

Ābād, Wajīh al-Mulk, should be his [i.e. my] substitute. We
then continued our journey from this city and alighted at the
post-station of Hanawl, then that of Wazīr-būr, then that of al-
Bajāliṣa, and then came to the town of Mawrī, a small place
with good bazaars.[34] I met there the pious and venerable
shaikh Quṭb al-Dīn, called by the title of Ḥaidar of Farghāna;
he was suffering from an illness but he gave me his blessing
and supplied me with a loaf of barley bread. He told me that
he was more than a hundred and fifty years old and his
companions related to me that he used to fast continuously |
and for many days on end. He used to make frequent retreats 28
and often remained in his cell for forty days, during which he
would eat forty dates, one on each day. I had myself seen at
Dihlī the shaikh known by the name of Rajab al-Burquʿī go
into his cell with forty dates and remain in it for forty days
after which he came out with thirteen of them still in his
possession.[35]

We went on from there and came to the town of Marh, a
large town, inhabited chiefly by infidels under Muslim
control.[36] It is well fortified and produces an excellent wheat,
the like of which is not found elsewhere, and which is exported from there to Dihlī; its grains are long, very yellow, and
large. I have never seen wheat like it except in China. This
town takes its name from the Mālawa, a tribe of Hindus, of
powerful build, great size and fine figures; their women espe-
cially are exceedingly beautiful and | famous for their charms 29
in intercourse and the amount of pleasure that they give. So
also are the women of the Marhata and of the Maldive Islands.

From Marh we travelled to ʿAlābūr, a small town most of
whose inhabitants are infidels under Muslim control.[37] A day's

[34] Mžik (p. 263, n. 27) remarks that it is extremely difficult to determine I.B.'s route from Kanauj to Gwalior. No names resembling Hanaul, Wazirpur or Al-Bajalisa are to be found in the Etawah district through which he must have passed. He suggests that Mawri may be Umri. I.B. mentions below (p. 787) a previous visit to Gwalior, but he nowhere describes the route he took then; it is possible that he has confused two different journeys.

[35] See I, pp. 227–8.

[36] Mžik suggests that this may be a scribal error for Mauh.

[37] Alapur, some 7 km south-east of Gwalior. Mžik (p. 264, n. 28) notes that there is another place of the same name, 37 km west-north-west of Gwalior, which would be away from any route from Kanauj.

journey from there lived an infidel Sultan, named Qatam, who was Sultan of Janbīl and was killed after besieging Guyālyur [Gwalior].[38]

His history. This infidel Sultan had besieged the town of Rābarī, which is on the river Jūn and has many villages and cultivated lands.[39] Its governor was Khaṭṭāb the Afghānī, who was one of the stalwarts. The infidel Sultan sought the aid of an infidel Sultan like himself called Rajū, whose town is called
30 | Sulṭān-Būr.[40] When the two of them invested the city of Rābarī, Khaṭṭāb sent a message to the Sultan asking him for help, but the reinforcements were slow in reaching him, as he was at a distance of forty days' journey from the capital. Khaṭṭāb therefore, fearing that the infidels should overpower him, gathered about three hundred men of the tribe of the Afghan and a similar number of mamluks and about four hundred of the other troops. They wound their turban-cloths on the necks of their horses, this being the custom of the people of India when they seek death and sell their souls to God. Khaṭṭāb and his tribesmen led the way followed by the rest of the party; they opened the gate at dawn and charged as one man upon the infidels, who numbered about 15,000. By the grace of God they routed them, and killed their two Sultans Qatam and Rajū, whose heads they sent to the Sultan and none of the infidels escaped but some scattered remnants. |

31 *Account of the governor of ʿAlābūr and of his death in battle.* The governor of ʿAlābūr was the Abyssinian Badr, a slave of the Sultan's, a man of the kind whose bravery becomes proverbial. He was continually making raids on the infidels alone and single handed, killing and taking captives, so that his fame spread far and wide and the infidels went in fear of him. He was tall and corpulent, and used to eat a whole sheep at a meal, and I was told that after eating he would drink about a pound and a half of ghee, following the custom of the Abyssinians in their own country. He had a son nearly as brave as himself.

[38] Mžik (p. 264, n. 29) suggests that the reference is to the Raja of Dholpur, and explains the name as that of the Chambal river.

[39] Rābarī has not been identified; the river is the Jumna (Yamuna). The governor is mentioned below (p. 794).

[40] Sultanpur, another name for Irijpur in Bundelkhand.

It happened that he raided a village of the infidels on one occasion with a company of his slaves and his horse fell with him into a matamore. The villagers gathered around him and one of them struck him with a *qattāra*, which is a piece of iron resembling a ploughshare into which a man inserts his hand |
so that it covers his forearm leaving a projection two cubits in 32
length.[41] A blow with this is mortal, so he killed Badr with that blow. His slaves put up a vigorous fight, took possession of the village, killed its men, seized its women and everything in it, and got the horse out of the matamore safe and sound and brought it to his son. By a strange coincidence he was mounted on that same horse and had set out for Dihlī when the infidels came out against him; he fought with them until he was killed and the horse returned to his companions who handed it over to his household. Later on a brother-in-law of his was riding the same horse when the infidels killed him on it also.

We journeyed next to Gālyūr or Guyālyūr, a large town with an impregnable fortress isolated on the summit of a lofty hill. Over its gate is the figure of an elephant with its mahout
carved in stone, | as has been mentioned previously in con- 33
nection with the Sultan Quṭb al-Dīn.[42] The governor of this town, Aḥmad b. Sīrkhān, was a man of upright character, and he treated me very honourably when I stayed with him on a previous occasion.[43] One day I came before him as he was about to have an infidel cut in two. I said to him: 'By God I beseech you, do not do this, for I have never seen anyone put to death in my presence'. He ordered the man to be put in prison so my intervention was the means of his escape.

From Gālyūr we went on to Parvan, a small town belonging to the Muslims, but situated in the land of the infidels.[44] Its governor was Muḥammad ibn Bairam, a Turk by origin.

[41] Urdu *katar*, defined as 'a dagger having a broad straight blade, the hilt of which comes up on either side of the wrist, while it is grasped by a crossbar in the centre' (S. W. Fallon, *A New Hindustani-English Dictionary*, Banaras, 1879, 2 vols).

[42] See III, p. 645.

[43] There has been no reference to I.B.'s former visit to Gwalior.

[44] 'Parwán is almost certainly Narwar in Gwalior State (Ibn Battúta here as elsewhere rendering a strange name by one more familiar, namely Parwan in Afghanistan)' (Gibb, *Selections*, p. 363, n. 5). He notes that there is a place called Parwai about 40 km north-east of Gwalior.

There are many tigers there, and one of the inhabitants told
me that a certain tiger used to enter the town by night,
although the gates were shut, and used to seize people.[45] It
34 killed | quite a number of the townsfolk in this way, and they
used to wonder how it made its way in. One of the inhabitants
of the town, Muḥammad al-Tawfīrī, who was a neighbour of
mine there, told me that it came into his house by night and
carried off a boy who was lying on his bed. Another told me
that he was with a party at a wedding celebration and one of
them went out to relieve nature, when the tiger seized him;
his companions went out in search of him and found him lying
in the bazaar. The tiger had drunk his blood but not eaten his
flesh and they say that this is the way it does with men. Here
is an amazing thing; a certain man told me that it was not a
tiger who did this but a human being, one of the magicians
known as *jūgīs* [yogis], appearing in the shape of a tiger. When
I heard this I refused to believe it, but a number of people told
me the same thing so let us give at this point some of the
stories about these magicians. |
35 *Account of the magicians called Jūgīs.* The men of this sect do
some marvellous things. One of them will spend months
without eating or drinking, and many of them have holes dug
for them under the earth which are then built in on top of
them, leaving only a space for air to enter. They stay in these
for months, and I heard tell of one of them who remained thus
for a year. In the town of Manjarūr [Mangalore] I saw a man of
the Muslims, one of these who learn the arts of these people,
for whom a platform had been put up, on top of which he
stayed without eating or drinking for a space of not less than
twenty-five days. I left him at that point and I do not know
how long he remained after I had gone. The people say that
they make up pills, one of which they take for a given number
36 of days or months, and during that time they require no | food
or drink. They can tell what is happening at a distance. The
Sultan holds them in esteem and admits them to his company.
Some eat nothing but vegetables, and others, the majority, eat

[45] The Arabic word, *sabʿ*, often denotes a lion, but can be used of other large predators. Its ability to climb and its blood-sucking propensity suggest a leopard rather than a tiger.

no meat; it is obvious that they have so disciplined themselves in ascetic practices that they have no need of any of the goods or vanities of this world. There are amongst them some who merely look at a man and he falls dead under their glance. The common people say that if the breast of a man killed in this way is cut open, it is found to contain no heart, and they assert that his heart has been eaten. This is commonest in the case of women, and a woman who acts thus is called *kaftār*.[46]

An anecdote. When the great famine was caused in the land of
India by the drought, during the Sultan's absence in the
province of Tiling,[47] he despatched an order that the inhabi-
tants of Dihlī should be given | an allowance of food at the rate 37
of a pound and a half per person per day. The vizier assembled them and distributed the indigent inhabitants amongst
the amirs and qāḍīs so that these latter should be responsible
for supplying them with food. My share of them was five
hundred souls; I built for them galleries in two houses and
lodged them there, and I used to give them provisions for five
days every five days. One day they brought me a woman, one
of their number, saying that she was a *kaftār* and had eaten the
heart of a boy who was beside her, and they also brought the
dead body of the boy. I ordered them to take her to the
Sultan's lieutenant, who commanded that she should be put
to the test. They filled four jars with water, tied them to her
hands and feet and threw her into the river Jūn. As she did not
sink she was known to be a *kaftār*; had she not floated she
would not have been one. He ordered her then to be burned
with fire. The people of the town came | and collected her 38
ashes, men and women alike, for they believe that anyone
who fumigates himself with them is safe against a *kaftār*'s
enchantments during that year.

Anecdote. The Sultan sent for me once when I was with him at Dihlī, and on entering I found him in a private apartment with some of his intimates and two of these *jūgīs*. They were wearing long cloaks and had their heads covered, because they remove all their hair with ashes as people generally remove the hair of the armpits. After the Sultan had ordered me to sit

[46] A Persian word for a hyena.
[47] See III, p. 644, n. 98.

down and I had done so, he said to them: 'This distinguished man comes from a far country, so show him something that he has not seen', to which they replied: 'Yes'. One of them squatted on the ground, then rose from the ground into the air above our heads, still sitting. I was so astonished and frightened that I fell to the floor in a faint. The Sultan gave orders |
39 to administer to me a potion that he had there and I revived and sat up. Meantime this man remained in his sitting posture. His companion then took a sandal from a sack he had with him, and beat it on the ground like one infuriated. The sandal rose in the air until it came above the neck of the sitting man and then began hitting him on the neck while he descended little by little until he sat down alongside us. The Sultan said to me: 'The man sitting is the pupil of the owner of the sandal'. Then he said: 'If I did not fear for your reason I would have ordered them to do still stranger things than this you have seen'. I took my leave but was affected with palpitation and fell ill, until he ordered me to be given a draught which removed it all.

To return to our subject. We travelled from the town of Parwan to the post-station of Amwārī and on to the post-
40 station of Kajarrā.[48] Here there is a large tank, about | a mile in length, on the sides of which there are temples containing idols which have been mutilated by the Muslims.[49] In the centre of the tank there are three pavilions of red stone, three stories high, and on each of the four corners another pavilion. There live there a company of *jūgīs* who have matted their hair and let it grow until it has come to be as long as themselves. They are generally of a yellow colour because of their mortifications, and many Muslims become their disciples in order to learn their secrets. They say that if a man suffering from some bodily disease such as leprosy or elephantiasis resorts to them for a long time, he will be cured by the grace of God.

The first time that I saw the men of this company was in the

[48] Gibb (*Selections*, p. 363, n. 5) had no doubt that Kajarrā was Khajuraho, famous for the erotic sculptures on the temple walls, but it is far from the route from Gwalior to Cambay. Amwārī cannot be identified with any confidence. Yule (*Cathay*, IV, p. 22) comments that I.B. may have been forced to follow a very devious route 'owing to the interposition of insurgent districts'.

[49] Much greater damage has been caused in more recent times by dealers breaking off erotic sculptures to sell to prurient tourists.

maḥalla of Sultan Tarmashīrīn, king of Turkistan. There were
about fifty of them for whom a cave had been dug under the
earth, and they used to stay in it, never coming out except to
satisfy a need. They had a sort of horn | which they used to 41
sound at the beginning and end of the day and after the first
third of the night. Everything about them is marvellous. It
was one of them who made for the Sultan of the land of
Maʿbar, Sultan Ghiyāth al-Dīn al-Dāmaghānī pills, to take as
an aphrodisiac.[50] Amongst their ingredients were iron filings,
and he was so pleased with their effect that he took more of
them than was necessary and died. He was succeeded by his
brother's son Nāṣir al-Dīn, who showed high consideration for
that *jūgī* and raised him in dignity.[51]

We went on next to the city of Chandīrī, a large town with
magnificent bazaars, and the residence of the supreme governor of that province, ʿIzz al-Dīn al-Banatānī, who has the
title of Aʿẓam Malik.[52] He was a liberal and worthy man who
used to invite the men of learning to his company. Amongst
those who frequented his company were the jurist ʿIzz | al- 42
Dīn al-Zubairī,[53] the jurist and theologian Wajīh al-Dīn al-
Bayānī (from the town of Bayāna which we have already
mentioned),[54] the jurist and qāḍī known by the title of Qāḍī
Khāṣṣa, and their imam Shams al-Dīn. His deputy for the
business of the treasury was called Qamar al-Dīn, and his
deputy for the affairs of the army Saʿāda of Telingana, one of
the principal champions; it is before him that the troops pass
in review, Aʿẓam Malik himself not appearing except on
Fridays or rarely on other days.

From Chandīrī we continued our journey to the city of Ẓihār, which is the chief city of Mālwa, the largest district in that province.[55] It is thickly cultivated, especially with wheat, and from this city betel leaves are exported to Dihlī. The distance between them is twenty-four days' journey, and all along the road between them there are pillars on which is

[50] See below, p. 862.
[51] See below, p. 864.
[52] See n. 16 above.
[53] See n. 16 above.
[54] See p. 775.
[55] Mentioned in III, p. 715, but not identified. It must be Dhar, but, as Mžik noted (p. 275, n. 41) I.B. must have passed through Ujjain before reaching Dhar.

engraved the number of miles from each pillar to the next.
43 When the traveller wishes to know how many miles | he has gone that day and how far it is to the post-station or to the town that he is making for, he reads the inscription on the pillars and so finds out. The city of Ẓihār is held in fief by Shaikh Ibrāhīm, who comes from the Maldive Islands.

Anecdote. This Shaikh Ibrāhīm came originally to this city and settled outside it, where he restored to cultivation some dead lands. He used to cultivate melons, and they produced fruits of superlative sweetness, the like of which were not to be found in that region. Other people used to cultivate melons on the neighbouring lands, but they were not like his. He used to supply food to the poor brethren and the indigent, and when the Sultan made his expedition to the land of Maʿbar this Shaikh sent him some melons as a gift. He accepted them, found them excellent, gave him the city of Ẓihār in fief and commanded him to build a hospice on a hill overlooking the
44 town. He erected a very fine hospice there and used | to supply food in it to travellers of every sort. After he had continued this practice for some years he presented himself before the Sultan and brought him thirteen laks, saying: 'This is the surplus of the money from which I used to supply food for the people, and the public treasury has a better claim to it than I'. So the Sultan accepted it from him, but did not approve of his action because of his amassing the money and not spending it all in providing food.

It was in this city that the sister's son of the vizier Khwāja Jahān attempted to murder his uncle, to seize his treasures, and to join the rebel in the province of Maʿbar.[56] His plot was denounced to his uncle, who seized him together with a number of the amirs, and sent them to the Sultan. The Sultan put the amirs to death but sent his sister's son back to the vizier, who executed him.

Anecdote. When the vizier's sister's son was sent back to him he gave orders that he should be executed in the same manner as
45 | his associates. The young man had a concubine whom he loved; he asked her to come and gave her betel, she gave him

[56] See I, p. 262 and n. 62. Khwāja Jahān was the title conferred by the Sultan on Aḥmad b. Aiyās. There are a number of references to him in vol. III.

betel in return and he embraced her saying farewell. He was then thrown to the elephants and flayed, and his skin was stuffed with straw. That night the girl went out of the house and threw herself into a well close by the place in which he was killed. She was found dead in the morning and taken out and his flesh was buried with her in the same grave, which they call *qubūr-i-ʿāshiqān* meaning in their language 'The lovers' graves'.[57]

We travelled from the town of Ẓihār to the town of Ujain, which is a fine and populous city.[58] It was the residence of the malik Nāṣir al-Dīn son of ʿAin al-Mulk, an upright, generous and learned man, who suffered martyrdom in the island of Sandābūr at the time of its conquest. I have visited his grave there and shall describe it in due course.[59] In this town too |
lived the jurist and physician Jamāl al-Dīn al-Maghribī, who 46
came originally from Gharnāṭa.[60]

From the town of Ujain we continued our journey to Dawlat Ābād, the enormous and important city which rivals Dihlī, the capital, in standing and in the spaciousness of the planning. It is divided into three sections; one is Dawlat Ābād proper, and is reserved for the Sultan and his troops, the second is called Kataka,[61] and the third is the citadel, which is unrivalled and unequalled for its strength and is called Duwaygīr.[62]

At Dawlat Ābād resides the Great Khan Quṭlū Khān, the Sultan's preceptor, who is governor of the town, and the Sultan's lieutenant there and in the lands of Ṣāghar, Tiling, and their dependent territories.[63] This province extends for
three | months' march, is well-populated, and wholly under 47
his authority and that of his lieutenants. The fortress of Duwaygīr mentioned above is a rock situated in a plain; the rock has been excavated and a castle built on its summit. It is

[57] Persian.

[58] Ujjain.

[59] I.B. does not keep his promise. For the Muslim capture of Sandābūr, i.e. Goa, see below pp. 819–20.

[60] See I. p. 183, and III, p. 685.

[61] A Sanskrit word for a royal camp.

[62] Deogiri.

[63] There are several references to Qutlū Khān in vol. III; see especially pp. 617, 718 and 720. On Ṣāghar, see below p. 796. On Tiling see III, p. 644 and n. 98.

reached by a ladder made of leather, which is taken up at night. It is occupied by the troops called *mufrad*, that is to say, who are on the register, together with their sons.[64] There is a prison there, in whose dungeons are imprisoned those convicted of serious crime, and in these dungeons there are huge rats, bigger than cats – in fact, cats run away from them and cannot defend themselves, for these rats are too strong for them, so they can be captured only by means of ingenious devices which are employed to deal with them. I saw them there and marvelled at them.[65]

Anecdote. The malik Khaṭṭāb al-Afghānī[66] told me that he had once been imprisoned in a dungeon in this fortress, which went by the name of 'the pit of the rats'. He said: 'They used
48 to collect together by night | to devour me and I fought against
them, which I could only do with great difficulty. I then saw in a dream a man who said to me: "Recite the sura of *al-Ikhlāṣ* a hundred thousand times and God will deliver you".[67] So I recited it and when I had completed this number I was released. The reason for my release was that the malik Mall was imprisoned in a dungeon adjacent to mine; he fell sick and the rats ate his fingers and his eyes and he died. When this was reported to the Sultan he said "Fetch out Khaṭṭāb in case the same thing happens to him".' It was to this fortress that Nāṣir al-Dīn, the son of this same Malik Mall, and the qāḍī Jalāl fled for refuge when the Sultan defeated them.[68]

The inhabitants of Dawlat Ābād belong to the tribe of the Marhata, whose women God has endowed with special beauty, particularly in their noses and eyebrows.[69] They have in inter-
49 course | a deliciousness and a knowledge of erotic movements
beyond that of other women. The infidels of this city are

[64] The word means 'singular' or 'detached'.

[65] Mžik (p. 274, n. 43) thinks it probable that I.B. saw brown rats for the first time at Deogiri.

[66] Mentioned above (p. 786) as governor of Rābarī.

[67] Qur'ān, sūra cxii. It is the shortest sūra in the Qur'ān and is an assertion of the unity and uniqueness of God.

[68] On the persons mentioned and their revolt, see III, pp. 730–35. Mahdi Husain (284) has noted that, by his own account, I.B. must have left India before this rebellion.

[69] The Mahrattas. Other travellers have shared I.B.'s opinions on their womenfolk.

merchants dealing principally in jewels, and their wealth is enormous. They are called the *Sāha*, each one of them being a *Sāh*, and are like the Kārimīs in Egypt.[70] At Dawlat Ābād there are grapes and pomegranates, both of which produce fruit twice in the year. It is one of the largest and most important of the provinces in respect of taxes and land revenue, on account of its dense population and the extent of its territory. I have been told that a certain Hindu contracted for the farm of the taxes of the town and its province together (and the latter is, as we have said, a three months' journey) for seventeen crores, the crore being a hundred laks and the lak a hundred thousand dinars. But he was unable to fulfil his obligation; a part of it remained outstanding and his property was seized and he was flayed. |

Description of the bazaar of the singers. In the city of Dawlat 50
Ābād there is an exceedingly fine and spacious bazaar for
singers and singing-girls, called Ṭarab Ābād,[71] containing
numerous shops, each of which has a door leading to the
house of its proprietor. Each house has another door as well.
The shop is beautified with carpets, and in the centre of it
there is a sort of large cradle on which the singing-girl sits or
reclines. She is adorned with all kinds of ornaments and her
attendant girls swing her cradle. In the centre of the bazaar
there is a large carpeted and decorated pavilion in which the
chief musician sits every Thursday after the afternoon
prayer, with his servants and slaves in front of him. The
singing-girls come in relays and sing and dance before him
till the sunset prayer, when they withdraw. | In the same 51
bazaar there are mosques for the prayer-services, in which
the imams hold the *tarāwīḥ* services during the month of
Ramaḍān.[72] One of the infidel rulers in India used, on
passing through this bazaar, to alight at the pavilion and the
singing-girls used to sing before him. One of the Muslim
Sultans, too, used to do the same.

[70] *Sah*, or *Sahu*, is a Hindi word for a merchant or banker. The Kārimīs were a guild of merchants prominent in the trade of the Red Sea and Indian Ocean. Mžik was wrong in connecting the name with Kanem near Lake Chad (p. 275, n. 67).

[71] 'The Abode of Joy' (Persian).

[72] Additional prayers recited during the nights of Ramaḍān.

We continued on our way to Nadharbār, a small town inhabited by the Marhatas,[73] who possess a great skill in the arts, and are physcians and astrologers. The nobles of the Marhatas are Brahmans and also Katris [Kshatriyas].[74] Their food consists of rice, vegetables, and oil of sesame, and they do not hold with giving pain to or slaughtering animals. They wash themselves before eating, like our major ablution, and do not marry among their relatives, unless those who are cousins six times removed. Neither do they drink wine, for this in their
52 eyes is the greatest of vices. | The Muslims in India take the same view, and any Muslim who drinks is punished with eighty stripes, and shut up for three months in a matamore which is opened only when he is given food.

From this town we journeyed on to Ṣāghar [Songarh], which is a large town on a great river called by the same name of Ṣāghar.[75] There are large water-wheels on the river, and there are orchards in which they grow mangoes, bananas and sugarcane. It inhabitants are upright, religious, and trustworthy, and all their ways are praiseworthy. They have orchards in which there are hospices for all travellers. Anyone who builds a hospice gives it the orchard as its endowment and appoints his sons as its supervisors, and if they die out the supervision reverts to the qāḍīs. It is densely populated and people go there to participate in the blessing conveyed by inhabitants, and because the town is exempted from taxes and dues. |

[73] Nandurbar. Mžik (p. 276, n. 50) notes that I.B. left Daulatabad in the direction from which he came, and suggests that the embassy may have been heading for Calicut by land, but had learnt in Daulatabad that the journey would not be safe, especially because of the value of the presents it was carrying.

[74] The Mahratta Khatris claim to be descended from Kshatriyas, the warrior caste in the fourfold division of ancient Indian society (R. E. Enthoven, *The Tribes and Castes of Bombay*, II, p. 207).

[75] Songarh; the river is the Tapti. It may or may not be the place mentioned above (p. 793), for which I.B. uses the same spelling, but which could be Songir, also south of the river but further to the east and beyond Nandurbar.

CHAPTER XVI

South India

From the aforesaid Ṣāghar we travelled on to the town of 53
Kinbāya [Cambay] which is situated on an arm of the sea resembling a river;[1] it is navigable for ships and its waters ebb and flow. I myself saw the ships there lying on the mud at ebb-tide and floating on the water at high tide. This city is one of the finest there is in regard to the excellence of its construction and the architecture of its mosques. The reason is that the majority of its inhabitants are foreign merchants, who are always building there fine mansions and magnificent mosques and vie with one another in doing so. Amongst the great mansions in the town is the house of the sharif al-Sāmarrī with whom I was involved in the incident of the sweetmeats, and to whom the 'king' of the intimate courtiers gave the lie.[2] I have never seen heavier baulks of wood than those which I saw in this house, and its gate is like that of a city. Beside it
there is | a large mosque which is known by his name.[3] Other 54
mansions are those of the 'king of the merchants' al-Kāzarūnī, alongside which is his mosque also, and that of the merchant Shams al-Dīn *Kulāh-Dūz*, which means the sewer of caps.

Anecdote. On the occasion of the revolt of the qāḍī Jalāl the Afghānī, which we have related earlier,[4] this Shams al-Dīn, together with the ship-owner Ilyās (who was one of the principal men of this city) and the 'king of the physicians' previously mentioned, attempted to defend themselves against him in this city. They set about digging a trench around it, since it

[1] Cambay, then an important port, which declined because of the silting of the harbour.

[2] See III, pp. 756–7.

[3] His tomb is in the congregational mosque, which had been recently built with the fragments of Hindu and Jain Temples.

[4] See III, pp. 730–34.

had no wall, but he overcame them and entered the city. These three went into hiding in a house together, and fearing that they should be discovered, they made a pact to kill one
another. Each one of them struck the other with a *qattāra* (we
55 have already described [p. 787] | the nature of this instrument),
and two of them died but the 'king of the physicians' survived.

Among the chief merchants there was also Najm al-Dīn of Jīlān, a man of fine figure and immensely wealthy. He built there a great mansion and a mosque. Some time later the Sultan sent for him and made him governor of the city, assigning him the ceremonial honours, but the outcome of this was the loss of his own life and of his fortune.

The governor of Kinbāya at the time of our arrival was Muqbil of Telingana, who was held in high consideration by the Sultan.[5] In his company was the Shaikh-Zāda of Iṣfahān, acting as deputy for him in all his affairs. This shaikh had great riches and was distinguished by knowledge of the affairs of government. He was continually sending money to his own country and devising plans for his escape. This came to the ears of the Sultan, it being reported of the shaikh that he was planning to take flight, whereupon he sent written instructions to Muqbil to dispatch him [to Dihlī]. Muqbil despatched
56 him by the post | and he was brought before the Sultan who
placed him under guard. Now customarily at his court when anyone is placed under surveillance, he rarely escapes death, but this shaikh made a pact with his guard for a sum which he would pay him, and the two of them fled together. A trustworthy person told me that they had seen him by a pillar in a mosque in the city of Qalhāt,[6] and that he subsequently reached his own country, obtained possession of his moneys and lived in security, having nothing more to fear from that quarter.

Anecdote. The malik Muqbil gave a banquet for us one day in his mansion. By an amusing chance the qāḍī of the city, who was blind in the right eye, on taking his seat had opposite him a sharif from Baghdad with a marked resemblance to him in his features and his blindness, except for the fact that he was

[5] See III, pp. 730–34.

[6] In ʿOmān.

blind in the left eye. The sharif kept looking at the qāḍī and laughing, and when the qāḍī rebuked him he replied: 'Do not reprove me, for I am more handsome than you.' 'How's that?' asked the qāḍī. 'Because you are blind in the right eye and I 57
am blind in the left', he replied, whereupon the governor and all those present laughed and the qāḍī was put to shame, but he was unable to make a rejoinder because sharifs are treated in India with the greatest veneration.

One of the devotees in this city was the Ḥājj Nāṣir, of the people of Diyār Bakr, who lived in one of the pavilions of the cathedral mosque. We went to visit him there and ate his food. It happened that when the qāḍī Jalāl entered the city of Kinbāya at the time of his rebellion, he came to this saint, and the Sultan was informed that the latter had prayed for a blessing on him. For this reason he fled, to avoid being put to death as al-Ḥaidarī had been.[7] Another of the devotees there was the merchant Khwāja Isḥāq, who has a hospice in which he supplies food to travellers of every sort. He makes large donations to the poor brethren and the indigent, yet his wealth for all that continues to grow and to multiply.

We journeyed from this city to the town of Kāwī, which is
on a tidal bay also,[8] | and is in the territories of the infidel raja 58
Jālansī, of whom we shall speak later.[9] Thence we went on to Qandahār, a large town belonging to the infidels and situated on a bay of the sea.[10]

Account of its Sultan. The Sultan of Qandahār is an infidel called Jālansī, who is under Muslim suzerainty and sends a gift to the king of India every year. When we reached Qandahār he came out to welcome us and showed us the greatest honour, himself leaving his palace and installing us in it. The principal Muslims at his court came to visit us, such as the children of the Khwāja Buhra.[11] One of these is the shipowner Ibrāhīm, who possesses six vessels of his own. From this city we continued our journey by sea. |

[7] See III, pp. 705–6.

[8] Kava, now a mile from the sea.

[9] Probably the Rajput tribal name Jhalas, preserved in the name of Jhalawar district in Kathiawar (Gibb, *Selections*, p. 363, n. 10).

[10] An arabicization of Gandhar, now a fishing village near the mouth of the Dhandar river. It was formerly a port of some importance, Barbosa's Guindarim and Linschoten's Gandar.

59 *Account of our embarkation*. We embarked on a ship belonging to the Ibrāhīm mentioned above, called *al-Jāgir*. On this ship we put seventy of the horses of the Sultan's present, and the rest we put with the horses of our companions on a ship belonging to this Ibrāhīm's brother, called *Manūrt*. Jālansī gave us a vessel on which we put the horses of Ẓahīr al-Dīn and Sunbul and their party, and he furnished it for us with water, provisions and forage. He sent his son with us on a ship called *al-ʿUkairī*, which resembles a grab, but is rather broader; it has sixty oars and is covered with a roof during battle in order to protect the rowers from arrows and stones. I myself went on board *al-Jāgir*, which had a complement of fifty rowers and fifty Abyssinian men-at-arms. These latter are
60 the guarantors of safety | on this sea; let there be but one of them on a ship and it will be avoided by the Indian pirates and idolaters.

Two days later we called at the island of Bairam, which is uninhabited and at a distance of four miles from the mainland.[12] We disembarked on this island and took a supply of water from a tank there. The reason for its devastation is that the Muslims captured it by force from the infidels and it has not been inhabited since. The 'king of the merchants' afore-mentioned wishes to repopulate it and after constructing a wall for it and setting up mangonels he settled some Muslims on it.

We continued our journey thence and on the following day arrived at the city of Qūqa, a large town with important bazaars.[13] We anchored four miles from shore on account of the low tide. I went down into a skiff with some of my associates at the time of low tide, with the object of going into
61 the town, but the skiff stuck | in the mud when we were about a mile distant from it. When we sank into the mud I was leaning upon two of my companions, and the men of the place

[11] The Bohras of Gujerat and Bombay are a branch of the Ismāʿīlīs, prominent as traders and money-lenders. Other Bohras in northern Konkan are Sunnīs, often peasants, and retain many Hindu practices (*Hobson-Jobson*, s.v. Bora).

[12] Perim or Piram, a small island near the mouth of the Gulf of Cambay, a pirate stronghold until its capture by the Muslims shortly before I.B.'s visit.

[13] Goga. It has been objected to this identification that it is not on the route from Gandhar to Goa, but the ship may have needed to take on supplies or have been forced by contrary winds (Mžik, p. 283, n. 64).

gave me to fear the turn of the tide before I should reach it, since I was not a good swimmer. But finally I did get to it and made the circuit of its bazaars and saw there a mosque attributed to al-Khiḍr and Ilyās (on them both be peace), in which I made the sunset prayer. I found in the mosque a number of poor brethren of the Ḥaidarī order along with a shaikh of theirs.[14] I then returned to the ship.

Account of its Sultan. The Sultan of Qūqa is an infidel called Dunkul, who used to profess submission to the king of India but was in reality a rebel.

On setting sail from this town we arrived after three days at the island of Sandābūr [Goa], an island in which there are
thirty-six | villages.[15] It is surrounded by a gulf, the waters of 62
which are sweet and agreeable at low tide but salt and bitter at high tide. In the centre of the island are two cities, an ancient one built by the infidels, and the other built by the Muslims when they first captured the island.[16] In the latter there is a great cathedral mosque, resembling those of Baghdād, built by the shipowner Ḥasan, the father of the Sultan Jamāl al-Dīn Muḥammad of Hinawr, who will be mentioned hereafter, as well as my presence with him on the occasion of the second capture of this island, if God will.[17] [On this occasion] we did not stop at this island when we passed by it, but anchored at a smaller one near the mainland, in which there was a temple, an orchard, and a water-tank, and on which we found one of the *jūgīs*.[18]

The story of this jūgī. When we landed on this smaller island we
found | there a *jūgī* leaning against the wall of a *budkhāna*, that 63
is an idol-temple;[19] he was between two of its idols and showed the traces of continuous practice of religious austerities. When we spoke to him he did not say a word, and we looked to see if there was any food with him but did not see

[14] See II, p. 274 and n. 15, and III, p. 583 and n. 175.

[15] According to Barros, Goa was formerly known as Ticuari (Marathi: Tiswadi, i.e. 30 villages).

[16] Goa was first captured by the Muslims in 1312, but subsequently changed hands more than once.

[17] See below pp. 803–5 and 819–21.

[18] Anjidiv.

[19] Notwithstanding its etymology the word is applied to any temple with idols, whether Buddhist, Hindu or Jain.

any. While we were still looking he uttered a great shout, and as he shouted a coconut fell from a coco-palm in front of him. He handed it to us and we in astonishment gave him some dinars and dirhams, which he would not accept, and when we brought him provisions he refused them also. There was a cloak of camel-hair lying on the ground in front of him; I took it in hand to examine it and he gave it to me. I had in my hand a chaplet of Zailaʿ;[20] he examined it in my hand so I gave it to him. He rubbed it between his fingers, smelt it, kissed it, and pointed first to the sky and then in the direction of Mecca. My companions did not understand his signs, but I for my part understood him to indicate that he was a Muslim who was
64 concealing his Muslim belief from | the people of that island and living on those coconuts. When we were about to leave him I kissed his hand; my companions disapproved of that, but he perceived their disapproval and taking my hand kissed it and smiled and signed to us to go. So we left, I being the last of my party to go out, when he tugged at my cloak; I turned my head towards him and he gave me ten dinars. When we came out of the place my companions said to me: 'Why did he pull you?' and I told them that he had given me those dinars. I gave three of them to Ẓahīr al-Dīn and three to Sunbul, saying to them: 'The man is a Muslim; do you not see how he pointed to the sky to indicate that he knew God, and then to Mecca to indicate his knowledge of the Apostle (peace be upon him)? And his taking of the chaplet confirms the fact.' They went back when I said this to them but they could not find him.

We set out again immediately and on the next day reached
65 | the town of Hinawr, which is on a large inlet into which large ships enter.[21] The town itself is half a mile from the sea. During the *bushkāl*, which is the rainy season,[22] this bay is so stormy and boisterous that for four months it is impossible for anyone to sail on it except for fishing.

On the day of our arrival at this place one of the Hindu *jūgīs*

[20] The Arabic could also be translated as 'a chaplet of cowries'. This is perhaps more likely. I.B. called Zailaʿ 'the dirtiest, most disagreeable, and most stinking town in the world' and avoided spending the night on shore (II, p. 373).

[21] Honavar.

[22] Hindi, *pashkal*, the rainy season.

came to me secretly and gave me six dinars saying to me: 'The Brahman has sent this to you', meaning the *jūgī* to whom I had given the chaplet. When he gave me the dinars I took them from him and offered him one of them, but he declined it and withdrew. I told my companions what had happened and said to them: 'If you wish your share of them [you may have it].' They both refused but were full of astonishment at the ways of this person and said to me: 'The six dinars which you gave
us we left with six others between the two idols | in the place 66
where we found him.' I was greatly astonished at our adventure with this person and kept with special care those dinars that he had given me.

The people of the city of Hinawr are Shāfiʿites in doctrine, upright, religious, engaged in warfare on the sea, and mighty. They were celebrated in this respect until time brought them low after their conquest of Sandābūr, which we shall relate. Amongst the devotees whom I met in this city was the shaikh Muḥammad al-Naqawrī, who entertained me in his hospice. He used to cook the food with his own hand, regarding it as defiled by the maidservant and the manservant. I met there also the jurist Ismāʿīl, the instructor in the Book of God, who was a scrupulous man of good disposition and generous nature, also the qāḍī there, Nūr al-Dīn ʿAlī, and the preacher, whose name I do not remember.

The women of this town and of all these coastal districts
wear no | sewn garments but only unsewn lengths of cloth, 67
one end of which they gird round their waists, and drape the rest over their head and chest. They are beautiful and virtuous, and each wears a gold ring in her nose. One peculiarity amongst them is that they all know the Qur'ān by heart. I saw in the town thirteen schools for girls and twenty-three for boys, a thing which I have never seen elsewhere. Its inhabitants live by maritime commerce, and have no cultivated land. The people of Mulaibār pay a fixed sum annually to Sultan Jamāl al-Dīn, through fear of his sea-power. His army consists of about six thousand men, horse and foot.

Account of the Sultan of Hinawr. He is the Sultan Jamāl al-Dīn
Muḥammad ibn | Ḥasan, one of the best and most powerful 68
Sultans. He is under the suzerainty of an infidel Sultan named

Haryab, of whom we shall speak later.[23] The Sultan Jamāl al-Dīn is assiduous in attending the congregational prayers. It is his custom to come to the mosque before daybreak and to read the Qur'ān until the rising of the dawn, when he prays at the earliest moment. He then rides outside the city and returns about the middle of the forenoon, when he goes first to the mosque and prostrates himself there before going into his palace. He fasts regularly during the 'white days' [when the moon is at the full]. During my stay with him he used to invite me to break my fast in his company; I and the jurist ʿAlī and the jurist Ismāʿīl would present ourselves, and four small stools would be placed on the ground, on one of which the Sultan would sit and each of us on another. |

69 *Account of the order observed in his banquet.* The order of this was as follows. A brass table (which they call *khawanjah*)[24] is brought in and there is set on it a brass platter (which they call *ṭālam*).[25] A beautiful slave-girl wrapped in a silk robe then comes and sets in front of him the pots of food; she carries a large brown ladle and with it she ladles out a single spoonful of rice and puts it into the *ṭalam*, then sprinkles over it ghee and puts along with this bunches of salted peppers and green ginger, salted lemons, and mangoes. One eats a mouthful [of rice] and follows it up with some of these preserves, and when the first ladleful which she placed in the *ṭālam* is finished she takes out another ladleful of rice and puts a cooked fowl into a bowl, and the rice is eaten with this also. When the second ladleful is finished she ladles out again and puts out another
70 kind of fowl, which one eats with it. When | the different kinds of fowls are finished they bring various sorts of fish, with which they eat rice also, and when the different fish dishes are emptied they bring vegetables cooked with ghee and preparations of milk, and they eat rice with these too. When all these are done with they bring *kūshān*, which is curdled milk, with which they end up their service of food. When this is served it is a signal that there is nothing else to be eaten after it. Finally they drink warm water on top of this, for cold water would be harmful to them in the season of the rains.

[23] He is not mentioned again.
[24] Persian, *khwāncheh*.
[25] Arabic *ṭulm*, a pastry board.

On another occasion I stayed for eleven months at the court of this Sultan without ever eating bread, for their sole food is rice. I lived also in the Maldive Islands, Ceylon, and on the Maʿbar and Mulaibār coasts for three years eating nothing but rice, until I could not swallow it except by taking water with it.

The clothes worn by their Sultan are cloaks of silk and fine
linen; he ties a waist-cloth round his middle and puts on two
cloaks, one on top of | the other. He plaits his hair and winds 71
on a small turban. When he rides out he puts on a military
jacket and wears two cloaks above it, and drums and trumpets
are carried by men and sounded before him. On this occasion
we stayed with him for three days; he supplied us with provisions, and we left him to continue our journey.

Three days later we reached the land of Mulaibār [Mala-
bar], which is the pepper country. It extends for two months'
journey along the coast from Sandābūr to Kawlam [Quilon].
The road over the whole distance runs beneath the shade of
trees, and at every half-mile there is a wooden shed with
benches on which travellers of every kind, whether Muslims
or infidels, may sit. At each shed there is a well for drinking
and an infidel who is in charge of it. If the traveller is an infidel
he gives him water in vessels; if he is a Muslim he pours the
water into his hands, | continuing to do so until he signs to him 72
to stop or stops him. It is the custom of the infidels in the
Mulaibār lands that no Muslim may enter their houses or eat
from their vessels; if he does so they break the vessels or give
them to the Muslims. If a Muslim goes into a place there in
which there is no house belonging to Muslims, they cook food
for him, putting it on banana leaves, and put the condiments
over it, and birds eat what is left. At all the halting-places on
this road there are houses belonging to Muslims, at which
Muslim travellers alight, and where they buy all that they
need, and food is cooked for them. Were it not for these
Muslims, no Muslim would travel by this road.

On this road, which, as we have said, extends for a two
months' march, there is not a span of ground or more but is |
cultivated. Every man has his own separate orchard, with his 73
house in the middle and a wooden palisade all round it. The
road runs through the orchards, and when it comes to a palisade

there are wooden steps to go up by and another flight of steps down into the next orchard. So it goes on for two months. No one travels on an animal in that country, and only the Sultan possesses horses. The principal vehicle of the inhabitants is a *dūla* carried on the shoulders of slaves or hired porters;[26] those who do not travel in a *dūla* go on foot, be they who they may. If a man has baggage or merchandise or anything of the kind, it is transported by hired carriers on their backs, and you may see a single merchant with a hundred such or less or more carrying his goods. Each porter has in his hand a stout staff, with an iron ferrule, and at the upper end an iron crook. When
74 he is tired out, and finds no | bench on which to rest, he sticks his staff in the ground and hangs his load from the crook, and after resting resumes his load without assistance and goes on with it. I have never seen a safer road than this, for they put to death anyone who steals a single nut, and if any fruit falls no one picks it up but the owner. I was told that some Hindus travelled by this road, and one of them picked up a nut. When the governor was informed of this, he ordered a stake to be fixed in the ground; its upper end was sharpened and inserted into a wooden spar so that it protruded from it. The man was stretched on the spar, belly downwards, and transfixed on the stake until it came out of his back, and he was left like that as an example to the beholders. There are many such stakes on this road, so that people may see them and be warned. We
75 sometimes | met infidels during the night on this road, and when they saw us they stood aside to let us pass. Muslims are shown the highest consideration on it except that, as we have said, they do not eat with them nor allow them into their houses.

In the Mulaibār lands there are twelve infidel Sultans, some of them strong with armies numbering fifty thousand men, and others weak with armies of three thousand. Yet there is no discord whatever between them, and the strong has no ambition to seize the possessions of the weak. At the boundary of the territories of each ruler there is a wooden gateway, on which is engraved the name of the ruler whose territories begin at that point. This is called 'The Gate of Security' of

[26] Hindi *doli*, a litter.

such-a-such prince. If any Muslim or infidel criminal flees from the territories of one and reaches the Gate of Security of another, his life is safe and the prince from whom he has fled cannot seize him, even though he be a powerful prince | with 76
a great army. The Sultans in these lands transmit their sovereignty to their sisters' sons, to the exclusion of their own children. I have seen this practice nowhere else except among the veiled Massūfa, who will be mentioned later.[27] When a Sultan in the land of Mulaibār wishes to stop people from buying and selling he orders one of his manservants to hang over the shops branches of trees with their leaves, and no one either sells or buys so long as these branches remain hanging. *Description of pepper.* The pepper-trees resemble grape-vines; they are planted alongside coco-palms and climb up them in the same way that vines climb, except that they have no shoots, that is to say tendrils, like those of vines. The leaves of the trees resemble | those of stocks [*or, according to a variant* 77
reading, horses' ears], and some of them resemble the leaves of briar. It produces its fruit in small clusters, the grains of which resemble the grains of *abū qinninah*[28] when they are green. In the autumn they gather the grains and spread them on mats in the sun, just as is done with grapes in order to obtain raisins; they keep on turning them until they are thoroughly dried and become black, and then sell them to the merchants. Most people in our country suppose that they roast them with fire and that it is because of that they become crinkled, but it is not so since this results only from the action of the sun upon them. I have seen pepper grains in the city of Qāliqūṭ being poured out for measuring by the bushel, like millet in our country.

The first town in the land of Mulaibār that we entered was the town of Abū Sarūr [Barcelore], a small place on a large inlet and abounding in coco-palms. The chief of the Muslims here is Shaikh Jumʿa, known as *Abū Sitta*, | a most charitable 78

[27] See below pp. 951–2. The Massūfa, Berbers of the western Sahara, were distinguished by a matrilineal social structure. The name was often given by medieval Muslim writers to the Tuaregs, among whom the lower part of the face is veiled.

[28] I.e. the date palm, *Phoenix dactylifera*, L. The word *qinnina*, 'flask', is used in the Sahara for a semispherical scoop made from the wood of the date palm, which is therefore called the 'father of the scoop'.

man, who spent all that he had on the poor brethren and the indigent. Two days' journey from there brought us to Fākanūr [Bacanor], a large town on an inlet;[29] here there is a large quantity of fine-flavoured sugar-canes, which are unexcelled in the rest of that country. There is a Muslim community here, whose chief is called Ḥusain al-Salāṭ, and it has a qāḍī and a preacher. This Ḥusain built a mosque in the town for the holding of the Friday prayer.

Account of its Sultan. The Sultan of Fākanūr is an infidel called Bāsadaw. He possesses about thirty warships, commanded by a Muslim called Lūlā, who is an evildoer and a pirate and a
79 robber of merchants. When we anchored at Fākanūr | the Sultan sent his son to stay on board the ship as a hostage. We went on shore to visit him and he treated us with the utmost hospitality for three nights, as a mark of respect for the Sultan of India and acknowledgement of what was due to him, and also from a desire to make some profit by trading with the personnel of our vessels. It is a custom of theirs that every ship that passes by a town must needs anchor at it and give a present to the ruler. This they call the 'right of *bandar*'.[30] If anyone omits to do this, they sail out in pursuit of him, bring him into the port by force, double the tax on him, and prevent him from proceeding on his journey for as long as they wish.

Three days after leaving Fākanūr we reached Manjarūr [Mangalore], a large town on the inlet called *Khaur al-Dunb*,
80 which is the largest inlet in the land of Mulaibār. | This is the town at which most of the merchants from Fārs and al-Yaman disembark, and pepper and ginger are exceedingly abundant there.

Account of the Sultan of Manjarūr. He is one of the principal rulers in that land, and his name is Rāma Daw.[31] There is a colony of about four thousand Muslims there, living in a suburb alongside the town. Warfare frequently breaks out between them and the townspeople, but the Sultan makes peace between them on account of his need of the merchants.

[29] Now Barkur.

[30] Mžik (p. 295, n. 75) argues that the word *bandar* in this phrase is not the common word for a port in Persian and Arabic, but is the Sanskrit *bhandara*, meaning a storehouse or treasury, and that the customs dues are intended.

[31] Ram Deo.

There is a qāḍī there, a distinguished and generous man of the Shāfi'ī *madhhab*, called Badr al-Dīn of al-Maʿbar, who also teaches religious science. He came on board the vessel to meet us and invited us to go ashore to visit his town, but we said: 'Not until the Sultan sends his son to stay on board the vessel.' He answered: 'This is done only by the Sultan of Fākanūr because the Muslims in his town are powerless, but as for us the Sultan | is afraid of us', but we refused to land 81
until the Sultan sent his son. When he had done so, as the previous Sultan had done, we went on shore and were treated by them with great consideration.

After staying with them for three days, we set sail for the town of Hīlī, which we reached two days later.[32] It is large and well-built, situated on a big bay which is navigable for large vessels. This is the farthest town reached by ships from China; they enter only this port, the port of Kawlam, and Qāliqūṭ. The town of Hīlī is venerated both by Muslims and infidels on account of its cathedral mosque, for it is of great blessedness, and resplendent with radiant light. Seafarers make many votive offerings to it,[33] and it has a rich treasury under the supervision of the preacher Ḥusain and the chief of the Muslim community, Ḥasan al-Wazzān. | In this mosque also there are 82
a number of students of religious science who receive stipends from its revenue, and it has a kitchen from which all travellers and the poor Muslims of the town are supplied with food. I met in this mosque a pious jurist from Maqdashaw,[34] called Saʿīd, of fine figure and character. He used to fast continually, and I was told that he had studied at Mecca for fourteen years and for the same length of time at al-Madīna, had met Abū Numayy the Amir of Mecca[35] and Manṣūr b. Jammāz, the Amir of al-Madīna, and had travelled in India and China.

We then continued our journey from Hīlī to the town of

[32] This name survives in that of Mount Dely. 'The medieval port is probably now represented by the village of Nileshwar, a few miles north of the promontory' (Gibb, *Selections*, p. 364, n. 14).

[33] There is a small mosque on the summit, which is a conspicuous landmark for sailors, and is visited by pilgrims.

[34] Mogadishu, in Somalia.

[35] Abū Numayy, ruler of Mecca 652–701/1254–1301. For an anecdote about him, see I, p. 223.

Jurfattan[36] between which and Hīlī there is a distance of three farsakhs. I met there a highly estimable jurist from Baghdād,
83 called al-Ṣarṣarī after the name of a township ten miles | from Baghdād on the Kūfa road, the name of which is the same as the Ṣarṣar in our country in the Maghrib. He had a brother in this city, a wealthy man with small children, who had died leaving them in his charge, and when I left he was preparing to take them to Baghdād. It is the custom of the people of India, like that of the negroes, not to interfere with the estate of any deceased person, even though he leaves thousands, but his property remains in the hands of the leader of the Muslim community until his legal inheritor takes it over.

Account of the Sultan of Jurfattan. He is called Kuwail, and is one of the most powerful Sultans of Mulaibār. He possesses a large fleet of vessels which sail to ʿOmān, Fārs, and al-Yaman, and his territories include Dahfattan and Budfattan[37] |
84 which we shall describe. We went on from Jurfattan to the town of Dahfattan which is a large town on an inlet with many orchards, in which there are coco-palms, pepper trees, areca palms and betel plants, as well as great quantities of colocasia which they cook along with meat. As for bananas, never have I seen any place in which they are more numerous or cheaper. At Dahfattan there is an immense *bā'in*, five hundred paces in length and three hundred in breadth, cased with red stones squared. On its sides are twenty-eight stone pavilions, each of which contains four stone loggias, and is approached by a flight of steps in stone. In the middle of the tank there is a large pavilion three stories high, with four loggias on each story. It was told me that it was the father of the present Sultan Kuwail who constructed this *bā'in*. Alongside it is a cathedral mosque of the Muslims, which has a flight of steps by which one goes down to the tank, and the people make
85 their ablutions | and bathe in it. The jurist Ḥusain told me that the builder of both the mosque and the *bā'in* was a certain

[36] Yule (*Cathay*, IV, p. 76) identifies it as 'probably' Cannanore, Mžik (p. 297, n. 79) as either Baliapatam or Cannanore, and Gibb (*Selections*, p. 234) as Cannanore, without comment. Yule connects the name given to the Sultan by I.B., Kuwail, with Kolatiri, the name of the Rajas of Cannanore.

[37] Dharmapatam and Puduppattana, of which the latter has disappeared from modern maps.

ancestor of Kuwail and that he was a Muslim whose conversion was due to a strange event which we shall relate here.

Account of the marvellous tree which is alongside the mosque. I saw that the mosque was by a tender green tree with leaves like fig leaves, but smooth, surrounded by a wall. Beside it was a *miḥrāb* in which I made a prayer of two *rakʿas*. This tree is known amongst them as *dirakht al shahādah*.[38] I was told there that in the autumn of each year a single leaf falls from this tree after it has turned first yellow and then red, and that written on it by the pen of the divine power there are the words *There is no god but | Allah, Muḥammad is the apostle of Allah.* The jurist 86
Ḥusain and a number of trustworthy persons told me that they had seen this leaf with their own eyes and had read that which was written on it. He told me also that at the time of its falling trustworthy persons from among both the Muslims and the infidels sit underneath the tree, and when the leaf falls the Muslims take half of it and the other half is placed in the treasury of the infidel Sultan, and they use it for the healing of the sick. This tree was the cause of the conversion to Islam of Kuwail's ancestor who constructed the mosque and the tank. He was able to read the Arabic script and when he read and understood the meaning of what was written on the leaf he embraced Islam and lived as a good Muslim. His story has been handed down amongst them by many witnesses. The jurist Ḥusain related to me that one of his sons reverted to idolatry after his father's death and governed with violence. He ordered | that the tree should be pulled out by the roots, 87
which was done so that no trace was left of it, and afterwards it sprouted up again and became as fine as it had ever been, and the infidel perished swiftly.

From there we continued our journey to the city of Budfattan, a large town on a large inlet. Outside it and close to the sea there is a mosque to which Muslim strangers repair, for there is no Muslim in this city. Its port is very fine indeed and its water is sweet; the areca nut grows there in profusion and is exported from it to India and China. The majority of its inhabitants are Brahmans, who are venerated amongst the

[38] 'The tree of testimony' (Persian).

infidels and who hate the Muslims, and it is for this reason that there is no Muslim living amongst them.

Anecdote. I was told that the reason why they leave this mosque undestroyed is that one of the Brahmans demolished its roof to
88 use it for a roof for his own house, | and afterwards his house caught fire and he and his children and his goods were all burnt up. So they respect this mosque and have not molested it since, but they serve it, placing outside it water from which all sorts of travellers may drink, and putting a net over its door so that the birds should not go into it.

From Budfattan we continued our journey to Fandaraynā [Panderani], a large and fine town with orchards and bazaars.[39] The Muslims occupy three quarters in it, each of which has a mosque. The cathedral mosque is on the sea front, a magnificent building with gazebos and loggias overlooking the sea. Its qāḍī and preacher is a man from ʿOmān, and he has a brother, a worthy man. It is at this town that the Chinese vessels pass the winter. Thence we travelled to the town of
89 Qāliqūṭ [Calicut], which is one of the chief ports in | Mulaibār. It is visited by men from China, Jāwa, Ceylon, the Maldives, al-Yaman and Fārs, and in it gather merchants from all quarters. Its harbour is one of the largest in the world.

Account of its Sultan. The Sultan of Qāliqūṭ is an infidel, known as '*the Sāmarī*'.[40] He is an aged man and shaves his beard, as some of the Greeks do. I saw him there and we shall speak of him later, if God will. The amir of the merchants there was Ibrāhīm Shāhbandar,[41] of the people of Baḥrain, a worthy man, of generous habits, at whose house the merchants used to gather and to eat at his table. The qāḍī of the place was Fakhr ad-Dīn ʿOthmān, a worthy and charitable man, and the superior of the hospice there was the shaikh Shihāb al-Dīn of Kāzarūn, to whom are paid the offerings made in vows by the people of India and China to the shaikh Abū Isḥāq al-

[39] Vasco da Gama anchored here before reaching Calicut; the site is now deserted.

[40] Malayalam *samutira* or *samuri*, a vernacular form of the Sanskrit for 'sea king', converted by the Portuguese into Samorin or Zamorin, which became the usual word in European languages.

[41] 'The title of ... the chief authority with whom foreign traders and shipmasters had to transact. He was often also head of the Customs' (*Hobson-Jobson*, s.v. Shahbunder). See above p. 808 n. 30.

Kāzarūnī, God profit us by him.[42] In this | town too lives the 90
famous shipowner Mithqāl, who possesses vast wealth and
many ships for his trade with India, China, al-Yaman, and
Fārs. When we reached the city, the *shāhbandar* Ibrāhīm, the
qāḍī, the Shaikh Shihāb-al-Dīn, the principal merchants and
the infidel Sultan's deputy, by the name of Qulaj, all came out
to welcome us, with drums, trumpets, bugles and standards
on their ships. We entered the harbour in great pomp, the like
of which I have never seen in those lands, but it was a joy to
be followed by distress. We stopped in the port of Qāliqūṭ, in
which there were at the time thirteen Chinese vessels, and
disembarked. Every one of us was lodged in a house, and we
stayed there three months as | the guests of the infidel, await- 91
ing the season of the voyage to China. On the sea of China
travelling is done in Chinese ships only, so we shall describe
their arrangements.

Description of the Chinese vessels. The Chinese vessels are of
three kinds; large ships called *junks*, middle sized ones called
zaws, and small ones called *kakams*.[43] The large ships have
anything from twelve down to three sails, which are made of
bamboo rods plaited like mats. They are never lowered, but
they turn them according to the direction of the wind; at
anchor they are left floating in the wind. A ship carries a
complement of a thousand men, six hundred of whom are
sailors and four hundred men-at-arms, | including archers, 92
men with shields and arbalists, that is men who throw naphtha.
Each large vessel is accompanied by three smaller ones, the
'half', the 'third', and the 'quarter'. These vessels are built
only in the town of Zaitūn in China [Ch'üan-chou], or in Ṣīn-Kalān, which is Ṣīn al-Ṣīn [Canton].

Their method of building the ships is to construct two walls of timber, the space between which they fill up with immensely large baulks of wood fastened both in length and breadth by huge nails each of which is three cubits in length. When the two walls are firmly joined together by these baulks they build

[42] See II, pp. 319–20 and n. 151. At Quilon I.B. was to stay at the hospice of shaikh Fakhr al-Dīn, the son of Shihāb al-Dīn (below, p. 818). He mentions another hospice of the same fraternity at Ch'üan-chou (below, p. 895).

[43] I.e. junk, dhow and *hoa-ch'üan* or trade ship. Cordier (Yule, *Cathay*, IV, p. 25 n. 1) suggests that *kakam* may be a corruption of old Italian *cocca*.

on top of them the bottom flooring of the vessel, and launch them into the sea, where they complete the construction of the ship. Since these baulks and side-walls remain in contact with the water, they go down to them in order to wash themselves and to relieve nature. At the sides of these baulks are their oars, which are as large as masts, ten or fifteen men
93 joining together to work each of them, | and they row standing on their feet. In the vessel they build four decks, and it has cabins, suites and salons for merchants; a set of rooms has several rooms and a latrine; it can be locked by its occupant, and he can take along with him slave-girls and wives. Often a man will live in his suite unknown to any of the others on board until they meet on reaching some town. The sailors have their children living on board ship, and they cultivate green stuffs, vegetables and ginger in wooden tanks. The owner's factor on board ship is like a great amir. When he goes on shore he is preceded by archers and Abyssinians with javelins, swords, drums, bugles and trumpets. On reaching the house where he is to stay they stand their lances on both
94 sides of the door, and continue thus | during his stay. Some of the Chinese own large numbers of ships on which their factors are sent to foreign countries. There is no people in the world wealthier than the Chinese.

Account of our preparations for the voyage to China, and how it all ended. When the time came for the voyage to China, the Sultan al-Sāmarī equipped for us one of the thirteen junks in the port of Qāliqūṭ. The factor on the junk was called Sulaimān of Ṣafad, in Syria. I had made his acquaintance previously and I said to him: 'I want a set to myself because of the slave-girls, for it is my habit never to travel without them.' He replied: 'The merchants from China have hired the sets for the outward and return journey. My son-in-law has one which
95 I can give you, but it has no lavatory; | perhaps you may be able to exchange it for another.' So I ordered my companions to take on board all my effects, and the male and female slaves embarked on the junk. This was on a Thursday, and I stayed on shore in order to attend the Friday prayers and join them afterwards. The malik Sunbul and Ẓahīr al-Dīn also went on board with the present. Early on the Friday morning a slave-boy I had named Hilāl came to me and said that the set we had

taken on the junk was small and unsuitable. When I spoke of this to the captain he said: 'It cannot be helped, but if you like to transfer to the *kakam* there are sets of rooms on it at your choice.' I agreed to this and gave orders accordingly to my companions, who transferred the slave-girls and effects to the *kakam* and were settled in it before the hour of the Friday prayer.

Now it is usual for this sea to become stormy every day in
the late afternoon, and no one can embark then. | The junks 96
had already set sail, and none of them were left but the one which contained the present, another junk whose owners had decided to pass the winter at Fandaraynā, and the *kakam* referred to. We spent the Friday night on the seashore, we unable to embark on the *kakam*, and those on board unable to disembark and join us. I had nothing left but a carpet to spread out. On the Saturday morning the junk and *kakam* were both at a distance from the port, and the junk whose owners were making for Fandaraynā was driven ashore and broken in pieces. Some of those who were on board died and some escaped. In it there was a slave-girl who belonged to one of the merchants, and a favourite of his. He offered to give ten dinars in gold to anyone who would rescue her (for she had clung to a spar in the stern of the junk). A sailor from Hurmuz undertook to do it, and brought her ashore but would not take
the dinars, saying: 'I did this only | for the sake of God.' 97

That night the sea struck the junk which carried the Sultan's present, and all on board died. In the morning we went to the scene of their disaster; I saw Ẓahīr ad-Dīn with his head smashed and his brains scattered, and the malik Sunbul had a nail driven through one of his temples and coming out at the other, and having prayed over them we buried them. I saw the infidel, the Sultan of Qāliqūṭ, wearing a large white cloth round his waist, folded over from his navel down to his knee, and with it a small turban on his head, bare-footed, with the parasol carried by a slave over his head and a fire lit in front of him on the beach; his police officers were beating the people to prevent them from plundering what the sea cast up. In all the lands of Mulaibār, except in this one land alone, it is the custom that whenever a ship is wrecked all that is taken from it belongs to the treasury. At Qāliqūṭ, however, it is retained

by its owners, and for that reason Qāliqūṭ has become a
98 flourishing and | much frequented city. When those on the *kakam* saw what had happened to the junk they spread their sails and went off, with all my goods and slave-boys and slave-girls on board, leaving me alone on the beach with but one slave whom I had enfranchised. When he saw what had befallen me he deserted me, and I had nothing left with me at all except the ten dinars that the *jūgī* had given me and the carpet I had used to spread out.

As I was told that the *kakam* would have to put in at the port of Kawlam,[44] I decided to travel thither, it being a ten days' journey either by land or by the river, if anyone prefers that route.[45] I set out therefore by the river, and hired one of the Muslims to carry the carpet for me. Their custom when travelling on that river is to disembark in the evening and pass the night in the villages on its banks, returning to the boat in the
99 morning. | We used to do this too. There was no Muslim on the boat except the man I had hired, and he used to drink wine with the infidels when we went ashore and annoy me with his brawling, which made things all the worse for me. On the fifth day of our journey we came to Kunjī-Karī, which is on top of a hill there;[46] it is inhabited by Jews, who have one of their own number as their governor, and pay a poll-tax to the Sultan of Kawlam.

Account of the cinnamon and brazil trees. All the trees along this river are cinnamon and brazil trees. They use them for firewood in these parts and we used to light fires with them to cook our food on this journey.

On the tenth day we reached the city of Kawlam [Quilon], one of the finest towns in the Mulaibār lands. It has fine
100 bazaars, and its merchants are called Ṣūlīs.[47] | They are

[44] Quilon.

[45] It is not possible to make the entire journey by inland waterways.

[46] On the Jewish communities in Kerala, see J. B. Segal, *A History of the Jews of Cochin*, London, 1993. Professor Segal writes: 'Kunjakari has been plausibly identified with the section of the river called Kanjirapuzha to the east of the island of Chennamangalam where there was a very old Jewish settlement' (p. 10).

[47] '*Chulia* is a name given in Ceylon and in Malabar to a particular class of Mahommedans, and sometimes to Mahommedans generally. There is much obscurity about the origin and proper application of the term' (*Hobson-Jobson*, s.v. Choolia).

immensely wealthy; a single merchant will buy a vessel with all that is in it and load it with goods from his own house. There is a colony of Muslim merchants there, the chief of whom is ʿAlāʾ al-Dīn al-Āwajī, from Āwa in al-ʿIraq.[48] He is a Rāfiḍī,[49] and has a number of associates belonging to his sect, and they proclaim it openly. The qāḍī of the town is a worthy man from Qazwīn, and the head of the Muslim community there is Muḥammad Shāhbandar, who has a worthy and open-handed brother named Taqī al-Dīn. The cathedral mosque is a magnificent building, constructed by the merchant Khwāja Muhadhdhab. This city is the nearest of the Mulaibār towns to China and it is to it that most of the merchants [from China] come. Muslims are honoured and respected there.

Account of its Sultan. The Sultan of Kawlam is an infidel called
Tīrawarī;[50] | he respects the Muslims and he judges severely 101
thieves and profligates.

Anecdote. Amongst the events which I witnessed at Kawlam was the following. One of the Iraqi archers killed another and then fled to the house of al-Āwajī. He was a man of considerable wealth, and when the Muslims wished to bury the murdered man the Sultan's officers stopped them saying: 'He cannot be buried until you deliver his murderer to us that he may be put to death for him.' They left him in his coffin at al-Āwajī's gate until he stank and decomposed, whereupon al-Āwajī gave them possession of the murderer and desired them to let him go alive in return for surrendering his properties to them. But they refused to accept this and put him to death and thereafter the murdered man was buried. |

Anecdote. I was told that the Sultan of Kawlam rode out into 102
the environs of the town one day. His road lay between the orchards, and he had with him his son-in-law, his daughter's husband, one of the sons of the maliks. This man picked up a mango which had fallen from one of the orchards. The Sultan

[48] Aveh in Persia.

[49] I.e. Turncoats, a pejorative word applied to some Shīʿīs, and on occasion to Shīʿīs in general. The Muslims of Kerala are now Sunnīs, but names like the Karbalāʾ Maidān in Quilon may indicate the presence of a Shīʿī community in the past.

[50] A title, perhaps meaning 'sacred lord', rather than a personal name.

was watching him and gave orders that he should be cut in two on the spot. He was divided into two halves and each half was put on a cross on the right and on the left of the road and the mango also was cut in two, one half of it being placed above each half of him, and he was left there as an example to the beholders.

Anecdote. There was an incident of the same kind at Qāliqūṭ, when the brother's son of the Sultan's deputy forcibly seized a sword belonging to one of the Muslim merchants. The mer-
103 chant laid a complaint before his uncle | who promised him to investigate his case. He sat down at the gate of his house; and by-and-bye his nephew appeared wearing that sword, whereupon he called him and said: 'This is the sword of the Muslim.' He replied: 'Yes.' He said: 'Did you buy it from him?', and when his nephew said 'No' he bade his guards seize him, and then gave orders that he should be executed with that very sword.

I stayed at Kawlam for some time in the hospice of the shaikh Fakhr al-Dīn, son of the shaikh Shihāb al-Dīn of Kāzarūn, the shaikh of the hospice of Qāliqūṭ,[51] but heard no news of the *kakam*. During my stay there the ambassadors from the king of China who had been with us arrived there also. They had embarked on one of the junks which was wrecked like the others. The Chinese merchants provided them with clothes and they returned to China, where I met them again later.

I intended at first to return from Kawlam to the Sultan to
104 tell him what | had happened to the present, but afterwards I was afraid that he would find fault with what I had done and ask me why I had not stayed with the present. I determined therefore to return to Sultan Jamāl al-Dīn of Hinawr and stay with him until I should obtain news of the *kakam*. So I went back to Qāliqūṭ and found there a vessel belonging to the Sultan [of India], on which he had despatched an Arab amir known as the sayyid Abu'l-Ḥasan. He was one of the *bard-dārs*, that is the private door-keepers,[52] whom the Sultan had despatched with sums of money with which to enlist in his

[51] See above, p. 812.
[52] For Persian *pardehdār*, a chamberlain.

service all whom he could of the Arabs from the land of
Hurmuz and al-Qaṭīf,[53] because of his affection for the Arabs.
I went to visit this amir and found him decided to winter at
Qāliqūṭ, after which he would continue his journey to the land
of the Arabs. I asked him to advise me about returning to the
Sultan and he did not support this suggestion, so I travelled
with him in his ship from Qāliqūṭ. It was then the end of the
season for voyaging, | and we used to sail only during the first 105
half of the day, then anchor until the next day. We met four
fighting vessels on our way and were afraid of them but after
all they did us no harm. On reaching Hinawr, I went ashore to
visit the Sultan and saluted him; he assigned me a lodging,
but without a servant, and asked me to recite the prayers with
him. I spent most of my time in his mosque and used to read
the Qur'ān through every day, and later twice a day, beginning the first recital after the dawn prayer and ending it in the
early afternoon, then after making fresh ablutions I would
begin the second recital and end it about sunset. I continued
to do this for the space of three months, during which I went
into retreat for forty days. |

Account of our going out on an expedition and conquest of Sandābūr. 106
Sultan Jamāl al-Dīn had fitted out fifty-two vessels for an
expedition to attack Sandābūr [Goa]. A quarrel had broken out
there between the Sultan and his son, and the latter had
written to Jamāl al-Dīn inviting him to seize the town and
promising to accept Islam and marry his sister. When the ships
were made ready it occurred to me to set out with them to the
Holy War, so I opened the Qur'ān to take an augury, and
found at the top of the page: '*In them is the name of God
frequently mentioned, and verily God will aid those who aid Him.*'[54]
I took this as a good omen, and when the Sultan came for the
afternoon prayer I said to him: 'I wish to join the expedition.'
'In that case', he replied, 'you will be their commander.' I
related to him the incident of my augury from the Qur'ān,
which so delighted him that he resolved to join the expedition
| himself, though previously he had not intended to do so. He 107
embarked on one of the vessels, I being with him, on a

[53] See II, p. 410 and n. 145, where I.B. specifies the unusual spelling al-Quṭaif.
[54] Qur'ān, sūra xxii, 40.

Saturday, and we reached Sandābūr on the Monday evening. When we entered its bay, we found its inhabitants prepared for the battle, with mangonels already set up. So we spent that night near the place, and on the next morning, when the drums, trumpets and bugles were sounded, the vessels moved in to the attack, and the defenders bombarded them with the mangonels. I saw a stone hit one of the men who was standing close to the Sultan. The men on the ships jumped into the water, shields and sword in hand, and the Sultan went down into an *ʿukairī*, which is like a *shillīr*.[55] I too jumped into the water with the rest of the men. We had with us two tartans, open at the stern, carrying horses; they are so constructed that the horseman mounts his horse inside the vessel, puts on his
108 armour and comes out. | They did this and God permitted its conquest and sent down victory to the Muslims. We entered the city at the point of the sword and the greater part of the infidels took refuge in their Sultan's palace, but when we set fire to it they came out and we seized them. The Sultan thereafter gave them quarter and restored their wives and children to them. They were about ten thousand in number and he assigned to them as residence a suburb of the town and himself occupied the palace, giving the houses in its neighbourhood to his courtiers. He gave me a Marhata (?) slave-girl called Lamkī – I called her Mubāraka, and when her husband wished to ransom her I refused – and also gave me a *farajīya*[56] of Egyptian manufacture which was found in the treasuries of the infidel.

I stayed with him at Sandābūr from the day of its capture, which was the 13th of Jumādā I, until the middle of Shaʿbān;[57] I then asked him for permission to travel and he made me
109 promise to return to him. So I sailed | to Hinawr, continued thence to Fākanūr, Manjarūr, Hīlī, Jurfattan, Dahfattan, Budfattan, Fandaraynā and Qāliqūṭ – all of which places have been mentioned above – and finally to al-Shāliyāt, a most beautiful town, in which the fabrics called by its name are

[55] Dozy (*Supplément*, s.v.) defines *ʿukairi* as 'sorte de grande galère' and *shillīr* as 'espèce de barque'; the boat in question was evidently of shallow draught.

[56] An ample robe to wear over other clothing.

[57] I.e. from 15 October 1342 to mid January 1343.

manufactured.[58] After a long stay in this town I returned to Qāliqūṭ. Two slaves who had been with me on the *kakam* arrived at Qāliqūṭ and told me that the slave-girl who had been pregnant, and on whose account I was much upset, had died, and that the ruler of Jāwa had taken the rest of my slave-girls, that my goods had been seized by various hands, and that my companions were scattered to China, Jāwa and Bengal. On hearing this I returned to Hinawr and thence to Sandābūr, reaching it at the end of Muḥarram, and I stayed there until the 2nd of RabīʿII.[59]

The infidel Sultan of Sandābūr, | from whom we had cap- 110
tured the town, now advanced to recapture it. All the infidels fled to join him, and the Sultan's troops, who were dispersed in the [outlying] villages, abandoned us. We were besieged by the infidels and reduced to great straits. When the situation became serious, I left the town during the siege and returned to Qāliqūṭ, where I decided to travel to Dhībat al-Mahal, of which I had heard.

[58] Chaliyam, opposite Beypur on the south side of the river of that name. Many fabrics of different kinds were made there, and there are many kinds with names recalling the place, but their precise identity has not been established (*Hobson-Jobson*, s.v. Chalia, and Mžik, p. 314, n. 102).

[59] I.e. from 24 June to 24 August 1343. These dates cannot be reconciled with his statement (below, p. 846) that he left the Maldives on 26 August 1344.

CHAPTER XVII

The Maldives

Ten days after embarking at Qāliqūṭ we reached the islands of Dhībat al-Mahal [the Maldives] (*Dhība* being pronounced like the feminine of *dhīb*).[2] These islands are one of the wonders of the world and number about two thousand in all.[3] Each hundred or less of them form a circular cluster resembling a ring, this ring having one entrance like a gateway, and only through this entrance can ships reach the islands.[4] When a vessel arrives at any one of them it must
111 needs take one of the inhabitants | to pilot it to the other
islands. They are so close-set that on leaving one island the tops of the palms on another are visible. If a ship loses its course it is unable to enter and is carried by the wind to al-Maʿbar or to Ceylon.

The inhabitants of the Maldives are all of them Muslims, pious and upright. The islands are divided into twelve districts, each under a governor whom they call the *kardūī*.[5]

[1] I.B.'s description of the Maldives is of great interest, being far more detailed than any earlier surviving account. Early notices of the islands, including I.B.'s, were collected and translated by Albert Gray, assisted by H. C. P. Bell, in Appendix A to their translation of the narrative of François Pyrard of Laval, published by the Hakluyt Society, 1887–90. In the notes to this chapter their spellings of Maldivian words have been adopted except that long vowels have been indicated by a macron instead of an acute accent. I am grateful to Mr C. H. B. Reynolds (hereafter C.H.B.R.) for much help with some of the notes to this and the following chapter.

[2] *Dhi'b* is the Arabic word for a wolf, or, in Africa, a jackal; *dhībat* is from Sanskrit *dvīpa* 'island'.

[3] The number of islands has been variously estimated, some being mere sandbanks which may be temporarily submerged; rather more than 200 are inhabited.

[4] The islands are coral atolls raised on a submarine ridge.

[5] 'The Divehi (Maldivian) word is *karudā-veri*, an old equivalent of the modern *atoḷu-veri* or atoll chief' (C.H.B.R.).

Amongst the districts are Pālipūr, Kannalūs, Mahal (which has given its name to the whole archipelago, and in which is the residence of their Sultans), Talādīb, Karāydū, Al-Taim, Taladummatī, | Haladummatī, Baraidū, Kandakal, Mulūk, and 112
Suwaid, which is the most remote of them.[6] There is no agriculture at all on any of the islands, except that a cereal resembling *anly*[7] is grown in the district of Suwaid and carried thence to Mahal. The inhabitants live on a fish resembling the *līrūn*,[8] which they call *qulb al-mās*;[9] it has red flesh and no grease, and smells like mutton. On catching it, they cut the fish in four, cook it lightly, then smoke it in palm-leaf baskets. When it is quite dry, they eat it. Some of these fish are exported to India, China and al-Yaman. |

Description of their trees. Most of the trees on these islands are 113
coco-palms, and they provide food for the inhabitants along with fish. We have already spoken of the coco-palm. These trees are quite extraordinary; each palm bears twelve bunches a year, one coming out every month; some are small, some large, some dry and some green, it is always so. They make milk, oil and honey from it, as we have related in the first journey. From its honey they make sweetmeats which they eat along with the dried coconut. All these products of the coco-palm and the fish which they live on have an amazing and unparalleled effect in sexual intercourse, and the people of these islands perform wonders in this respect. I had there

[6] Gray and Bell identified these as Fādiffolu, Kinalos, Mālē, Nilandū, Kārhidu, Utimu, Tiladummati, Haddumati, Falidu, Kedīkolu, Mulaku, and Suadiva: *The Voyage of François Pyrard*, II, p. 457, n. 3. These are all atolls except Kārhidu, Utimu and Kedīkolu, which are islands; they suggest that I.B. used the name of the most important island for the whole atoll. They see his Talādīb as a copyist's error for Nilādīb, itself standing for Nilandū. They also note that Utimu island is in Tiladummati atoll, which is listed separately. I.B. later states (pp. 833–4) that he landed in Kannalūs and then sailed by way of al-Taim to Mālē. They remark that this would be a circuitous route, Utimu lying well to the north of Kinalos and Mālē to the south. However, I.B. did not hire his own vessel but took ship with someone who may well have had reasons of his own for going to Utimu.

[7] A Berber word for a small-grained millet. In West Africa I.B. probably refers to *Pennisetum typhoideum*, here to *Panicum miliaceum* or *Setaria italica* both of which grow in the southern atolls.

[8] D. and S. read *līrūn* but note that MS Bib. Nat. 910 reads *l. bīrūn*, which is certainly the better reading, representing the Berber word for the tunny fish. See E. Destaing, *Vocabulaire français-berbère*, Paris, 1935, under *poisson* and *thon*.

[9] Maldivian *kaḷu bili mas*, i.e. black bonito, *Scomber pelamis* L.

myself four wives, and concubines as well, and I used to visit
114 all of them every day and pass the night with | the wife whose turn it was, and this I continued to do the whole year and a half that I was there.

Among their trees also are the *jamūn*,[10] the citron, orange and colocasia.[11] From the roots of this last they grind a flour, with which they make vermicelli, and they cook this in the milk of the coconut. This is one of the most delicious dishes; I was very fond of it, and used to eat it often.

Account of the people of these islands, and of some of their customs, and description of their dwellings. The people of these islands are upright and pious, sound in belief, and sincere in purpose; they keep to lawful foods, and their prayers are answered. When one of them sees a man he says to him: 'God is my Lord and Muḥammad my Prophet, and I am an ignorant and miserable creature.' Their bodies are weak, they are unused to fighting and warfare, and their armour is prayer. Once when I
115 ordered | a thief's hand to be cut off, a number of those who were in the room fainted. The Indian pirates do not raid or molest them, as they have learned from experience that anyone who seizes anything from them speedily meets misfortune. When the enemies' ships come this way, they seize any whom they find other than the natives, but do not offer any injury to any of the latter. If one of the idolaters takes but a single lemon, the chief of the infidels punishes him and beats him severely through fear of the consequences of that action. Were it not for this they would be the easiest prey for those who should come to fight them because of the weakness of their physique. In each island of theirs there are beautiful mosques, and most of their buildings are made of wood. They are very cleanly and avoid filth; most of them bathe twice a day to cleanse themselves, because of the extreme heat there and their profuse perspiration. They make plentiful use of |
116 perfumed oils, such as oil of sandalwood, and they smear themselves with *ghāliya* brought from Maqdashaw.[12] It is their custom when they have prayed the dawn prayer that every

[10] *Eugenia jambolana*.

[11] The reference is to *Dioscorea oppositifolia*, Maldivian *hittala*, not to a colocasia.

[12] A perfume of musk and ambergris.

woman comes to her husband or her son, bringing the antimony jar, rose water and *ghāliya*; she then paints his eyes with the antimony so that his skin shines and the traces of fatigue are removed from his face. Their garments are simply aprons; they tie one round their waists in place of trousers, and on their backs they place cloths called *al-wilyān*, resembling the *iḥrām* garments.[13] Some wear a turban, others a small kerchief instead. When any of them meets the qāḍī or preacher, he removes his cloth from his shoulders, uncovering his back, and accompanies him thus to his house. |

It is one of their customs that when one of their men marries 117
and goes to his wife's house, cotton cloths are spread on the ground for him from the outer door of her house to her chamber, and on them, to right and to left of his way to the chamber, are placed handfuls of cowries. The woman is standing at the door of her apartment awaiting him, and when he comes to her she throws over his feet a garment, which is taken by his servants. Should it be the woman who goes to the man's place of residence, his house is carpeted in the same way with cowries placed on the cloths, and when she reaches him the woman throws the garment over his feet.[14] The same custom is observed by them in saluting the Sultan; each one must throw a garment on that occasion, as we shall describe later.

Their buildings are of wood and they raise the floors of their houses high above the ground as a protection from the damp, for their soil is humid. Their procedure in doing so is | to cut 118
stones, each of them two or three cubits long, and lay them in rows, and to place upon these transversely planks of coco-palms, and then make the walls of planks. They show a remarkable skill in this. In the vestibule of the house is a room which they call the *mālam*, where the owner sits with his friends.[15] This *mālam* has two doors, one of them opening on the vestibule, by which his visitors come in. At the entrance to

[13] Gray and Bell suggest that this is probably a corruption of Maldivian *fèliya*, waist cloth. The *iḥrām* refers to the seamless garments worn by pilgrims at Mecca.

[14] Evidently at this time two kinds of marriage practised in Ceylon were also prevalent in the Maldives. In one the groom went to the bride's house, which became the marital home and remained her property; in the other the bride went to the groom's house and the situation was reversed.

[15] Not identified. 'Reception rooms are currently called *aṛī*' (C.H.B.R.).

this room is a jar filled with water and a scoop of coconut shell which they call *walanj*, with a handle two cubits long.[16] They use this scoop to draw water from the wells because of their shallowness. All of them high or low, are bare-footed; their lanes are kept swept and clean and are shaded by trees, so that
119 to walk in them is like walking in an orchard. In spite of | that, every person entering a house must wash his feet with water from the jar kept at the entrance to the *mālam*, and wipe them with a rough towel of fibre matting which he finds there, after which he enters the room. The same practice is followed on entering a mosque.

It is a custom of theirs when a vessel arrives at their island that *kanādir*, that is to say small boats, go out to meet them,[17] loaded with people from the island carrying betel and *karanbah*, that is green coconuts.[18] Each man of them gives these to anyone whom he chooses on board the vessel, and that person becomes his guest and carries his goods to his host's house as though he were one of his relatives. Any of the visitors who wishes to marry may do so, but when it is time for him to leave he divorces the woman, because their women never leave the country. If a visitor does not marry, the woman in the house
120 where he lodges | cooks for him, serves him and gives him provisions when he sets out on his journey. In return for that she is content to receive from him the smallest pittance of charity. The profit of the treasury (which they call the *bandar*)[19] consists in its purchase at a fixed rate of a proportion of every kind of merchandise in the vessel, whether the goods are worth that or more than that; they call this the 'right of the *bandar*'. In every island there is a *bandar* house made of wood, which they call the *bajanṣār*,[20] and in which the governor, who is called the *kardūrī*,[21] stores all the goods, and buys and sells

[16] 'There is a Sinhalese word *valaňda* or *valanj*, meaning a cooking vessel . . . A well-scoop is now called *dāni*' (C.H.B.R.).

[17] An Arabic plural of *kundura*. 'The word is, or was, used in Sinhalese for a Maldivian boat, but not, as far as I am aware, in Maldivian . . . The normal Maldivian word for a sailing boat is *oḍi* or *dōni*' (C.H.B.R.).

[18] Maldivian *kuruňbā*.

[19] Sanskrit *bhānḍāra*, 'storehouse', 'treasury', which I.B. has confused with Persian *bandar*, 'port'. (Mžik, p. 295, n. 75.)

[20] For *bangaṣār* (*Hobson-Jobson*, s.v. Bankshall).

[21] Previously written *kardūī*, p. 822.

with them. The people buy pottery, when it is brought to them, with chickens, so that a cooking pot is sold amongst them for five or six chickens.

From these islands there are exported by ship the fish we have mentioned, coconuts, waist cloths, *wilyān*, and cotton turbans, as well as brass utensils, of which they have a great
many, | cowrie shells and *qanbar*.[22] This is the hairy integu- 121
ment of the coconut, which they tan in pits on the shore, and afterwards beat out with bars; the women then spin it and it is made into cords for sewing [the planks of] ships together. These cords are exported to India, China, and al-Yaman, and are better than hemp. The Indian and Yemenite ships are sewn together with them, for that sea is full of reefs, and if a ship is nailed with iron nails it breaks up on striking the rocks, whereas if it is sewn together with cords, it is given a certain resilience and does not fall to pieces.

The inhabitants of these islands use cowrie shells as money. This is an animal which they gather in the sea and put into pits there where its flesh disappears, leaving its white shell. They call a hundred of these by the name of *siyāh*, and seven
hundred by the name of *fāl*, | twelve thousand *kuttā* and a 122
hundred thousand *bustū*.[23] They buy and sell with these at the rate of four *bustūs* for a gold dinar, but they often fall in value to ten *bustūs* for a dinar. They sell them in exchange for rice to the people of Bengal, who also use them as money, as well as to the Yemenites, who use them instead of sand [as ballast] in their ships. These cowries are used also by the negroes in their lands; I saw them being sold at Māllī and Gawgaw at the rate of 1,150 for a dinar.[24]

Account of their women. Their womenfolk do not cover their
heads, not even at one side. | Most of them wear only one 123
apron from the navel to the ground, the rest of their bodies being uncovered. It is thus that they walk abroad in the bazaars and elsewhere. When I was qāḍī there, I tried to put an end to this practice and ordered them to wear clothes, but I met with no success. No woman was admitted to my presence in a lawsuit unless her body was covered, but apart from

[22] The Arabic form of the Tamil *kayiṛu* (*Hobson Jobson*, s.v. 'Coir).

[23] Maldivian *hiya*, *fālē*, *kottē* and *bastā*.

[24] Mali and Gao, which I.B. visited in West Africa.

that I was unable to effect anything.[25] Some of them wear shirts in addition to the waistcloth, their shirts having short and wide sleeves. I had some slave-girls who wore garments like those worn at Dihlī and who covered their heads, but it was more of a disfigurement than an ornament in their case, since they were not accustomed to it.

The women's ornaments consist of bracelets, of which each woman wears so many on her forearm as to cover the arm from wrist-bone to elbow. They are made of silver, and no one wears
124 bracelets of gold | except the Sultan's wives and relatives. They wear anklets also, which they call *bāyil*,[26] and necklaces of gold on their chests, and these they call *basdarad*.[27] A singular custom amongst them is to hire themselves out as servants in houses at a fixed wage of five dinars or less, their employer being responsible for their upkeep; they do not look upon this as dishonourable, and most of their girls do so. You will find ten or twenty of them in a rich man's house. Every utensil that a girl breaks is charged up against her. When she wishes to transfer from one house to another, her new employers give her the sum which she owes to her former employers; she pays this to the latter and remains so much in debt to her
125 new employers. The chief occupation of these | hired women is spinning *qanbar*.

It is easy to get married in these islands on account of the smallness of the dowries and the pleasure of their women's society. The majority of people do not specify a dowry; only the act is witnessed and a wedding gift conformable to the bride's station is given. When ships arrive the crews marry wives and when they want to sail they divorce them; it is really a sort of temporary marriage, and the women never leave their country. I have never found in the world any women more agreeable to consort with than they are. Amongst these people the woman never entrusts the service of her husband to anyone but herself; it is she who brings him his food and removes it from his presence, who washes his hand and brings him the

[25] By the time of Pyrard's stay in the Maldives female dress approximated to I.B's minimum requirements.

[26] Mr Reynolds suggests that, as Maldivian formerly used *p* where it now has *f*, there might have been a word like *pai aḷa*, which could mean 'worn on the feet'.

[27] Not identified.

water for his ablutions, and who covers his feet when he
sleeps. It is one of their customs that the woman does not eat
with her husband, nor does the man even know what she eats.
I married several women there, and some of them ate with me
after some effort on my part, | but some of them never did so, 126
nor was I able to see them eating and no ruse of mine for this
purpose succeeded.

*Account of the reason for the conversion to Islam of the inhabitants of
these islands and of the evil spirits of the jinn which used to do injury
to them every month.* A number of trustworthy persons among
the population such as the jurist ʿĪsā of al-Yaman, the jurist
and teacher ʿAlī, the qāḍī ʿAbdallāh and others told me that
these islanders were infidels[28] and that every month there
would appear to them an evil spirit of the jinn, coming from
the direction of the sea and resembling a ship filled with
lights. On seeing him it was their custom to take a virgin girl
and, after dressing her in finery, to conduct her to the
Budkhānah,[29] that is the idol-temple, which was built on the
seashore and had a window looking out on the sea. There they
would leave her | for a night and when they came back in the 127
morning they would find her violated and dead. So they went
on drawing lots every month amongst themselves, and the one
on whom the lot fell gave up his daughter. Then there came
amongst them a man from the Maghrib called Abu'l Barakāt
al-Barbarī, who could recite by heart the Holy Qur'ān, and he
lodged in the house of an old woman of their people in the
island of Mahal. One day when he visited her he found that
she had called together all her kinswomen and they were
weeping as though they were at a funeral ceremony. He asked
them what was the matter with them but they did not explain
it to him. Then an interpreter came and told him that the lot
had fallen on the old woman, and she had but one daughter
whom the evil spirit would kill. Abu'l Barakāt said to her: 'I
shall go in place of your daughter tonight', for he was beardless, having no hair at all on his face. So they took him that
night and brought him into the *Budkhānah*, he having previously made his ablutions, and he stayed there reciting the

[28] The Maldivians were formerly Buddhists.

[29] Persian. *Bud*, from Buddha, is widely used in Islamic languages for an idol.

Qur'ān. Then the evil spirit appeared to him from the window
but he continued his recitation and when the spirit came so
128 near as to hear the recital | he plunged into the sea. In the
morning the Maghribī was still occupied in his recitation when
the old woman came with her kinsfolk and the people of the
island to bring out the girl, as they had been accustomed to
do, and burn her body. They found the Maghribī reciting,
took him to their king who was called Shanūrāza, and told the
latter his story. The king was astonished at it and when the
Maghribī expounded Islam to him and interested him in it he
replied: 'Stay with us until the next month; then if you repeat
this action and escape the evil spirit I shall become a Muslim.'
So he stayed with them and God opened the breast of the king
to Islam and he was converted before the end of the month,
and his children and his court also.[30]

When the next month opened the Maghribī was taken to
the *Budkhānah*, but the demon did not come; he continued to
recite the Qur'ān till dawn, and when the Sultan came along
with the people and found him occupied in recitation they
129 broke up the idols and destroyed the *Budkhānah*. | The popu-
lation of the island embraced Islam and sent word to all the
other islands, whose populations were converted also. The
Maghribi settled down among them, greatly venerated, and
they adopted his rite, namely the rite of the Imam Mālik, may
God be pleased with him,[31] and to this day they continue to
hold the Maghribīs in high respect because of him. He built a

[30] There is confusion about the conversion of the Maldives to Islam. The *Ta'rīkh*, the history of the islands from then to 1821, is accessible only in Bell's abridged translation. It ascribes the conversion to miracles performed by Shaikh Yūsuf Shams al-Dīn of Tabrīz and gives the date as 12 Rabīʿ II 548, i.e. July 1153. A wooden inscription in Arabic from the Hukuru Miskit, the Friday mosque, in Male attributes the conversion to Abu'l Barakāt Yūsuf of Tabrīz and gives the same year and month. Confusion between Barbarī and Tabrīzī would not be inconceivable in Arabic MSS. (Andrew D. W. Forbes, 'The Mosque in the Maldive Islands; a Preliminary Historical Survey', *Archipel*, 26, 1983, where a photograph of the inscription is reproduced.) No Maldivian Sultan named Shanūrāza is recorded. The inscription in the Hukuru Miskit refers to the role of the Wazīr Shanfiraz ʿAlī ibn Abi'l Faraj al-Ṣalāḥī in the reconstruction of the mosque in 738/1338. Mr Reynolds reads the name as Shanavirāzā and connects it with the Sinhalese *senevirājā*, 'Commander-in-chief'. The first Muslim Sultan was Muḥammad al-ʿĀdil, 'the just'.

[31] As Mr Forbes has noted, if Abu'l Barakāt came from the Maghrib and not from Tabrīz it is probable that he was a Mālikī.

mosque which is known by his name and I read the following words on the grille (*maqṣūrah*) of the cathedral mosque carved in wood: 'The Sultan Aḥmad Shanūrāza accepted Islam at the hand of Abu'l Barakāt al-Barbarī al-Maghribī.'[32] This Sultan assigned the third of the tax receipts of the islands as alms for travellers, since it was through them that his conversion to Islam had happened, and for that reason his name is remembered to the present day.

On account of that demon many of these islands were
uninhabited before the introduction of Islam. When we came
to them I was still ignorant of this event. One night when I was
engaged in some business or other I heard the people shouting
tahlīls and *takbīrs*[33] and saw | the boys carrying copies of the 130
Qur'ān on their heads and the women beating on basins and
copper utensils. Greatly astonished at all this I asked what was
afoot and they said: 'Just look out to sea', so I looked and there
was something like a great ship which seemed as though it were
full of lamps and torches. They said: 'That is the demon, whose
habit it is to appear once a month, but when we do what you
have seen he goes away without doing any harm to us.'

Account of the Sultana of these islands. It is a strange thing about
these islands that their ruler is a woman, Khadīja, daughter of
the Sultan Jalāl al-Dīn ʿOmar, son of the Sultan Ṣalāḥ al-Dīn
Ṣāliḥ of Bengal. The sovereignty belonged to her grandfather,
then to her father, and after his death to her brother Shihāb al-
Dīn, who was a minor. The Wazīr ʿAbdallāh b. Muḥammad
of Haḍramaut married | his mother and took control of him.
This is the same ʿAbdallāh who married also the present 131
Sultana Khadīja after the death of her [first] husband, the
Wazīr Jamāl al-Dīn, as we shall relate. When Shihāb al-Dīn
came to manhood he drove out his father-in-law, the Wazīr
ʿAbdallāh, exiled him to the islands of al-Suwaid and ruled
as sole sovereign.[34] As Wazīr he appointed one of his dependants [mawālī] named ʿAlī Kalakī,[35] whom he afterwards

[32] This may be the inscription published by Mr Forbes despite the discrepancies. The reigning Sultan at the time of I.B.'s visit was Aḥmad Shihāb al-Dīn.

[33] The formulas 'There is no God but God' and 'God is most great'.

[34] I.B.'s narrative is confirmed by the *Ta'rīkh* except that Ṣalāḥ al-Dīn of Bengal is not named, Jalāl al-Dīn ʿOmar is called Umaru-vīru and Khadīja is called Rehendi Kambādikilagē.

[35] Kilage, a Maldivian title implying authority, Pyrard's *Quilague*.

removed from office three years later and exiled also to al-Suwaid. It is told of this Sultan Shihāb ad-Dīn that he used to frequent the wives of his nobles and chief courtiers at night, on account of which they deposed him, exiled him to the region of Haladutanī,[36] and sent someone there who killed him.

None of the royal house was now left but his sisters Khadīja the eldest, and Maryam and Fāṭima, so they raised Khadīja to the throne. She was married to their preacher,[37] and promoted
132 his son | Muḥammad to the office of preacher in his place, but orders are executed in her name only. They write the orders on palm leaves with a curved iron instrument resembling a knife; they write nothing on paper but copies of the Qur'ān and works of theology. The preacher mentions her name at the Friday prayer and on other occasions, saying: 'Oh God aid Thy maidservant whom Thou hast chosen in Thy knowledge of the world, and hast made her a mercy for the whole people of the Muslims, that is, this Sultana Khadīja, daughter of the Sultan Jalāl ad-Dīn, son of the Sultan Ṣalāḥ al-Dīn.'

When a stranger comes to the islands and visits the audience-hall which they call the *dār*,[38] custom demands that he take two pieces of cloth with him. He makes obeisance towards this Sultana, and throws down one of these cloths, then to her Wazīr, who is her husband Jamāl al-Dīn, and throws down the other. Her army comprises about a thousand men, recruited from abroad, though some are natives. They
133 come to the *dār* every day, | make obeisance and retire, and their pay consists of rice, which is issued to them from the *bandar* every month. At the end of each month they come to the *dār*, make obeisance and say to the Wazīr: 'Transmit our homage and make it known that we have come for our pay', whereupon orders are given for it to be issued to them. The qāḍī and the officials, whom they call Wazīrs, also present their homage daily at the *dār* and after the eunuchs have transmitted it they withdraw.

[36] Haddummati.

[37] The office of *katibu* in Male was one of great dignity (Pyrard, I, pp. 131–3). The Maldivian word, Pyrard's *Catibe*, represents Arabic *khaṭīb*, 'preacher', not, as Gray and Bell supposed (Pyrard, I, p. 70, n. 2) *kātib*, 'scribe'.

[38] Arabic *dār*, 'house'.

Account of the officials and their comportment. These people call
the principal Wazīr, the Sultan's deputy, by the name of
Kalakī, and the judge *Fandayārqālū*.[39] All their judgments are
referred to the qāḍī; he is held in greater respect among the
people than anyone else; | his orders are obeyed as those of 134
the ruler or even more so. He sits on a carpet in the *dār*, and
enjoys the entire revenue of three islands, according to an
ancient custom, established by the Sultan Aḥmad Shanūrāza.
They call the preacher *Handījarī*, the chancery officer [ṣāḥib
al-dīwān] *Fāmaldārī*, the finance officer *Māfākalū*, the police
commandant *Fitnāyak*, and naval commander *Mānāyak*.[40] All
these persons have the title of Wazīr. There is no prison in
these islands; criminals are confined in wooden chambers
intended for merchandise, and each of them is secured by a
piece of wood, as is done amongst us [in Morocco] with
Christian prisoners. | 135

*Account of my arrival at these islands and of the course of my fortune
there.* When I arrived at these islands I disembarked at the one
called Kannalūs, a fine island containing many mosques, and I
put up at the house of one of the pious persons there. I was
hospitably entertained by the jurist ʿAlī, a worthy man who
has sons engaged in religious studies. On this island I met a
man called Muḥammad, belonging to Ẓafār al-Ḥumūḍ,[41] who
showed me hospitality and told me that if I entered the island
of Mahal the Wazīr would detain me there, because they had
no qāḍī. Now my design was to sail from there to Maʿbar,
Sarandīb, and Bengal, and thence on to China. I had come to
the islands in the vessel of the captain ʿOmar of Hinawr, a
worthy man and a pilgrim, and when we reached Kannalūs he
stayed there for ten days, and then hired a *kundura* to go to
Mahal with a present for the Sultana | and her husband. I
wanted to go with him, but he said: 'the *kundura* has no room 136

[39] Faḍiyāru Kalōge-fānu, Pyrard's *Pandiare*.

[40] Other authorities give lists of the principal ministers in which some of these words appear, though not necessarily with the same meaning. *Handījarī* is Bell's *hadēgiri*, designating 'chief treasurer'. *Fāmaldārī* is Pyrard's *Pammedery*, which Bell takes to be *Fāmudēri*, for Pyrard a great lord but not a minister. *Māfākalū* is Pyrard's *Manpas*, Bell's *Māfai*, 'chancellor'. Mžik connects *Fitnāyak* with Sanskrit *nāyaka* 'commander' and Mānāyak with Sanskrit *mahānāyaka*, 'grand commander'. They are discussed in a long note in *The Voyage of François Pyrard*, I, pp. 210–13.

[41] See vol. II, p. 382, n. 68.

for you and your companions, but if you wish to come by yourself without them it is up to you.' I refused to do this and he set out, but the wind played tricks with him and four days later he returned to us, sorely tried. He then made his excuses to me and insisted that I should go with him and take my companions. We used to set sail in the morning and disembark at midday on one of the islands, then set off | again and spend the night on another. After four days we reached the district of al-Taim; the *kardūī* there was called Hilāl and he made his salutations to me and entertained me. He came to visit me accompanied by four men, two of whom carried four fowls suspended from a staff across their shoulders, and the other two about ten coconuts suspended from a similar staff. I was surprised at the importance they gave to this miserable affair
137 but I was told that they had done it | by way of showing honour and respect.

After leaving them we disembarked on the sixth day on the island of ʿOthmān, a worthy man, one of the best of men, who received us honourably and showed us hospitality, and on the eighth day we disembarked on an island belonging to a Wazīr called al-Talamdī. On the tenth day we arrived at the island of Mahal, the seat of the Sultana and her husband and anchored in its harbour. The custom of the islanders is that no one may go ashore without their permission. When permission was given to us to disembark I wished to repair to one of the mosques, but the attendants on shore prevented me, saying that I must visit the Wazīr. I had previously enjoined the captain of the ship to say, if he were asked about me: 'I do not know him', fearing that I should be detained by them, and I was ignorant of the fact that some gossip had written to them telling them about me and that I had been qāḍī at Dihlī. On reaching the *dār*, that is, the audience-hall, we halted in some
138 porticoes | by the third gateway. The qāḍī ʿĪsā of al-Yaman came up and greeted me and I greeted the Wazīr. The captain Ibrāhīm[42] brought ten pieces of cloth and made obeisance towards the Sultana, throwing down one piece, then to the Wazīr, throwing down another in the same way. When he had thrown them all down he was asked about me and answered:

[42] Previously (p. 833) called ʿOmar.

'I do not know him.' Afterwards they brought out betel and rose-water to us, this being their mark of honour, and lodged us in a house, where they sent us food, consisting of a large platter of rice surrounded by plates containing salted meat, chickens, ghee, and fish.

On the following morning I went with the captain and the qāḍī ʿĪsā of al-Yaman to visit a hospice which had been built at the extremity of the island by the pious Shaikh Najīb,[43] and we returned during the night. In the morning following that night the Wazīr sent to me a robe and a hospitality gift |
including rice, ghee, salted meat, coconuts and the honey 139
made from them which they call *qurbānī* (the meaning of which is 'eater of sugar'),[44] and along with this they brought 100,000 cowries for my expenses.

When ten days had passed a ship arrived from Ceylon bringing some poor brethren, Arabs and Persians, who recognized me and told the Wazīr's attendants who I was. This made him still more delighted to have me, and at the beginning of Ramaḍān[45] he sent for me. I found the amirs and Wazīrs present and when the food was brought in on tables, each table serving for a number of guests, the Wazīr made me sit beside him, the others in his company being the qāḍī ʿĪsā, the Wazīr *fāmaldārī* and the Wazīr ʿOmar *daharad*, which means 'commander of the army'.[46] Their dishes are rice, fowls, ghee, fish, salted meat, and cooked banana, and after eating they drink coconut honey mixed with spices which facilitates digestion of the food.

On | the ninth of Ramaḍān the Wazīr's son-in-law, his 140
daughter's husband, died. She was previously married to the Sultan Shihāb al-Dīn, but neither of her husbands had consummated the marriage because of her youth, and the Wazīr brought her back to his house and gave me her house, which was a very fine one. I asked his permission to give a banquet

[43] The Habshīgefānu Magan, in memory of Shaikh Najīb, was in the precincts of the Lonu Ziyāre at Male, but both have now disappeared. It may have included a mosque. (Andrew Forbes, 'The Mosque in the Maldive Islands', p. 62).

[44] *Hakurpani*, jaggery water.

[45] 17 January 1344.

[46] I.B. does not specify the vowels of this word, which seems to be Bell's *Dāharā*, one of three chief ministers, but who had come to have no particular department to direct.

to the poor brethren who had come from visiting the Foot [of Adam, in Ceylon]. He gave permission, and sent me five sheep, which are rarities among them because they are imported from Maʿbar, Mulaibār, and Maqdashaw, together with rice, chickens, ghee, and spices. I sent all this to the house of the Wazīr Sulaimān the *manāyak*, who had it excellently cooked for me, and added to it, besides sending carpets and brass utensils. We broke our fast, according to the custom, in the Sultana's palace, in company with the Wazīr, and I asked his permission for some of the ministers to attend my
141 banquet, and he said to me: 'And I shall come too.' | So I thanked him and on returning home to my house found him already there with the ministers and high officials. The Wazīr sat in an elevated wooden pavilion, and all the amirs and ministers who came greeted him and threw down an unsewn cloth, so that there were collected about a hundred cloths, which were taken by the poor brethren. The food was then served, and when the guests had eaten, the Qur'ān readers chanted in beautiful voices. The poor brethren then began their ritual chants and dances. I had made ready a fire and they went into it, treading it with their feet, and some of them ate it as one eats sweetmeats, until it was extinguished.

Account of part of the Wazīr's generosity towards me. When the night came to an end, the Wazīr withdrew and I went with him. As we passed by an orchard belonging to the treasury he said to me: 'This orchard is yours, and I shall build a house in it for you to live in.' I thanked him and prayed for his happiness. Then |
142 on the next day he sent me a slave-girl and his servant said to me: 'The Wazīr says to you that if this girl is agreeable to you she is yours, but if not he will send you a Marhata girl.' Now the Marhata girls were much to my liking, so I said to him: 'I should prefer the Marhata', and he sent her to me. Her name was Qulistān, which means 'Flower of the Garden',[47] and she knew the Persian language, so she pleased me, for the people of those islands have a language of their own which I did not understand.

Then on the following day the Wazīr sent me a Maʿbarī slave-girl called ʿAnbarī,[48] and on the night of the same day

[47] Persian *gulistān*, 'rose garden'.
[48] I.e. perfumed with ambergris.

he came to me after the last evening prayer with a small number of his friends and came into the house accompanied by two small slave-boys. When I greeted him he asked how things were with me, and I thanked him and prayed for his happiness, whereupon one of the slave-boys laid a bundle down before him rather like a clothes bag and took out | of it 143
some silk cloths and a box containing pearls and jewellery. The Wazīr gave these to me saying: 'If I had sent them to you with the slave-girl she would have said that they were her own property which she had brought from her master's house; but now they are your property so give them to her as a present', whereupon I thanked him and prayed for his happiness for he was entitled to thanks, God's mercy on him.

Account of his displeasure and my intention to leave and subsequent stay. The Wazīr Sulaimān the *manāyak* had sent to me proposing that I should marry his daughter, and I sent to the Wazīr Jamāl al-Dīn to ask his permission for my acceptance. The messenger returned to me and said: 'The proposal does not find favour with him, for he wishes to marry you to his own daughter when her period of widowhood comes to an end.'[49] But I for my part refused that, in fear of the ill-luck attached to her, for she had already had two husbands who had died before consummating the marriage. Meanwhile I was seriously attacked by fever, | for every person who comes to this island 144
inevitably contracts fever. I firmly determined therefore to leave it, sold some of the jewellery for cowries, and hired a vessel to take me to Bengal. When I went to take leave of the Wazīr, the qāḍī came out to me and said: 'The Wazīr says to you: "If you wish to go, give us back what we have given you and go".' I replied: 'I have bought cowries with some of the jewels, so do what you like with those.' He came back to me and said: 'He says "We gave you gold, not cowries".' I said to him: 'I shall sell them and bring you the gold.' So I sent for the merchants, asking them to buy back the cowries from me, but the Wazīr forbade them to do so, his purpose in all this being to prevent my leaving him. Afterwards he sent one of his courtiers to me to say: 'The Wazīr says "Stay with us, and

[49] Under Islamic law, as a widow who was not pregnant, she could remarry after four months and ten days.

you shall have what you will".' So reasoning with myself that
145 I was in their power and that if I did not stay | of my own free will I should be kept by main force, and that it was better to stay of my own choice, I said to his messenger: 'Very well, I shall stay with him.' When the messenger returned to him he was overjoyed at this and summoned me. As I entered he rose and embraced me saying: 'We wish you to stay near us and you wish to go away from us!' I made my excuses, which he accepted, and said to him: 'If you wish me to stay I have some conditions to make.' He replied: 'Granted. Name them.' I said: 'I cannot walk about on foot.' Now it is their custom that no one rides there except the Wazīr, and when I had been given a horse and rode out on it, the population, men and boys, used to follow me in amazement. At length I complained to him, so he had the *dunqura* beaten and a public proclamation made that no one was to follow me. The *dunqura*
146 is a sort of brass basin | which is beaten with an iron rod and can be heard at a great distance;[50] after beating it any proclamation which it is desired to make is publicly announced. The Wazīr said to me: 'If you wish to ride in a palanquin, do so; if not we have a stallion and a mare – choose which of them you wish.' So I chose the mare and it was brought to me on the spot along with a robe. Then I said: 'What shall I do with the cowries I bought?' He replied: 'Send one of your companions to sell them for you in Bengal.' I said: 'I shall, on condition that you too send someone to help him in the transaction.' He agreed to that, so I sent off my travelling companion Abū Muḥammad b. Farḥān and they sent with him a man named al-Ḥājj ʿAlī. It happened that the sea became stormy and they threw overboard all that they had even down to the provisions, water, mast, and waterskins, and remained for sixteen nights without sails or rudder or anything else. At
147 length | after suffering hunger and thirst and hardship they came out at the island of Ceylon. My companion Abū Muḥammad returned to me a year later having visited the Foot [of Adam], which he visited a second time with me.

Account of the Festival which I attended in their company. When

[50] '*Kurā* means a water pot; *dun* or *dum* means 'smoke'; alternatively, *don* means 'pale or ripe-coloured' . . . A brass pot would be *lo kurā*' (C.H.B.R.).

the month of Ramaḍān ended, the Wazīr sent me a robe and we went out to the *muṣallā*; the road by which the Wazīr would pass from his house to the *muṣallā* was decorated and spread with cloths, and *kuttās* of cowries were placed right and left of it. Every one of the amirs and principal men who had a house on his way had planted beside it little coco-palms, areca trees and bananas, and had stretched from one tree to the next cords from which he hung green nuts. The owner of the house would then stand beside its door and as the Wazīr passed |
would throw down in front of him a piece of silk or cotton 148
cloth, which his slaves picked up together with the cowries placed along the road. All this time the Wazīr walked on his own feet, wearing an Egyptian *farajīya* of goat's hair and a large turban, with a silk cloth round his shoulders, and four parasols over his head. He had sandals on his feet while everybody else was barefoot. He was preceded by trumpets, bugles and drums, and in front of and behind him were troops all of whom were shouting the *takbīr* until they came to the *muṣallā*.

After the prayer the Wazīr's son delivered the *khuṭba*, then a litter was brought in which the Wazīr took his seat and the amirs and the Wazīrs did homage to him and threw down cloths according to the custom. He had not ridden in a litter before this because it is a thing which is not done except by the kings. The bearers then lifted him up and I rode my horse, and so we entered the palace, where the Wazīr took his
seat in an elevated place, attended by the Wazīrs | and amirs, 149
and the slaves stood with shields, swords and staves. After the food had been served followed by the areca-nut and the betel, a small plate containing Macassar sandalwood[51] was carried round and when a group of those present had eaten they rubbed themselves with sandalwood. I saw that day on one of their dishes some sardines, salted but uncooked, which had been brought to them as a gift from Kawlam, for they are plentiful in the land of Mulaibār. The Wazīr took a sardine and as he was eating it he said to me: 'Eat some of these for they are not found in our country.' I replied: 'How can I eat

[51] *m.qāṣ.rī*, probably referring, not to the town of Macassar (Ujung Pandang), but to the island of Celebes (Sulawesi).

them when they are uncooked?' He said: 'But they are cooked.' I replied: 'I know better for they are common in our country.'

Account of my marriage and my appointment as qāḍī. On the second of Shawwāl[52] I made an agreement with the Wazīr Sulaimān the *manāyak* to marry his daughter, so I sent to the
150 Wazīr Jamāl | al-Dīn requesting that the ceremony might be held in his presence at the palace. He gave his consent, and sent the customary betel and sandalwood. The guests arrived but the Wazīr Sulaimān delayed. He was sent for but still did not come, and on being summoned a second time excused himself on the ground of his daughter's illness. The Wazīr then said to me privily: 'His daughter has refused and she is her own mistress. The people have assembled, so what do you say to marrying the Sultana's mother-in-law?' (It was her daughter to whom the Wazīr's son was married.) I said: 'Very well', so the qāḍī and notaries were summoned, and the profession of faith recited. The Wazīr paid her dowry, and she was conducted to me a few days later. She was one of the best of women, and was so affectionate that when I married her she used to anoint me with perfume and cense my garments, laughing all the while and without showing any displeasure.

After this marriage the Wazīr forced me to take the office of
151 qāḍī. | The reason for this was that I had reproached the qāḍī for his practice of taking a tenth of all estates when he divided them amongst the heirs, saying to him: 'You should have nothing but a fee agreed upon between you and the heirs.' Besides he never did anything properly. When I was appointed, I strove my utmost to establish the prescriptions of the Sacred Law. Lawsuits there are not like those in our land. The first bad custom I changed was the practice of divorced wives of staying in the houses of their former husbands, for they all do so till they marry another husband. I put a stop to that. About twenty-five men who had acted thus were brought before me; I had them beaten and paraded in the bazaars, and the women put away from them. Afterwards I gave strict injunctions that the prayers were to be observed, and ordered
152 men | to go swiftly to the streets and bazaars after the Friday

[52] 17 February 1344.

service; anyone whom they found not having prayed I had beaten and paraded. I compelled the salaried prayer-leaders and muezzins to be assiduous in their duties and sent letters to all the islands to the same effect. I tried also to determine how women dressed, but I could not manage this.

Account of the arrival of the Wazīr ʿAbdallāh ibn Muḥammad of Ḥaḍramaut, whom the Sultan Shihāb al-Dīn had exiled to al-Suwaid, and of what took place between us. I had married his step-daughter, the daughter of his wife, and I was exceedingly fond of her. When the Wazīr sent for him to return to the island of Mahal, I sent him presents, went out to meet him and accompanied him to the palace. He saluted the Wazīr who assigned him as his residence a fine house, where I used to visit him. It happened that I went into retreat during the feast of Rama-
ḍān, and | all the people came to visit me except him, until the 153
Wazīr Jamāl al-Dīn visited me when he came with him by way of keeping him company. A coolness grew up between us, and when I came out of retreat the maternal uncles of my wife who was his step-daughter, that is to say the sons of the Wazīr Jamāl al-Sinjarī, laid a complaint before me. Their father had appointed the Wazīr ʿAbdallāh as their guardian and their property was still in his hands although they had emerged from his tutelage under the provisions of the Law, and they demanded that he should be brought before the tribunal. It was my custom when I sent for any of the parties to a case to send him a scrap of paper, with or without writing on it, on receipt of which he would at once come to the tribunal of the Law, and if he did not I punished him. I sent for him accordingly in the usual way, but he was indignant at my action, made it a grudge against me and became secretly hostile to me. He sent an agent to speak on his behalf, and I was informed that he had used some unseemly language.

It was the custom of the people, both small and great, | to 154
do homage to him as they did to the Wazīr Jamāl al-Dīn. Their manner of doing homage is to put the forefinger to the ground, then to kiss and lay it on their heads. I ordered the crier to announce in the Sultan's palace, in the presence of witnesses, that anyone who did homage to the Wazīr ʿAbdallāh in the same way as to the great Wazīr would be visited by severe penalties, and I took an engagement from him that he would

not permit the people to do this, all of which made him still more hostile. I also married another wife, the daughter of a Wazīr, a man highly respected among them whose grandfather was the Sultan Dā'ūd, the descendant of Sultan Aḥmad Shanūrāza. Afterwards I married a wife who had formerly been married to the Sultan Shihāb al-Dīn, and I built three houses in the garden which the Wazīr had given me. My fourth wife, who was the daughter-in-law of the Wazīr ʿAbdallāh, used to live in her own house, and she was my favourite amongst
155 them. After | I had become allied by marriage to these persons whom I have mentioned the Wazīr and the islanders stood in awe of me, because of their weakness, and they exerted themselves to turn the Wazīr against me by slanders, Wazīr ʿAbdallāh taking the largest part in this, until our relations became strained.

Account of my separation from them and the reason for it. It happened one day that a slave belonging to the Sultan Jalāl al-Dīn was complained of to the Wazīr by his wife who informed him that he was at the house of one of the Sultan's concubines and committing adultery with her. The Wazīr sent witnesses who entered the concubine's house, found the slave sleeping with her in one bed, and arrested them both. On the following morning, when I learned of the event I went to the audience hall and sat in my usual place without saying a word about the affair. One of the courtiers came out to me and said: 'The
156 Wazīr asks you if there is anything you want', | to which I said: 'No.' It was his intention that I should speak of the affair of the concubine and the slave, since it had been my custom to let no case arise without passing judgment in it, but when the estrangement and hostility intervened I had omitted to do so. After this I went back to my house and took my seat in the place of judgments, when one of the Wazīrs appeared and said to me: 'The Wazīr informs you that yesterday there took place such and such (referring to the case of the concubine and the slave) so give your decision in regard to them according to the law.' I replied: 'This is a case in which it is not fitting to give judgment except in the Sultan's palace', and returned to it where there was a concourse of people. After having the concubine and the slave brought in I gave orders that both of them should be beaten because of their intimacy, and then set

the woman at liberty and imprisoned the slave. On my return
to my house the Wazīr sent some of his principal attendants |
to ask me to set him at liberty. I said to them: 'Are you going 157
to intercede for a negro slave who has violated his master's
honour, when you yourselves but yesterday deposed the Sultan Shihāb al-Dīn and put him to death because he had
entered the house of one of his slaves?' Thereupon I sent for
the slave and had him beaten with bamboo rods, which give
heavier blows than whips, and paraded round the island with a
rope round his neck. When they went to the Wazīr and told
him of this he was much agitated and fell into a violent rage,
assembled the ministers and army commanders and sent for
me. I came to him, and though I usually made obeisance to
him, I did not make obeisance but simply said: '*Salām
'alaikum*'. Then I said to those present: 'Be my witnesses
that I resign the office of the qāḍī because of my inability to
carry out its duties.' The Wazīr addressed me, whereupon I
mounted [to the dais], sat down in a place facing him, | and 158
answered him in the most uncompromising manner. At this
point the muezzin chanted the call to the sunset prayer and he
went into his palace saying: 'They say that I am Sultan, but I
sent for this fellow to vent my wrath on him and he vented his
wrath on me.' The respect in which I was held amongst them
was due solely to the Sultan of India, for they were aware of
the regard in which he held me, and even though they are far
distant from him yet the fear of him is in their hearts.

When the Wazīr entered his house he sent the former qāḍī
who had been removed from office to see me. This man had
an arrogant tongue, and said to me: 'Our master asks you why
you violated his dignity in the presence of witnesses, and did
not make obeisance to him.' I answered: 'I used to make
obeisance to him only because I was on good terms with him,
but when his attitude changed I gave that up. The greeting of
Muslims is the *Salām* and nothing more, and I said *Salām*.' He
sent him to me a second time to say: 'You are aiming only at
leaving us; give back your wives' dowries and pay your debts |
and go, if you will.' On hearing this I made obeisance to him, 159
went to my house, and acquitted all the debts I had con-
tracted. He had given me just before then the upholstery and
other furnishings of a house, such as brass utensils and so

forth, for he used to give me everything that I asked for, and show me affection and honour, but he had changed his attitude and been made to feel afraid of me. Then when he heard that I had acquitted my debt and was bent upon going, he repented of what he had said and withheld his permission for my departure. So I swore with the most solemn oaths that I had no alternative but to leave, and removed all my possessions to a mosque on the coast and divorced one of my wives. Another of them was with child, so I fixed a term of nine months for my return to her, failing which she was her own mistress. I took with me my wife who had been married to the Sultan Shihāb al-Dīn, in order to hand her over to her father in
160 the island of | Mulūk, and my first wife, the one whose daughter was the sister of the Sultana.

I made a compact with the Wazīr ʿOmar *daharad* and the Wazīr Ḥasan, the commander of the sea,[53] that I should go to the land of Maʿbar, the king of which was the husband of my wife's sister, and fetch troops from there to bring the islands under his authority, and that I should be his representative in them. I arranged that the signal between us should be the hoisting of white flags on the ships; when they saw these they were to rise in revolt on the shore. I had never suggested this to myself until the Wazīr became estranged from me. He was afraid of me and used to say to others: 'This man will without doubt seize the Wazīrate, either in my lifetime or after my death.' He was constantly making enquiries about me and would say: 'I have heard that the King of India has sent him money to aid him to revolt against me.' He feared my departure, lest I should fetch troops from Maʿbar, and sent to me
161 asking me to stay until | he could fit out a vessel for me but I refused.

The Sultana's sister complained to her of her mother's departure with me. The Sultana therefore tried to stop her but could not do so, and when she saw her determination to go she said to her: 'All the jewels that you have come from the money of the *bandar*; if you have witnesses that Jalāl al-Dīn gave them to you, good and well, otherwise you must return them', and although the jewellery was of considerable value she

[53] He has previously (pp. 140, 143) called him Sulaimān.

returned it all to them. The Wazīrs and chief men came to me at the mosque and begged me to return. I said to them: 'If I had not sworn I should return.' They said: 'Go to one of the islands so as to keep your oath and then return', so I said: 'Very well', in order to satisfy them. When the night fixed for my departure came I went on to take leave of the Wazīr, and he embraced me and wept so copiously that his tears dropped on my feet. He passed the following night guarding the island
in person, for fear that my relatives by marriage | and my 162
friends would rise in revolt against him.

I now set sail and reached the island of the Wazīr ʿAlī. Here my wife was attacked by severe pains and wished to go back, so I divorced her and left her there, sending word to that effect to the Wazīr, because she was the mother of his son's wife. I divorced also the wife for whom I had set a fixed term, and sent for a slave-girl of whom I was very fond, and we continued to travel through the islands from one district to another.

Account of the women who have a single breast. In one of these islands I saw a woman who had only one breast. She had two daughters one of whom resembled her in having one breast, and the other had two breasts but one of them was large and full of milk while the other was small and had none. I was astonished at their condition.

We came to a little island in that archipelago in which there
was but one house, | occupied by a weaver. He had a wife and 163
family, a few coco-palms and a small boat, with which he used to fish and to cross over to any of the islands he wished to visit. His island contained also banana bushes, but we saw no land birds on it except two crows, which came out to us on our arrival and circled above our vessel. And I swear I envied that man, and wished that the island had been mine, that I might have made it my retreat until the inevitable hour should befall me.

I then came to the island of Mulūk where the ship belonging to the captain Ibrāhīm was lying. This was the ship in which I had decided to travel to Maʿbar. Ibrāhīm and his companions met me and showed me great hospitality. The Wazīr had written to me that I was to receive in this island 120 *bustūs* of *kūdah*, that is of cowries,[54] along with twenty bowls of

[54] Not identified. Cowries are *boli* (C.H.B.R).

164 *atwan*, that is | coconut honey,[55] and a stated quantity of betel, areca-nuts, and fish every day. I stayed seventy days at Mulūk and married two wives there.

This is one of the finest of the islands in greenness and fertility. One of the astonishing things that I saw there was that a branch cut from the trees that grow there and planted in the ground or in a garden hedge will throw out leaves and grow into a tree,[56] and I saw also that the pomegranates there never cease to carry fruit all the year round. The islanders were afraid that the captain Ibrāhīm would plunder them at the moment of sailing, so they proposed to seize all the weapons on his ship and keep them until the day of his departure. A dispute arose over this, and we returned to Mahal but did not enter the harbour. I wrote to the Wazīr to tell him what had occurred, whereupon he wrote to say that there was no cause for seizing the weapons. We returned to Mulūk and set sail
165 from there in the middle of Rabīʿ II, 45.[57] | In Shaʿbān of the same year the Wazīr Jamāl al-Dīn died – May God have mercy upon him. The Sultana was with child by him, she gave birth after his death and the Wazīr ʿAbdallāh married her.

[55] Not identified. 'Coconut honey is *diyā-hakurū*' (C.H.B.R.).

[56] Mžik (p. 351, n. 33) suggests that the pipal tree, *Ficus religiosa* L., may be meant, and that its presence may be a relic of Buddhism.

[57] 22 August 1344.

CHAPTER XVIII

Ceylon

We set sail without an experienced pilot on board, the distance between the islands and Maʿbar being a three days' journey, and travelled for nine days, emerging on the ninth day at the island of Ceylon. We saw the mountain of Sarandīb there, rising into the heavens like a column of smoke.[1] When we came to the island, the sailors said: 'This port is not in the territory of the Sultan whose country can safely be visited by merchants. It is a port in the territory of the Sultan Ayrī Shakarwatī who is an evildoing tyrant and keeps pirate vessels.'[2] We were afraid to put into this harbour, but as a gale arose thereafter and we dreaded drowning, I said to the captain: 'Put me ashore | and I shall get 166
you a safe-conduct from this Sultan.' He did as I asked and put me ashore, whereupon the infidels came to us and said: 'What are you?' I told them that I was the brother-in-law and friend of the Sultan of Maʿbar, that I had come to visit him, and that the contents of the ship were a present for him. They went to their Sultan and informed him of this. Thereupon he summoned me, and I visited him in the town of Baṭṭāla [Puttalam], which is his capital. It is a small and pretty town, surrounded by a wooden wall with wooden towers. The whole of its coasts are covered with branches of cinnamon trees brought down by torrents and heaped up like mounds on the shore. They are taken without payment by the people of Maʿbar and Mulaibār, but in return for this they give presents

[1] Adam's Peak, which is the most spectacular, though not the highest, mountain in the island.

[2] The title used by a dynasty from south India where they had been feudatories of the Pāṇdyas and as such had invaded Ceylon. With the Muslim conquest of the Pāṇdya realm they became independent rulers of northern Ceylon. The king I.B. visited was probably the sixth of the dynasty, Mārtāṇḍa Singai Āriyaṇ.

of woven cloth and similar articles to the Sultan. It is a day and a night's journey from this island to the land of Maʿbar. It
167 has also much brazil-wood and Indian aloes, | which is called *kalakhī*, but it differs from the *qamārī* and the *qāqulī* also, and we shall describe it later.[3]

Account of the Sultan of Ceylon. His name is Ayrī Shakarwatī, and he is a Sultan powerful on the sea. Once when I was in Maʿbar I saw a hundred vessels of his there, some small, some large. There were in the port at that time eight vessels belonging to the Sultan [of Maʿbar] which were about to make the voyage to al-Yaman, so the Sultan gave orders to make ready all equipment and called up troops to guard his vessels. When the men from Ceylon saw that they could not effect a surprise seizure of them they said: 'We have come only to protect some vessels of ours which are also on their way to al-Yaman.'

When I entered the presence of this infidel Sultan, he rose
168 to meet me, | seated me beside him, and spoke most kindly to me. He said: 'Your companions may land in safety and will be my guests until they sail, for the Sultan of Maʿbar and I are friends.' He then gave orders for my lodging and I stayed with him three days, enjoying great consideration which increased every day. He understood Persian and was delighted with the tales I told him of kings and countries. One day, when I came into his presence, he had before him a large quantity of pearls which had been brought from the pearl dives in his country, and his entourage were separating out the valuable ones from the others. He said to me: 'Have you seen pearl dives in the countries that you have come from?' I replied: 'Yes! I have seen them in the island of Qais and the island of Kish which belongs to Ibn al-Sawāmilī.'[4] He said: 'I have heard of them', then taking some pearls from those in front of him he said:
169 'Are there in that island pearls like | these?' I replied: 'I have seen [only] smaller ones', which so pleased him that he said: 'They are yours', and added: 'Do not be shy, but ask me for anything that you want.' I replied: 'Since reaching this island I have but one desire, to visit the blessed Foot, the Foot of

[3] See below pp. 881–2.

[4] By Kish is meant Kishm. See II, p. 403, n. 127.

Adam.' (They call him Bābā, and Eve they call Māmā.) 'That is simple', he answered. 'We shall send an escort with you to take you to it.' 'That is what I want', said I, then I added: 'And this ship that I came in can set out in safety for Maʿbar, and when I return [from the Foot] you will send me in your own vessels.' 'Certainly', he replied. When I related this to the captain, however, he said to me: 'I shall not set sail until you return, even if I wait a year on your account', so I told the Sultan this and he said: 'He will remain as my guest until you come back.'

The Sultan then gave me a palanquin, which was carried by his slaves on their shoulders, and sent with me four *jūgīs*, whose custom it is | to make an annual pilgrimage to the Foot, 170 three Brahmans, ten other persons from his entourage, and fifteen men to carry provisions. Water is plentiful along that road. On the first day we encamped beside a river, which we crossed on a raft, made of bamboo canes. Thence we journeyed to Manār Mandalī [Minneri-Mandel], a pretty town situated at the extremity of the Sultan's territories.[5] The inhabitants regaled us with a fine banquet of buffalo calves, which they hunt in a forest there and bring in alive, along with rice, ghee, fish, fowls and milk. We did not see a single Muslim in this town, except one man from Khurāsān, who was exhausted as the result of an illness, but who came on with us. We continued our journey to Bandar Salāwāt [Chilaw], a small town, | after which our way lay through rugged and well 171 watered country. In this part there are many elephants, but they do no harm to pilgrims and strangers, through the blessed virtue of the Shaikh Abū ʿAbdallāh b. Khafīf (God's mercy on him) who was the first to open up this road for the pilgrimage to the Foot. These infidels used formerly to prevent Muslims from making this pilgrimage and would maltreat them, and neither eat nor trade with them, but since the adventure that happened to the Shaikh Abū ʿAbdallāh, as we have related in the first journey, when the elephants killed his

[5] It is about ten miles from Puttalam. At this time central and southern Ceylon were ruled by Sinhalese kings who sometimes paid tribute to the Ārya Cakravarti. At this time two brothers ruled jointly, Bhuvanekabāhu IV and Parākramabāhu V from Gaṁpola and Dädigama respectively. It seems that the Aḷagakkōnāra (n. 8 below) also claimed to be independent.

companions and he alone of them escaped, and an elephant carried him on its back,[6] the infidels honour the Muslims, allow them to enter their houses, eat with them, and have no suspicions regarding their dealings with their wives and children.[7] To this day they continue to pay the greatest veneration to this Shaikh, and call him 'The Great Shaikh'.

172 After this we came to | the town of Kunakār, which is the capital of the principal Sultan in this land.[8] It is built in a narrow valley between two hills, near a great channel called the Channel of Rubies, because rubies are found in it. Outside this town is the mosque of Shaikh ʿOthmān of Shīrāz, known as the Shāwush; the Sultan and inhabitants of the town visit his tomb and venerate him. He was the guide to the Foot, and when his hand and foot were cut off, his sons and slaves took his place as guides. The reason for his mutilation was that he killed a cow. The Hindu infidels have a law that anyone who kills a cow is slaughtered in the same fashion or else put in its skin and burned. As Shaikh ʿOthmān was so highly revered by them, they cut off his hand and foot instead, and assigned to him the revenues of one of the bazaars. |

173 *Description of the Sultan of Kunakār.* He is called the Kunār, and possesses a white elephant, the only white elephant I have seen in the whole world. He rides on it at festivals and puts great rubies on its forehead. It happened that his officers of state revolted against him, blinded him, and made his son ruler, but he is still there, though blind.

Description of the rubies. The marvellous rubies called *bahramān* [carbuncles] are found only in this town. Some are taken from the channel, and these are regarded by them as the most

[6] See II, pp. 314–15.

[7] It has been suggested that Muslim ascetics helped to popularize the Arab traders trying to enter the gem market with the local people who for religious reasons favoured their Chinese Buddhist rivals (S. M. Yusuf, in *University of Ceylon History of Ceylon*, I, pt 2, p. 706).

[8] The name of the place and the title given below to the ruler, the Kunar, probably reflect Aḷagakkōnāra, a South Indian family which had achieved considerable power, and were related to, and rivals of, the Sinhalese kings of Gaṁpola. The location of Kunākār is disputed. It is often identified with Kurunägala, as by Gibb (*Selections*, p. 365, n. 6) but I.B.'s description requires somewhere closer to Adam's Peak; the reference to rubies suggests Ratnapura, but the archaeologist Mr Roland Silva objects that there was no route from Puttalam to Ratnapura.

valuable,[9] and some are obtained by digging. In the island of
Ceylon rubies are found in all parts. The land is private
property, and a man buys a parcel of it and digs for rubies. He
finds white stones, deeply-cracked, and it is inside these that
the rubies are formed. | He gives them to the lapidaries who 174
scrape them down until they split away from the ruby stones.
Some of them are red, some yellow, and some blue, which
they call *nailam*.[10] Their custom is that all rubies of the value
of a hundred *fanams* belong to the Sultan, who pays their price
and takes them; those of less value belong to the finders. A
hundred *fanams* equal in value six gold dinars.

All the women in the island of Ceylon have necklaces of
rubies of different colours and wear them also on their arms
and legs in place of bracelets and anklets. The Sultan's slave-
girls make a network of rubies and wear it on their heads. I
have seen on the forehead of the white elephant[11] seven ruby-
stones each larger than a hen's egg, and I saw in the possession
of the Sultan Ayrī Shakarwatī a bowl | as large as a man's hand 175
made of rubies, containing oil of aloes. When I showed my
astonishment he said: 'We have things larger than that.'

We then set out from Kunakār and halted at a cave called after Usṭā Maḥmūd the Lūr, a pious man who dug out this cave at the foot of a hill beside a small channel. From there we went on and halted at a channel called *Khōr Būznah*, the word *buznah* meaning 'monkeys'.[12]

Account of the monkeys. There are in these mountains vast
numbers of monkeys. They are black and have long tails, and
their males are bearded like men.[13] Shaikh ʿOthmān and his
son and others as well told me that these monkeys have | a 176
chief, whom they obey as if he were a Sultan. He fastens on
his head a fillet of tree leaves and leans upon a staff. On his
right and his left are four monkeys carrying staves in their
hands. When the chief monkey sits down the four monkeys

[9] Mžik (p. 360, n. 12) notes that the precious stones were found in the detritus deposited in the pools at the edge of the stream.

[10] Sapphires.

[11] A white elephant was 'the emblem of supreme power in those days' (S. Paranavitana in *University of Ceylon History of Ceylon*, I, pt 2, p. 640). See Plate II.

[12] Persian *būzīnah*, 'monkey'.

[13] Wanderoo monkeys, *Macacus silenus*, which are black with long tails and prominent beards.

stand behind him, and his female and young come and sit in front of him every day. The other monkeys come and sit at a distance from him, and then one of the four monkeys addresses them and all the monkeys withdraw. After this each one brings a banana or an orange or some such fruit, and the monkey chief with his young and the four monkeys eat. One of the *jūgīs* told me that he had seen the four monkeys in the presence of their chief beating a monkey with sticks and after the beating pulling out its hair. Some trustworthy persons told me as a fact that when one of these monkeys seizes a girl who
177 is unable to defend herself | he has intercourse with her. I was told by one of the inhabitants of this island that there was in his house a monkey of this kind; one of his daughters went into a chamber and the animal followed her in, and though she screamed at it, it got the better of her, and he added: 'When we came into the room after her it was between her legs and so we killed it.'

Then we journeyed to the Bamboo Pool, from which Abū ʿAbdallāh b. Khafīf took the two rubies he gave to the Sultan of this island, as we have related in the first journey.[14] We continued our journey to a place called 'The Old Woman's Hut', which is the end of the inhabited part, and went on to the cave of Bābā Ṭāhir, who was a devotee, and then to the cave of al-Sabīk. This al-Sabīk was a Sultan of the infidels, who became an anchorite in that place.[15] |

178 *Account of the flying leeches.* In this place we saw the flying leech, which they call *zulū*.[16] It is found in trees and in the vegetation near water. When a man approaches, it jumps out at him, and wheresoever it alights on his body the blood flows. The inhabitants keep a lemon in readiness for it; they squeeze this over it and it falls off them; then they scrape the place on which it alighted with a wooden knife which they have for the

[14] See II, p. 315.

[15] Identified in William Skeen, *Adam's Peak*, Colombo, 1870, p. 176; relying on Samuel Lee's translation Skeen calls the king Sībak.

[16] A Persian word. Mžik (p. 361, n. 14) identifies as *Haemobdella ceylanica*, one of the smallest and most common leeches, which can become dangerous. Robert Knox (*An Historical Relation of the island Ceylon*, 1681, ch. vi) writes: 'Some therefore will tie a piece of Lemon and Salt in a rag and fasten it unto a stick, and ever and anon strike it upon their Legs to make the Leeches drop off: others will scrape them off with a reed cut flat and sharp in the fashion of a knife'.

purpose. It is related that as a certain traveller was passing by this place the leeches fastened on him. He took no notice and did not squeeze lemons on them but he lost so much blood that he died. His name was Bābā Khūzī, and there is a cave there which is called by his name. We continued our journey to the seven caves, then to the pass of Iskandar,[17] the grotto of Al-Iṣfahānī | and a spring and an uninhabited castle, below 179
which is a hollow called the Hollow of Gāh-i-ʿĀrifān [Place of Mystics]. At the same place is the cave of the bitter orange and the cave of the Sultan and close by is the *darwāza* of the mountain, that is the place of access to it.[18]

Description of the mountain of Sarandīb. This is one of the highest mountains in the world.[19] We saw it from the sea when we were nine days' journey away, and when we climbed it we saw the clouds below us, shutting out our view of its base. On it there are many evergreen trees and flowers of various colours, including a red rose as big as the palm of a hand. They maintain that on these roses there is writing, in which can be read the name of Allah and the name of His Apostle (peace be upon him). There are two tracks on the mountain leading to the Foot, one | called Bābā track and the other Māmā track, 180
meaning Adam and Eve (peace be upon them). The Māmā track is easy and is the route by which the pilgrims return, but anyone who goes by that way is not considered by them to have made the pilgrimage at all. The Bābā track is difficult and stiff climbing. At the foot of the mountain where the *darwāza* is there is a cave, which is ascribed also to Iskandar, and a spring of water. Former generations cut a sort of stairway on the mountain, and fixed iron stanchions on it, to which they attached chains for climbers to hold on by.[20] There are ten such chains, two at the foot of the hill by the *darwāza*, seven successive chains farther on, and the tenth is the 'Chain of the Profession of Faith', so called because when one reaches it and looks down to the foot of the hill, he is seized by apprehensions and recites the profession of faith for fear of

[17] Identified by Skeen, p. 227.
[18] A Persian word.
[19] Its height is 7357 ft.
[20] The chains still exist; they have sometimes been attributed to Alexander the Great.

181 falling. When you climb past this | chain you find a badly kept track. From the tenth chain to the cave of Khiḍr is seven miles; this cave lies in a spacious place, where there is a spring which is also called by his name;[21] it is full of fish, but no one catches them. Close to this there are two tanks cut in the rock on either side of the path. At the cave of Khiḍr the pilgrims leave their belongings and ascend thence for two miles to the summit of the mountain where the Foot is.

Description of the Foot. The blessed Footprint, the Foot of our father Adam (God bless him and give him peace) is on a lofty black rock in a wide plateau. The blessed Foot sank into the rock far enough to leave its impression hollowed out. It is eleven spans long.[22] In ancient days the Chinese came here
182 and cut out of the rock the mark of the great toe | and the adjoining parts.[23] They put this in a temple in the city of Zaitūn [Ch'üan-chou], where it is visited by men from the farthest parts of the land. In the rock where the Foot is there are nine holes cut out, in which the infidel pilgrims place offerings of gold, rubies and pearls. You can see the faqīrs, after they reach the cave of Khiḍr, racing one another from there to take what there is in these holes. We, for our part, found nothing in them but a few small stones and a little gold,

[21] Identified by Skeen, p. 228.

[22] The footprint is ascribed to Adam, Buddha, Shiva and St Thomas by Muslims, Buddhists, Hindus and Christians respectively. Nothing resembling a footprint is visible in the rock, and observers have estimated very differently the dimensions of the irregular depression. 'These discrepancies remind one of the ancient Buddhist belief regarding such footmarks, that they seemed greater or smaller in proportion to the faith of the visitor' (Yule, *Cathay*, IV, p. 322, n. 1). The illustration in Gibb's *Selections*, taken from François Valentijn's *Oud en Nieuw Oost-Indien*, vol. V, 1726, shows twin peaks on one of which the footprint can be seen. The picture has the caption 'Adams Berg' and in the original 'Vertoning van Adams Voet, boven op den Berg'. Adam's Peak is not a twin peak and the illustration must be purely imaginative. Arasaratnam, in his annotated translation of the portion of Valentijn's book concerned with Ceylon (*Description of Ceylon*, Hakluyt Society, 1978, p. 49) has noted that part of his description of the Peak relates to quite a different mountain, Mulgirigala in Hambantota District. Diogo do Couto (*Asia*, dec. V, liv. vi, cap. 2), on whom Valentijn largely relied, says there are two peaks. It is not known that any European had climbed the Peak before the nineteenth century.

[23] According to Marco Polo, in 1284 the Great Khan sent an embassy to Ceylon which succeeded in bringing back to Khanbaliq two molars, some hair and a green porphyry bowl preserved on the Peak and believed to have belonged to the Buddha or to Adam.

which we gave to the guide. It is customary for the pilgrims to stay at the cave of Khiḍr for three days, visiting the Foot every morning and evening, and we followed this practice.

When the three days were over we returned by the Māmā track and halted at the cave of Shaim, that is Shaith, son of Adam,[24] (Peace be upon them both). From there we went on to the channel of the fish, then to the villages of Kurmula, Jabarkāwān, | Dildīnawa, and Ātqalanja,[25] where the Shaikh 183
Abūʿ Abdallāh b. Khafīf used to spend the winter. All these villages and stations are on the mountain. At the foot of the mountain on the same track, there is an ancient tree called *darakht rawān*, whose leaves never fall off.[26] I have never seen anyone who has seen its [fallen] leaves. They also give this tree the name of 'the walker', because if you look at it from the upper part of the mountain, it appears far away and close to the foot, whereas if you look at it from the foot of the mountain it is quite the opposite. I saw there a number of *jūgīs* who never quit the base of the mountain waiting for its leaves to fall, for it is in a spot where it cannot be reached at all. They | tell lying tales about it, one being that whoever 184
eats of its leaves regains his youth, even if he be an old man, but that is false. Beneath the mountain is the great channel from which the rubies are taken; its water is a bright blue to the sight.

We travelled thence for two days to Dīnawar, a large town on the coast, inhabited by merchants.[27] In this town there is an idol known as Dīnawar, in a vast temple, in which there are about a thousand Brahmans and *jūgīs*, and about five hundred women, daughters of the Hindus, who sing and dance every night in front of the idol. The city and all its revenues form an endowment belonging to the idol, from which all who live in the temple and who visit it are supplied with food. The idol itself is of gold, about a man's height, and in the place of its

[24] I.B. confuses Shem, the son of Noah, with Seth, the son of Adam.

[25] The name survives in that of the sub-district of Atakalan and the village of Atakalanpan.

[26] Mžik suggests that the tree may have been *Ficus religiosa*. The name is Persian, meaning 'wandering tree'.

[27] Devundara (Dondra), at the southernmost point of Ceylon. A temple for the image of the recumbent Buddha had been built there early in the century, and the village of Gäṭamāna assigned to it.

185 eyes it has two great rubies, | which, as I was told, shine at night like lamps.

We went on to the town of Qālī, a small place six farsakhs from Dīnawar,[28] where there was a certain Muslim, called the captain Ibrāhīm who gave us hospitality in his place. We then journeyed to the town of Kalanbū [Colombo], which is one of the finest and largest towns in Sarandīb. In it resides the Wazīr and ruler of the sea Jālastī,[29] who has with him about five hundred Abyssinians. On setting out again we came, after three days' journey, back to Baṭṭāla again and visited its Sultan of whom we have spoken above. I found the captain Ibrāhīm awaiting me and we set sail for the land of Maʿbar.

[28] Galle.

[29] S. M. Yusuf notes; 'It is almost certain that "Jālasti" is not a proper name, but a designation compounded of *jala*, "water", "sea", and a word signifying "prince", "lord", maybe *arasan*' (*University of Ceylon History of Ceylon*, p. 711, n. 25). Yule and Cordier think it probable that he was the Muslim eunuch whom Marignolli calls Coya Jaan, i.e. Khwāja Jahān (*Cathay*, III, p. 231, n. 5).

CHAPTER XIX

Coromandel, Malabar and the Maldives

During the voyage a gale sprang up and our ship nearly took in water. We had no knowledgeable pilot on board. We came to some rocks | on which the ship 186
narrowly escaped being wrecked, and then into some shallows where the ship ran aground. We were face to face with death, and people jettisoned all that they had, and bade farewell to one another. We cut down the mast and threw it overboard, and the sailors made a wooden raft. We were then about two farsakhs from the shore. I was going to climb down to the raft, when my companions (for I had two slave-girls and two of my companions with me) said to me: 'Are you going to go down and leave us?' So I put their safety before my own and said: 'You two go down and take with you the girl that I love.' The [other] girl said: 'I am a good swimmer and I shall hold on to one of the raft ropes and swim with them.' So both my companions (the one being Muḥammad b. Farḥān al-Tūzarī, and the other an Egyptian) and the one girl went on the raft, the other girl swimming. The sailors tied ropes to the raft, and swam with their aid. I sent along with them | all the things that 187
I valued and the gems and ambergris, and they reached the shore in safety because the wind was in their favour. I myself stayed on the ship. The captain made his way ashore on the rudder. The sailors set to work to make four rafts, but night fell before they were completed, and the ship took in water. I climbed on the poop and stayed there until morning, when a party of infidels came out to us in a boat and we went ashore with them to the coast of Maʿbar. We told them that we were friends of their Sultan, under whose protection they live, and they wrote informing him of this. He was then two days' journey away, on an expedition, and I too wrote to him telling

him what had happened to me. Those infidels took us into a great jungle and brought us some fruit resembling melons. This is produced by the *muql* tree and has inside it what
188 resembles cotton containing a honey-like substance | which they extract and from which they make a sweet called by them *tall*, resembling sugar.[1] They brought also some good fish.

We stayed there three days at the end of which an amir called Qamar al-Dīn arrived from the Sultan with a body of horse and foot, bringing a palanquin and ten horses. I and my companions, the captain of the ship, and one of the slave-girls rode, and the other was carried in the palanquin. We reached the fort of Harkātū [Arcot], where we spent the night, and where I left the slave-girls and some of my slaves and companions. On the following day we arrived at the camp of the Sultan.

Account of the Sultan of the country of al-Maʿbar.[2] He is Ghiyāth al-Dīn of Dāmaghān. At the outset of his career he was a horseman in the service of the malik Mujīr b. Abī-Rajā, one of the household of the Sultan Muḥammad. He then entered
189 the service of the amir Ḥājī, son of | the Sayyid Sultan Jalāl al-Dīn. Then he became a malik, and having previously been called Sirāj al-Dīn he now took the name of Ghiyāth al-Dīn. The land of Maʿbar had been under the rule of the Sultan Muḥammad, the king of Dihlī. Then my father-in-law the Sharif Jalāl al-Dīn Aḥsan Shāh revolted. After reigning there for five years he was killed and one of his amirs, ʿAlā al-Dīn Udaijī, ruled after him for a year. He then made an expedition against the infidels and after taking immense riches of theirs and enormous booty returned to his country. He raided them again the following year but, after defeating them with enormous slaughter, it chanced on the very day he killed them that he took his helmet from his head to drink, was hit by a chance arrow, and died on the spot. They appointed as ruler his son-in-law Quṭb al-Dīn, but after forty days disliking his conduct,

[1] *Muql* is the fruit of the doum palm or gingerbread tree, *Hyphaena thebaica*. The name I.B. gives to palm-sugar or jaggery is unaccountable.

[2] I.B. is one of the few sources for the history of the short-lived Muslim Sultanate of Madurai. According to the historian ʿIṣāmī Jalāl al-Dīn was merely the *kutwāl* (police chief or commandant of the fort) when he seized power. It has been suggested that I.B. exaggerated his relative's rank (A. K. Majumdar in R. C. Majumdar (ed.) *The Delhi Sultanate*, p. 244, n. 16).

| they killed him, and the Sultan Ghiyāth al-Dīn succeeded 190
him as ruler. He married the daughter of the Sultan Sharif Jalāl al-Dīn, and it was her sister that I had married in Dihlī.

Account of my coming to the Sultan Ghiyāth al-Dīn. When we reached the neighbourhood of his camp, he sent one of his chamberlains to welcome us. He himself was lodging in a fort made of wood. Now, it is a custom throughout India that no person enters the Sultan's presence without boots on. I had no boots with me so one of the infidels gave me a pair. There were a number of Muslims there and I was astonished to find an infidel show greater courtesy than they did. When I appeared before the Sultan he bade me be seated, summoned the qāḍī, al-Ḥājj Ṣadr al-Zamān Bahā' al-Dīn, and assigned to me three tents in his vicinity. They call these tents *khiyām*. He
also sent furnishings | and some of their food, that is rice and 191
meat. They have the same custom there as in our own country of serving curdled milk after the meat.

Afterwards I met him and proposed to him the business of the Maldives and that he should send troops there. He decided to do this and designated the ships for the purpose, the gift for the Sultana and the robes of honour and presents for the Wazīrs and amirs. He entrusted me with drawing up his contract of marriage with the Sultana's sister and ordered that three ships should be loaded with alms for the poor people of the islands. He said to me: 'You will come back after five days.' Khwāja Sarlak, the admiral, said to him: 'It is impossible to travel to the islands except after three months from now.' The Sultan said to me: 'If that is so, proceed to Fattan[3] so we can bring this expedition to an end. We shall return to
Mutra our capital[4] | and the expedition will start from there.' 192
So I stayed with him and in the meantime did not send for my slave-girls and companions.

Account of the Sultan's order of march and his abominable conduct in killing women and children. The country through which we

[3] This must represent *pattinam*, *patnam*, *patam*, etc., the last element in the name of many ports in south India. Kaveripattanam and Negapatam (Nagapattinam) were the most important on the Coromandel coast, but Yule and Cordier suggest somewhere nearer to Madurai, e.g. Devipattinam (*Cathay*, IV, p. 35, n. 1).

[4] Madurai.

were passing was one jungle of trees and reeds such that nobody could penetrate it. The Sultan ordered that everyone in the army, whether high or low, should carry an axe for cutting through it. When the camp was pitched he rode to the forest accompanied by the troops, and they cut down trees from morning till afternoon. Then food was brought and all the people ate, one party after another. Then they resumed cutting down trees till evening. Any infidel whom they found
193 in the jungle they took prisoner. They made | wooden stakes sharpened at both ends and put them on the prisoners' shoulders to carry. Their wives and children were with them and they brought them to the camp. It is their custom to make round the camp a wooden palisade with four gates, which they call a *katkar*.[5] They make another *katkar* round the Sultan's tent. Outside the peripheral *katkar* they make platforms about half a man's height and light fires on them at night. The slaves and sentinels pass the night there. Each of them has a handful of thin reeds and when some of the infidels come to attack the camp at night each one lights the bundle he has in his hand and the night becomes like day from the brightness of the illumination, and the horsemen ride out in pursuit of the infidels.

In the morning the infidels taken prisoner the day before
194 were divided into four groups which were taken | to each of the four gates of the *katkar*. The stakes they had carried the day before were fixed in them and driven through them. Their women were killed and tied by the hair to the stakes. The little children were killed in their laps and left there. [Another] camp was pitched, they busied themselves cutting down more jungle, and acted in the same way with those they made prisoners. This was an abomination which I have not known of any other king. That is why God hastened his death.

One day the qāḍī was seated on his right and I on his left, and he was eating with us, and I saw an infidel brought to him with his wife and seven year old son. He signed with his hand to the sword bearers that they should cut off the man's head. Then he said to them: 'Va zan-i ū va pesar-i-ū',[5] which means 'and his son and his wife' and their throats were cut. I looked

[5] Persian.

away from them | and when I arose I found their heads thrown 195
on the ground.

I was in his presence one day when an infidel man had been
brought to him. He said something I did not understand and
immediately some of his myrmidons drew their knives. I got
up at once and he said to me: 'Where are you going?' I said: 'I
am going to pray the afternoon prayer.' He understood and
laughed. He ordered his hands and feet to be cut off. When I
returned I found him wallowing in his blood.

*Account of his rout of the infidels, one of the greatest victories of
Islam*. Bordering on his country was an infidel Sultan named
Balāl Diyau.[6] He was one of the principal infidel Sultans. His
army exceeded one hundred thousand and he also had with
him twenty thousand Muslims, | rascals, criminals and run- 196
away slaves. He wanted to get control of the country of al-
Maʿbar. The Muslim army there comprised six thousand
men, of whom half were excellent and the other half worthless
and of no use. They met outside the city of Kubbān.[7] The
infidel routed them and they retreated to Mutra, their capital,
while he encamped at Kubbān, one of the greatest and
strongest of the Muslim cities. He besieged it for ten months
and they were left with provisions for only fourteen days. The
infidel proposed to them that they should leave under safe
conduct and abandon the town to him. They said to him: 'We
must submit this to our Sultan.' He promised them fourteen
days [to do this]. They wrote to Sultan Ghiyāth al-Dīn about
their situation. He read their letter to the people on Friday.
They wept and said: 'We shall sell our lives | for God. If the 197
infidel takes that city he will come and lay siege to us. It is
better for us to die by the sword.' They pledged one another
to face death and they marched out next day. They took off
their turbans from their heads and put them on their horses'
necks, this signifying someone who is willing to die. They
placed the most valiant and bravest in the van, to the number
of three hundred. On the right they placed Saif al-Dīn Bahādūr,
a scrupulous and courageous jurist, and on the left the malik

[6] The Hoysala king Ballāla III, whose capital was at Dvārasamudra (Dursamand).

[7] Konnanūrkoppam.

Muḥammad the Silaḥdār (Sword bearer). The Sultan rode in the centre with three thousand men. The remaining three thousand he made the rearguard under Asad al-Dīn Kaykhusrū the Persian. They made for the infidel's camp at the time of the siesta when people were relaxing and the horses were at pasture. They attacked it and the infidels thought they were
198 robbers | and came out against them in confusion and fought them. Sultan Ghiyāth al-Dīn came up and they were disastrously routed. Their Sultan wanted to mount his horse, though he was eighty years old. Nāṣir al-Dīn, who was the son of the Sultan's brother, and who succeeded him as king, seized him and was going to kill him, not recognizing him. One of his slaves said to him: 'He is the Sultan.' So he made him prisoner and took him to his uncle, who treated him with apparent respect until he had extracted from him his wealth, his elephants and his horses. He was promising to set him at liberty, but when he had extorted everything he possessed, he killed and flayed him, stuffed his skin with straw, and hung it on the wall of Mutra, where I saw it hanging.

Let us return to our story. I travelled from the camp and reached the city of Fattan, which is a large and fine city on the coast. Its harbour is wonderful. A big wooden pavilion has
199 been built in it, which stands on thick wooden piers | and is reached by a covered wooden causeway. When the enemy comes the ships in the harbour are moored by the pavilion, the infantry and archers climb up to it and the enemy has no chance. In this city is a fine mosque, built of stone, and there are plentiful grapes and good pomegranates. There I met the pious shaikh Muḥammad of Naisābūr, one of the distraught faqirs, who let their hair grow down to their shoulders. With him was a lion which he had brought up, which ate with the faqirs and sat with them. He had about thirty faqirs with him. One of them had a gazelle which was in the same place as the lion, which did not attack it.

I stayed in the city of Fattan. A *jūgī* made pills for Sultan Ghiyāth al-Dīn to give him strength in copulation. It was said
200 that the mixture | included iron filings and that he ate more of them than was necessary and fell ill. When he reached Fattan I went out to meet him and gave him a present. When he was

established there he sent for the admiral, Khwāja Sarūr, and said to him: 'Concern yourself with nothing else but the ships assigned to the expedition to the islands.' He wanted to give me the price of my present, but I refused. I regretted it later for he died and I received nothing. He stayed half a month in Fattan, then travelled to his capital. I stayed half a month after him, then travelled to his capital, the city of Mutra, a large city with wide streets. The first to choose it as his capital was my father-in-law the Sultan Sharif Jalāl al-Dīn Aḥsan Shāh, who made it similar to Dihlī and gave it fine buildings.

When I arrived there I encountered a plague from which people died suddenly. Whoever | fell ill died in two or three 201
days. If death was delayed it was only till the fourth day. When I went out I saw only the sick or the dead. I bought a slave-girl there on the understanding that she was healthy, but she died the next day. One day a woman came to me whose husband had been one of the Wazīrs of Sultan Aḥsan Shāh. She had with her her son who was eight years old, talented, clever and intelligent. She complained of her impoverished state and I gave them a sum of money. They were both healthy and fit. Next day she came asking for a shroud for the aforesaid son who had suddenly died. At the time of the Sultan's death I used to see in his audience hall hundreds of servant-girls who had been brought in to pound the rice from which food was made for others than the Sultan; they were ill and had thrown themselves down in the sun. |

When the Sultan came to Mutra he found his mother, his 202
wife and his son all ill. He stayed in the city for three days, then went to a river a farsakh away where there was an infidel temple. I followed him on the Thursday and he ordered that I should stay with the qāḍī. When the tents were pitched for me I saw people hurrying and pushing against each other. Some said: 'The Sultan is dead' and some said: 'It is his son who has died.' We found out the truth; it was the son who had died and he had no other. His death aggravated the Sultan's illness and his mother died on the Thursday.

Account of the Sultan's death, of the accession of his brother's son, and of my leaving him. On the third Thursday Sultan Ghiyāth al-Dīn died. I learnt this | and hurried to the city fearing there 203
would be disturbances. I met Nāṣir al-Dīn, his brother's son

and heir apparent, on his way to the camp, to which he had been sent, as the Sultan had left no son. He asked me to go back with him but I refused, which made an impression on him. This Nāṣir al-Dīn had been a household attendant in Dihlī before his uncle reigned. When his uncle became ruler he fled to him in the guise of a faqir. Fate determined that he should rule after him. When allegiance had been sworn to him, the poets eulogised him and he rewarded them generously. The first to rise and recite was the qāḍī Ṣadr al-Zamān; he gave him five hundred dinars and a robe of honour. Then came the Wazīr called Al-Qāḍī to whom he gave two thousand dinar dirhams. He gave me three hundred dinars and a robe of honour. He distributed alms among the faqirs and the poor. When the preacher delivered the first address in which he
204 mentioned | his name, dinars and dirhams were poured on him on gold and silver plates. The obsequies of Sultan Ghiyāth al-Dīn were celebrated. The whole Qur'ān was recited at his grave every day. Then the *ʿashshārs*[8] recited, food was brought and people ate. Then dirhams were given to everyone according to his status. This continued for forty days. Then they did the same every year on the anniversary of his death.

The first thing Sultan Nāṣir al-Dīn did was to remove his uncle's Wazīr from office and demand his wealth. As Wazīr he appointed the malik Badr al-Dīn whom his uncle had sent to receive me when I was at Fattan. He soon died and Khwāja Sarūr, the admiral, was appointed Wazīr. The Sultan ordered that he should be addressed as Khwāja Jahān, like the Wazīr in Dihlī. Anyone who addressed him in any other way was fined
205 a specified number of dinars. Then | Sultan Nāṣir al-Dīn killed the son of his paternal aunt, who was married to the daughter of Sultan Ghiyāth al-Dīn, and married her himself. The Sultan was told that the malik Masʿūd had visited him in prison before his death, so he killed him too. He killed the malik Bahādūr who was brave, generous and a distinguished man. He ordered that the ships which his uncle had designated for the expedition to the islands should be assembled for me but then a fever, fatal in that country, attacked me. I thought it meant death for me, but God inspired me to resort to the

[8] Those who recited one of the ten portions into which the Qur'ān is divided.

tamarind, which is abundant there. I took about a pound of it in water and drank it; it purged me for three days and God cured me of my illness. I became disgusted with that city and sought permission to leave it. The Sultan said to me: 'How should you leave when not a single month is left before the time for sailing to the islands? Stay till you are given everything that the Master of the World ordered for you.' I refused and he wrote on my behalf to | Fattan and found eight ships 206
going to al-Yaman in one of which I travelled. We met four ships which fought us for a little while and then withdrew. We reached Kawlam. I still had some of my illness left in me and I stayed there for three months and then embarked on a ship to go to Sultan Jamāl al-Dīn of Hinawr, but infidels attacked us between Hinawr and Fākanūr.

Account of how the infidels plundered us. When we reached the little island between Hinawr and Fākanūr[9] the infidels came out against us in twelve warships, fought fiercely against us and overcame us. They took everything I had preserved for emergencies; they took the pearls and rubies that | the king of 207
Ceylon had given me, they took my clothes and the supplies given me by pious people and saints. They left me no covering except my trousers. They took everything everybody had and set us down on the shore. I returned to Qāliqūṭ and went into one of the mosques. One of the jurists sent me a robe, the qāḍī a turban and one of the merchants another robe. I learnt there that the Wazīr ʿAbdallāh had married the Sultana Khadīja after the death of the Wazīr Jamāl al-Dīn and that the wife I had left pregnant had given birth to a male child. I thought of going to the islands but I remembered the enmity between me and the Wazīr ʿAbdallāh. I opened the Qur'ān and found: 'The angels will descend to them saying "Do not be afraid and do not grieve."'[10] I asked God's blessing and set out. After ten days I reached the Maldive islands and landed |
in Kannalūs. Its governor, ʿAbd al-ʿAzīz of Maqdashaw, 208
treated me with honour, offered me hospitality and prepared a *kundura* for me. After that I reached Hululī which is the island to which the Sultana and her sisters go to relax and swim.[11]

[9] Nitran or Pigeon Island.
[10] Qur'ān, sūra xli, 30.
[11] Hululē, now the airport.

They call this 'going to the sea'. They play games on the ships and when she is there the Wazīrs and amirs send her presents and gifts. I found there the Sultana's sister, her husband the preacher Muḥammad, the son of the Wazīr Jamāl al-Dīn, and her mother, who had been my wife. The preacher visited me and food was brought. One of the islanders went off to the Wazīr ʿAbdallāh and informed him of my arrival. He asked about me and about those who had come with me. He was told that I had come to fetch my son, who was about two years old. His mother came to the Wazīr and complained of this. He
209 said | to her: 'I shall not prevent him from fetching his son.' He importuned me to come to the [principal] island and lodged me in a house opposite the tower of his palace so as to be aware of my circumstances. He sent me a complete set of clothes, betel and rose water as is their custom. I came with two silk robes to throw down when greeting him. They took them both from me but the Wazīr did not come out to receive me that day. My son was brought to me, but it appeared to me that it would be best for him to stay with them, so I returned him to them and stayed for five days. I thought it best to hasten my journey and I asked permission to leave. The Wazīr summoned me and I went in to him. They brought me the two robes they had taken from me and I threw them down on greeting him, according to custom. He seated me beside him and asked me about my circumstances. I ate with him and washed my hands in the bowl with him, something he never does with anyone. Betel was brought and I left. He sent me
210 robes and *bustūs* | of cowries and behaved as well as possible.

CHAPTER XX

Bengal and Assam[1]

I left and we were at sea for forty-three days and then reached the country of Bengal. It is a spacious country, producing rice in abundance. Nowhere in the world have I seen cheaper produce than there, but it is gloomy and the people of Khurāsān say 'dūzakhast pur niʿma',[2] meaning 'it is a hell full of blessings'. I have seen rice sold in the bazaars there at twenty-five Dihlī pounds for a silver dinar, which is eight dirhams. Their dirham is precisely equal to the silver ingot. The Dihlī pound is twenty Maghribī pounds. I have heard them say that it was a high price. Muḥammad al-Maṣmūdī from the Maghrib, who was a truthful man, had lived there formerly, and who died in my house in Dihlī, told
me he had | a wife and a servant and used to buy provisions for 211
the three of them for a year for eight dirhams. He also said he used to buy eighty Dihlī pounds of rice in the husk for eight dirhams. When it had been pounded fifty pounds net were left, that is to say, ten qintars. I have seen a milch cow sold there for three silver dinars; their cattle are buffaloes. I have seen fat hens sold at eight for one dirham. Pigeon squabs are sold at fifteen for a dirham. I have seen a fat ram sold for two, a pound of sugar, the Dihlī pound, for four, of julep for eight, of ghee for four, and of sesame oil for two. I have seen a piece of fine, high quality cotton, measuring thirty cubits, sold for two dinars. I have seen a slave-girl, good looking and suited to

[1] The character of I.B.'s narrative changes to some extent in this and the next two chapters. He mentions few place names considering the great distances he claims to have travelled in Bengal and China, two other countries which he says he visited cannot be plausibly identified, and for various reasons some of what he relates cannot possibly be true. The problem of chronology and authenticity that arise will be discussed in vol. V.

[2] Persian.

212 be a concubine, sold for a single gold dinar, which | is two and a half Maghribī gold dinars. I bought a girl named ʿAshūra of outstanding beauty for about this price. One of my companions bought a pretty young slave boy named Lu'lu' (Pearl) for two gold dinars.

The first city we entered in Bengal was Sudkāwān, a very big city on the shore of the Great Sea.[3] The rivers Kank, to which the Indians go on pilgrimage, and Jūn unite there and flow into the sea. There are many ships on the river in which they fight the people of the country of al-Laknawtī.[4]

Account of the Sultan of Bengal. He is Sultan Fakhr al-Dīn, surnamed Fakhra, an excellent Sultan, a lover of strangers |
213 and specially of faqirs and sufis.[5] The kingship of this country belonged to Sultan Nāṣir al-Dīn, son of Sultan Ghiyāth al-Dīn Balban.[6] He it is whose son Muʿizz al-Dīn was made king in Dihlī. Nāṣir al-Dīn went to fight him. They met by the river and it was called 'the meeting of two auspicious stars'. We have already recounted this, and how he relinquished the kingdom for his son and returned to Bengal, where he stayed till he died.[7] Then his [other] son Shams al-Dīn ruled till he died.[8] Then his son Shihāb al-Dīn ruled until he was overthrown by his brother Ghiyāth al-Dīn Bahādūr Būr. Shihāb al-Dīn appealed for help to Sultan Ghiyāth al-Dīn Tughluq, who helped him and took Bahādūr Būr prisoner. Then when his

[3] Identified as Sātgāon (Sātgāmw) above Calcutta by Jadunath Sarkar, Ferrand and others, but Mžik and Gibb prefer Chittagong (Chātgāmw) which gives readier access to Sylhet which seems to have been his objective. Neither place is on the shore of the ocean. Sātgāon is near the confluence of the Ganges and the Yamuna, which does not here mean the great river which joins the Ganges at Allahabad, but a stream connecting it with the Brahmaputra.

[4] The ancient name of Gaur, often the capital of as much of Bengal as was under Muslim rule. I.B. uses the name to designate the independent principality ruled by ʿAlā al-Dīn ʿAlī from Pandua, which had been renamed Fīrūzābād.

[5] Fakhr al-Dīn Mubārak Shāh, the independent ruler of eastern Bengal from Sonārgāon (Sonārgāmw).

[6] The history of Bengal at this time is obscure and confused and must be largely reconstructed from fragmentary numismatic evidence. It has been evident from his history of the Sultans of Delhi that I.B. was a careless historian (III, pp. 629–56).

[7] III, pp. 635–7.

[8] It has been questioned whether Shams al-Dīn Fīrūz can have been the son of his predecessor Nāṣir al-Dīn Maḥmūd Bughrā Khān, since none of his coins bear the inscription *sulṭān bin sulṭān*, 'Sultan son of a Sultan'.

son Muḥammad came to rule he freed Bahādūr Būr on condition that he shared sovereignty with him. He reneged and
Sultan Muḥammad fought him till he killed him.[9] Thereupon
he put a brother-in-law of his in charge but the troops killed
him. | ʿAlī Shāh, then in the country of Laknawti, took over 214
the government. When Fakhr al-Dīn saw that rule had passed
from the sons of Sultan Nāṣir al-Dīn, whose client he was, he
rebelled in Sudkāwān and in Bengal and made himself independent. Fierce hostilities broke out between him and ʿAlī
Shāh. When winter came and the muddy season Fakhr al-Dīn
invaded Laknawtī by river, because he was strong there, but
when the dry season came ʿAlī Shāh invaded Bengal by land,
where he was strong.[10]

Anecdote. Sultan Fakhr al-Dīn's love for faqirs went so far that
he installed one of them as his deputy in the government of
Sudkāwān. He was called Shaidā. | Fakhr al-Dīn went away to 215
fight an enemy and Shaidā rebelled against him, wanted to
become an independent ruler, and killed his only son. When
he learnt this Fakhr al-Dīn returned to his capital. Shaidā and
his followers fled to the city of Sunarkāwān, which is strongly
fortified.[11] The Sultan sent for troops to besiege it, but the
inhabitants, fearing for their lives, seized Shaidā and sent him
to the Sultan's camp. They wrote to him about this and he
ordered them to send him his head, which they did. A large
number of faqirs were killed on his account.

When I first entered Sudkāwān I did not see the Sultan of
the city and did not meet him, because he was in revolt
against the ruler of India, and I was afraid of the conse-
quences. I left Sudkāwān for the mountains of Kāmarū, a
journey from Sudkāwān | of one month.[12] They are extensive 216
mountains which join China and also Tibet, where are the
musk gazelles. The people of these mountains are like
Turks.[13] They are strong workers and a slave of that race is
twice as good as a slave of another. They are famous for
resorting to magic and for their involvement in it. My object in

[9] III, p. 653.
[10] ʿAlī's cavalry were useless in the rains.
[11] Sonargaon.
[12] The Kamrup district in Assam.
[13] A reference to the Shan (Ahom) and related peoples.

going to these mountains was to meet a saint living there, Shaikh Jalāl al-Dīn of Tabrīz.[14]

Account of the Shaikh Jalāl al-Dīn. This Shaikh is among the greatest saints and most remarkable men, responsible for famous miracles and wonderful achievements. He was an aged man. He told me he had even set eyes on – God's mercy on him – the Caliph al-Mustaʿṣim billāh the ʿAbbāsid in Baghdād and was there when he was killed.[15] Later on his companions
217 told me | he had died at the age of a hundred and fifty and that he had fasted for about forty years, breaking the fast only after ten continuous days. He had a cow and used to break his fast with its milk. He used to stand up all night. He was thin, tall and had little hair on his cheeks. He converted the people of those mountains to Islam, and that is why he stayed among them.

One of his miracles. One of his companions told me that one day before his death he summoned them, commended the fear of God to them, and said: 'Tomorrow I shall leave you, if God wills. My successor for you will be God, than whom there is no other god.' Next day God took him when he prayed the noon prayer, during the last prostration. Beside the cave where they
218 lived they found a grave dug | with a shroud and aromatics for embalming. They enshrouded him, prayed over him, and buried him there, may God have mercy on him.

Another miracle of his. When I was on my way to visit this shaikh four of his companions met me two days' journey from the place where he lived. They told me that the shaikh had said to the faqirs who were with him: 'The traveller from the Maghrib has come to you. Go and receive him.' They had set out accordingly by his order. He had no knowledge whatever of me; this had been revealed to him. I went with them to the

[14] Jalāl al-Dīn of Tabrīz, one of the founders of the Suhrawardī order in India. He was particularly active in the neighbourhood of Lakhnauti and did not visit Assam. By this time he had been dead for about a century. I.B. confused him with Shāh Jalāl, the militant preacher responsible for the conversion to Islam of the Sylhet district, now part of Bangladesh. R. M. Eaton has remarked that Bengalis commonly make the same mistake (Ross Dunn, p. 263, n. 26). Even so it seems strange that I.B. should have travelled from Madurai to Sylhet to meet someone who had died about a hundred years before, and have spent three days there with someone else whom he still supposed to be the man he wanted to meet.

[15] In 1258, when the Mongols captured Baghdad.

shaikh and came to his hospice outside the cave. There is no
cultivated land there. The people of the country, Muslims
and infidels alike, come to the hospice with presents and gifts,
and the faqirs and visitors feed on them. The shaikh has only
a cow | with whose milk he breaks his fast after ten days, as we 219
have already explained. When I entered his presence he rose,
embraced me, and asked about my country and my travels,
about which I informed him. He said to me: 'You are the
traveller of the Arabs.' One of his companions who was present said: 'And of the non-Arabs, my master.' He said: 'And of
the non-Arabs. Treat him with respect.' They took me to the
hospice and gave me hospitality for three days.

Marvellous anecdote including miracles by him. The day he received me I saw he was wearing a goat-hair *farajīya*, which I
admired. I said to myself: 'I wish the shaikh would give it to
me.' When I went to take leave of him, he rose, went to the
side of the cave, took off the *farajīya*, and put it on me with a
skull-cap from his head. He put on a patched garment. The
faqirs told me that the shaikh did not usually wear | that 220
farajīya and had put it on only on the occasion of my arrival.
He had said to them: 'The Maghribī will want this *farajīya*, an
infidel Sultan will take it from him and give it to our brother
Burhān al-Dīn of Ṣāgharj,[16] to whom it belongs and for whom
it was intended.' When the faqirs told me that I said: 'I have
received the saint's benediction in that he has clothed me with
this garment. I shall not enter the presence of any Sultan,
infidel or Muslim, wearing it.' I left the shaikh and it happened that a long time after I entered the country of China
and reached the city of Khansā. I was separated from my
companions because of the great crowd. I was wearing the
farajīya. While I was in a certain street the Wazīr appeared
with a huge cortège. He noticed me, summoned me to him,
took me by the hand, asked me about my arrival, and did not
part from me till we reached the house of the Sultan. I wanted
to leave him but he prevented me and presented me to | the 221
Sultan. He asked me about the Muslim Sultans. While I was
replying he looked at the *farajīya* and admired it. The Wazīr
said to me: 'Take it off.' I could not refuse. The Sultan took it

[16] See III, p. 677 and n. 89.

and ordered me to be given ten robes of honour, a fully caparisoned horse and a sum of money. I was displeased about this, but then I recalled that the shaikh had said that an infidel Sultan would take it and I was much amazed. Next year I went into the residence of the king of China in Khān Bāliq [Beijing] and sought the hospice of the Shaikh Burhān al-Dīn of Ṣāgharj. I found him reading and wearing the identical *farajīya*. I was astonished at this and fingered it in my hand. He said to me: 'Why are you fingering it? Do you recognize it?' I said: 'Yes. It is the one which the Sultan of Khansā took from me.' He said: 'My brother Jalāl al-Dīn made this for me and
222 he wrote to me | saying "The *farajīya* will come to you by the hand of so-and-so."' Then he offered me the letter. I read it and was amazed at how exactly correct the shaikh had been. I told Burhān al-Dīn the first part of the story. He said: 'My brother Jalāl al-Dīn was greater than all that. He had power over all that exists, but he has gone to the mercy of God. I have been told', he said, 'that he prayed the dawn prayer every day in Mecca and made the pilgrimage every year, for he was absent on the two days of ʿArafa and the Feast and no one knew where he had gone.'

When I had said farewell to Shaikh Jalāl al-Dīn I travelled to the city of Habanq, one of the biggest and most beautiful cities.[17] It is divided by a river which flows from the mountains of Kāmarū, called the Blue River, by which one goes to Bengal and the country of al-Laknawtī. There are water wheels,
223 orchards | and villages on both banks as there are on the Nile in Egypt. The people are infidels under Muslim protection. They pay half of their produce and dues in addition. We travelled on this river for fifteen days among villages and orchards as if we were walking through a bazaar. There were innumerable ships on the river and on each ship there was a drum. When two ships met each one beat a drum and they greeted each other. The said Sultan Fakhr al-Dīn ordered that on that river no freight charges should be exacted from faqirs and that provisions should be supplied to any of them who was without them. If a faqir arrives in a city he is given half a dinar.

[17] The name survives as that of a small hill on the bank of the Chingra Khal river, near Sylhet (Yule, *Cathay*, IV, pp. 151–5). Gibb (*Selections*, 366, n. 10) contends that the Blue River can only be the Meghna.

IBN BAṬṬŪṬA LEAVES BENGAL

After travelling by river for fifteen days, as we have described, we reached the city of Sunarkāwān, the city whose people seized the faqir Shaidā | when he had taken refuge 224
there. When we arrived there we found a junk intending to go to the country of al-Jāwa[18] which is forty days' sail away, on which we embarked.

[18] Not Java but Sumatra, as often, though not invariably, in Arabic geographical texts, Java being Mul Jāwa.

CHAPTER XXI

South-east Asia

We embarked and after fifteen days we arrived at the country of the Barahnakār who have mouths like those of dogs.[1] They are sottish and do not adhere to the religion of the Indians or to any other. They live in houses of reeds roofed with dried grass on the seashore. They have many bananas, areca palms and betel bushes. Their men are like us except that their mouths are like those of dogs. Their women are not like that and are of outstanding beauty. The men are naked with no covering except that some of them put their male organs and testicles in a painted holder made of reeds and attached to their bellies. The women cover them-
225 selves with tree leaves. | There is a community of Muslims among them. They are people from Bengal and at Jāwa and live in a separate quarter. They told us that they copulate like beasts and do not hide what they are doing. A man has thirty wives, more or less, and they do not commit adultery. If one does commit adultery the penalty for the man is that he is fixed to a cross till he dies, unless his friend or slave is fixed to the cross in his stead, when he is freed. The penalty for the

[1] Most commentators except Gibb and Tibbetts have treated this as a toponym, but I.B. evidently refers to a people. They have not been satisfactorily identified. The Andamanese, whom Marco Polo describes as having heads like big mastiffs, and the Nicobarese have been suggested, but these are both incompatible with the elephants and the Muslim settlement. The direction and duration of the voyage from Sonargaon would indicate somewhere near Cape Negrais. At this time Arakan was independent of Burma, and Sandoway and the coastal area to the south were probably independent of Arakan, the capital of which was in the Akyab district. Yule (*Cathay*, IV, p. 93, n. 1) remarked that 'Caesar Frederic and some other sixteenth-century travellers' called the sea off Negrais the Sea of Bara, but this is a misunderstanding. Bara, as used by Federici, Gasparo Balbi, Bocarro and Fitch, is not a proper name, but the word for 'bar'. As with Ṭawālisī below, it is more relevant to identify sources from which I.B. could have taken his descriptions than locations that would validate them.

woman is that the Sultan orders all his household attendants to copulate with her, one after the other till she dies, in his presence. Then they throw her into the sea. This is why they do not allow anyone from the ships to stay among them unless he is settled there. They buy and sell only on the shore. They bring water for the traffickers on elephants because | it is to be 226
had a long way from the shore. They do not allow strangers to draw it themselves, being nervous about their women who are attracted by handsome men. Elephants are plentiful among them but only their Sultan can sell them; they are bought from him for pieces of cloth. They have a strange language which nobody understands unless he has lived among them and revisited them often. When we reached the shore they came to us in little boats each of which was a single log hollowed out. They brought bananas, rice, betel, areca nuts and fish.

Account of their Sultan. Their Sultan came to us riding on an elephant on which was a kind of pack saddle made of skins. He was dressed in a goatskin robe, the hair on which was turned outwards. On his head were three coloured silk fillets |
and in his hand was a javelin of reed. Some twenty of his 227
relatives accompanied him on elephants. He sent us a gift of pepper, ginger, cinnamon, the fish there is in the Maldives[2] and Bengali cloths. They do not wear these but deck the elephants with them on feast days. For every ship that docks in his country he takes a slave-girl, a male slave, elephant cloths, and gold ornaments which his wife puts in her girdle and on her toes. If anyone does not give them this tribute they use magic against him. The sea becomes rough for him and he perishes, or almost so.

Anecdote. It happened that one night while we were in their port a slave of the master of the ship, who had repeatedly visited these people, left the ship | one night for an assignation 228
with the wife of one of their chief men in a place like a cave on the shore. The husband knew of this and came to the cave with a party of his friends, found them there and they were taken to the Sultan. He ordered that the slave's testicles should be cut off and he should be crucified. By his orders people copulated with the woman till she died. Then the

[2] See p. 823.

Sultan came to the shore and excused himself for what had happened. He said: 'We have to enforce our laws', and excused himself for what had happened. He then gave the master of the ship a slave in place of the one he had crucified.

We left these people and after twenty-five days we reached
the island of al-Jāwa [Sumatra], from which Jāwī incense takes
its name.[3] We saw it at a distance of half a day's sail. It is green
and very well wooded with coconuts, areca palms, cloves,
229 Indian aloes, *shakī*, *barkī*,[4] | mango, *jamūn*,[5] orange, and cam-
phor reeds. These people buy and sell with little pieces of tin
or unrefined Chinese gold. Most of the aromatics there are in
the part which belongs to the infidels; they are less common in
the part belonging to the Muslims. When we reached the
harbour the people came out to us in little boats bringing
coconuts, bananas, mangoes and fish. It is their custom to
make a present of these to the merchants and each of the latter
gives what recompense he can. The vice-admiral[6] also came
on board. He inspected the merchants who were with us and
gave us permission to land. We landed at the port which is a
big village on the seashore with houses called Sarḥā[7] about
four miles from the town. Then Buhrūz the vice-admiral
230 wrote to the Sultan | informing him of my arrival. The Sultan
ordered the amir Daulasa to come to meet me with the noble
qāḍī Amir Sayyid of Shīrāz and Tāj al-Din of Iṣfahān and other
jurists. They came out accordingly and brought a horse from
the Sultan's stables and other horses. I and my companions
mounted and we entered the Sultan's capital, the city of
Sumuṭra, a fine, big city with wooden walls and towers.

Account of the Sultan of al-Jāwa. He is Sultan Al-Malik Al-

[3] Benzoin.

[4] See III, p. 609, and n. 56.

[5] *Eugenia jambolana*, Lamk., a small, sweet fruit, which the French translators confused with the rose-apple, or jambu, *Eugenia jambos*, L.

[6] Literally 'the deputy of the master of the sea', but Ferrand notes that the official in question is the *shāhbandar*, who was in charge of policing the port, collecting dues and often of presenting foreigners to the ruler (*Relations de voyages et textes géographiques arabes, persans et turcs relatifs a l'Extrême-Orient*, II, 1914, p. 439, n. 6).

[7] Not identified; the reading may be corrupt as there is no *ḥ* in Malay. A Muslim state had been established in northern Sumatra before the end of the thirteenth century; it included the towns of Pasai and Semudera, the second eventually giving its name to the whole island.

Ẓāhir,[8] one of the noblest and most generous of kings, a Shāfiʿī in *madhhab*, and a lover of jurists, who come to his audiences for the recitation of the Qur'ān and for discussions. He often fights against and raids the infidels. He is unassuming and walks to the Friday prayer on foot. The people of his country are Shāfiʿīs | who are eager to fight infidels and readily 231
go on campaign with him. They dominate the neighbouring infidels who pay *jizya* to have peace.

Account of our entry to his house and his generosity to us. When we went towards the Sultan's house and were near it we found spears fixed in the ground on either side of the road. This is a sign that people should dismount and that no one riding should go any further. We dismounted and went into the audience chamber where we found the Sultan's deputy, who is called ʿUmdat al-Mulk ['Support of the Kingdom'] He rose and greeted us. Their form of greeting is shaking hands. We sat with him and he wrote a slip of paper to the Sultan informing him about our coming, sealed it and handed it to one of the pages, who brought the answer written on the back. Then a page | brought a *buqsha*, which is a clothes bag.[9] The 232
deputy took it in his hand, took me by the hand and took me into a little apartment they call a *fardkhāneh*,[10] a word like *zardkhāneh*, except that the first letter is *f*. It was his daytime rest room because it is the custom that the Sultan's deputy comes to the audience hall at dawn and does not leave it till nightfall. It is the same with the Wazīrs and great amirs.

From the *buqsha* he took three aprons, one of pure silk, one of silk and cotton, and one of silk and linen, three pieces of clothing which they call underwear, of the apron type, three pieces of different types which they call 'middle-wear', three woollen mantles, | one of them white, and three turbans. I put 233
on an apron in place of my trousers, according to their custom,

[8] The Malay chronicle *Hikayat Raja Raja Pasai* calls him Al-Malik Al-Ṭāhir. N. J. Krom has shown that Al-Malik Al-Ẓāhir was borne as an honorific title by several rulers of Pasai (*Hindoe-Javaansche Geschiedenis*, 2nd ed., 's Gravenhage, 1931, p. 396). I.B. almost certainly refers to Aḥmad who reigned from 1326 till about 1360 (A. H. Hill, 'The Coming of Islam to North Sumatra', *Journal of Southeast Asian History*, 4, 1963, pp. 6–21).

[9] A Turkish word denoting a cloth or leather carrier for clothes, etc.

[10] A Persian word for a small private room. For *zardkhāneh* see below p. 958 n. 48.

and one of each kind of clothing. My companions took what was left. Then they brought food, which was mostly rice, then a kind of beer, and then betel, which is the signal for departure. We accepted it, we rose, and the deputy rose when we did.

We left the audience hall and mounted. The deputy rode with us and they brought us to a garden enclosed with a wooden wall in the middle of which was a house, built of wood and spread with the cotton velvet carpets they call *mukhmalāt*,[11] some of them dyed and some not. In the house were beds of bamboo on which were counterpanes of silk, light quilts, and the cushions they call *balishts*.[12] We seated ourselves in the house with the deputy. Then the amir Daulasa brought two
234 slave-girls | and two male domestics. He said to me: 'The Sultan says to you that these are in accordance with our means, not those of Sultan Muḥammad.' The deputy then left and the amir Daulasa stayed with me.

We knew each other because he had come to Dihlī as a messenger to the Sultan. I said to him: 'When shall I see the Sultan?' He said: 'It is our custom that a newcomer does not greet the Sultan for three days, so that the fatigue of the journey has gone and he has recovered his faculties.' We stayed for three days; they brought us food three times a day, fruit and delicacies evening and morning. On the fourth day, which was a Friday, the amir Daulasa came to me and said: 'You will greet the Sultan in the *maqṣūra* of the mosque after prayers.' I came to the mosque and prayed the Friday prayer
235 with the chamberlain | Qayrān. Then I went to the Sultan. I found the qāḍī Amir Sayyid and the men of learning on his right and left. He gave me his hand, I greeted him, and he made me sit on his left. He asked me about Sultan Muḥammad and my travels. I replied. He then resumed the discussion on jurisprudence according to the Shāfiʿī *madhhab*. This lasted till the afternoon prayer. After praying he went into a room where he removed the clothes he was wearing. These were jurists' clothes which he wears when he goes to the mosque on Fridays on foot. Then he put on his royal robes which are tunics of silk and cotton.

[11] Presumably meaning carpets with deep pile.
[12] A Persian word for a cushion or pillow.

Account of his departure for his house and of the ceremony of greeting him. When he left the mosque he found the elephants and horses at the door. The custom is that when | the Sultan rides 236
on an elephant his escort ride on horses, and when he rides on a horse they ride on elephants; the theologians are on his right. That day he rode an elephant and we rode horses. We went with him to the audience hall. We dismounted in the usual place; the Sultan rode in. The Wazīrs, the amirs, the secretaries, the officers of state and the army commanders were ranged in ranks in the audience hall. The Wazīrs, of whom there were four, and the secretaries made the first rank. They greeted the Sultan and withdrew to their places. Then came the rank of the amirs, who greeted him and passed on to their stations. So did each category of people. Then came the sharifs and the jurists, then his personal favourites, the scholars and the poets, then the army commanders, then the pages and the mamluks. The Sultan remained on his elephant opposite the pavilion for assemblies. Above | his head a parasol en- 237
crusted with precious stones was raised. There were fifty caparisoned elephants on his right and as many on his left. There were a hundred horses on his right and as many on his left. They were Nubian horses.[13] His privy chamberlains stood before him. Then male musicians came and sang before him. Then came horses with silk coverings, gold anklets and gold-embroidered silk halters and they danced before him. I wondered at their performance; I had seen something similar before the king of India. Towards sunset the Sultan went into his house and the people went home.

Account of the rebellion of his brother's son and the reason for it. His brother's son was married to his daughter and he made him governor of a province. The youth fell in love with the daughter of one of the amirs | and wanted to marry her. It is the 238
practice there that if one of the people, whether an amir or a commoner or whatever, has a daughter who reaches marriageable age, he asks for the Sultan's orders in respect of her. The Sultan sends a woman who examines the girl and if the description she gives of her pleases him he marries her; if not, he

[13] The French editors read *nauba* and translate 'chevaux de relais'; Ferrand agrees. Dulaurier read *nūba*; Nubian horses were much prized and were often exported to South Asia.

leaves her alone and her relations marry her to whomever they
wish. The people there are eager for the Sultan to marry their
daughters because of the prestige and honour they acquire
thereby. When the father of the girl whom the Sultan's
nephew loved applied to the Sultan he sent someone to examine her, and then married her. The youth's passion became
violent and he saw no way to obtain her. Then the Sultan
went on campaign; the infidels were a month's journey away.
His nephew rebelled against him and entered Sumuṭra which
239 at the time was without walls. | He laid claim to the kingdom.
Some people swore allegiance to him; others refused. His
uncle learnt of this and returned. His nephew took what
possessions and treasure he could, and the girl he loved, and
made for the country of the infidels in Mul Jāwa [Java]. This is
why his uncle built the walls round Sumuṭra.

I stayed in Sumuṭra with him for fifteen days. After that I
sought permission to travel for it was the season, since the
voyage to China is not organized at any time. The Sultan
prepared a junk for us, stocked it with provisions, and was
most generous and kind, May God reward him! He sent one of
his companions with us to be host to us on the junk. We sailed
along his country for twenty-one nights. Then we reached
240 Mul Jāwa, which is the country of infidels.[14] It extends | for
two months' travel. It has aromatics, and good aloes of
Qāqula[15] and Qamāra.[16] both places being in the country. In
the country of Sultan Al-Ẓāhir, in al-Jāwa, there are only
incense, camphor, some cloves and some Indian aloes. The
greatest quantity of these occur in Mul Jāwa. We shall relate

[14] Java, at this time the centre of the Hindu empire of Majapahit. Yule's contention that Mul-Jāwa is the Malay peninsula (*Cathay*, IV, pp. 155–7) has been refuted by Tibbetts (pp. 151–2).

[15] There are references to this place in Arabic geographical works and travel narratives but they are inconclusive and sometimes inconsistent. A Chinese reference suggests that it was on the Tenasserim coast, which would imply that I.B. visited it on his way to Sumatra, and that his description is out of place (P. Wheatley, *The Golden Khersonese*, 1961, pp. 224–8).

[16] Usually Qamar (i.e. Khmer), meaning Cambodia. Its history at this time is confused and obscure, but there is no reason to think that it was subject to any state in either Java or the Malay peninsula; the threat to Khmer independence came from the Thais. Tibbetts suggests that Javanese rule over Tenasserim and Cambodia 'is probably a fiction of the Javanese court', I.B.'s voyage coinciding with 'the greatest period of Javanese expansion' (pp. 151–2).

about them what we have seen ourselves, have examined with care and verified.

Account of the incense.[17] The incense tree is small, as tall as a man or less. Its branches are like those of the artichoke, its leaves small and thin. Sometimes they fall and the tree is left with none. The incense is a resin occurring in the branches. It is more plentiful in Muslim country than among the infidels. |

Account of camphor.[18] The camphor tree is a reed like the reed 241
of our country, except that the hollow tubes in which the camphor is found are longer and thicker. When a reed is broken the camphor is found inside the tube shaped like it. The wonderful mystery about it is that there will be no camphor in the reed until some sort of creature is killed at its root; if this is not done there will be none at all. The best kind, which attains the greatest degree of cold, a dirham's weight of which is fatal because it congeals the breath of life, is called among them *hardala*.[19] A human being is killed beside the reed. Young elephants replace human beings.

Account of Indian aloes. The Indian aloes tree is like the | oak; 242
except that the bark is thin. Its leaves are exactly like oak leaves. It gives no fruit, the trunk does not become very large, and the roots are long and extend far. The aromatic smell is in the roots; the wood of the trunk and the leaves have no aroma.[20] In Muslim country every tree is private property, but

[17] He is describing benzoin.

[18] 'The description here given of the production of camphor has no resemblance to the truth, and I suspect that he may have confounded with camphor either something that he had learned about the *Tabashir* . . . or siliceous concretion found in bamboo-joints . . . or *Spodium*, if that be not the same thing' (Yule, *Cathay*, IV, p. 99, n. 3). Yule goes on to quote Crawfurd *Descriptive Dictionary of the Indian Islands*: 'The Malay camphor tree . . . is a large forest tree, confined, as far as is known, to a few parts of the islands of Sumatra and Borneo, but in these abundant. The oil . . . is found in the body of the tree where the sap should be'. Yule adds: 'The description in the text is yet more inapplicable to the Chinese camphor'.

[19] Yule comments: 'The word . . . does not seem to be known. I suspect . . . that what he has got hold of is the Malay *Artal*, corresponding to the Hindustani *Hartal*, 'orpiment' (*Cathay*, IV, p. 99, n. 3).

[20] I am indebted to Dr David V. Field of the Royal Botanic Gardens, Kew, for the following comments on this passage: 'The species most probably involved . . . is *Aquilaria malaccensis*. In India the species most commonly producing this product is *Aquilaria agallocha*. The aromatic resin deposited in the wood of these species only occurs when the tree becomes infected by a fungus. The highest concentrations occur in old trees which are sometimes said to look diseased. The

in infidel country most of them are not. Those that are privately owned are in Qāqula and these are the best aloes. It is the same in Qamāra which has the best kind of aloes. They are sold to the people of al-Jāwa for cloths. From Qamāra comes a kind on which an impression can be made, as if on wax. The roots of the *ʿaṭṭās* are cut off and buried in the earth for months; they retain their strength and are some of the best aloes. |

243 *Account of the clove.* The clove trees are of a great age and huge. There are more of them in infidel than in Muslim country. They are not privately owned as they are so common. What is brought to our country is the wood. What people in our country call 'the flower of the clove' is what falls from the flowers and is like orange flowers. The fruit of the clove is the nutmeg, known among us as the perfume nut. The flower that is formed within it is mace. I have seen all this and been witness to it.[21]

We arrived at the port of Qāqula and found there an assemblage of junks prepared for piracy and to fight any junk which might oppose them, for a tax is imposed on each junk.
244 We disembarked and went to the city of Qāqula. It | is a fine city with a wall of cut stone wide enough to take three elephants. The first thing I noticed outside the city was elephants with loads of Indian aloes wood which they burn in their houses; it is the price of firewood among us, or even cheaper. That, however, is when they sell it to each other. When they sell to (foreign) merchants a load costs a robe of cotton, cotton being more expensive than silk among them.

---

age, lack of vigour, etc., may have been responsible for the odd comment on the lack of fruit. There is no good reason why these trees should not fruit under normal conditions. The height of these large evergreen trees is given as from 40 to 80 feet and up to 8 feet in girth. One would expect the roots of most trees to be long and to extend far. The tissues, including the wood, of uninfected trees have no aroma. The leaves of Aquilaria species are similar to certain tropical species of *Quercus* (oaks).'

[21] I.B.'s botany is as unreliable as his history. The clove tree, *Eugenia aromatica* L., is neither particularly long-lived nor particularly large. It does not live much more than seventy years and grows to some 40 ft high, or more in the wild. The branches tend to be erect so the shape of the canopy is roughly cylindrical. The clove is the unopened flower bud. Nutmeg is the seed of another tree. *Myristica fragrans*; mace is the integument of the seed.

Plate I. A devotee visiting an ascetic. From Bundi, Rajasthan. By courtesy of the Victoria and Albert Museum

PLATE II. A white elephant. From Qazwīnī, *ʿAjāʾib al-makhlūqāt*, Royal Asiatic Society MS 178. See p. 851.

By courtesy of the Royal Asiatic Society

PLATE III. A gigantic bird carries off a woman. From Qazwīnī, *ʿAjāʾib al-makhlūqāt*, Royal Asiatic Society MS 178. See p. 912.
By courtesy of the Royal Asiatic Society

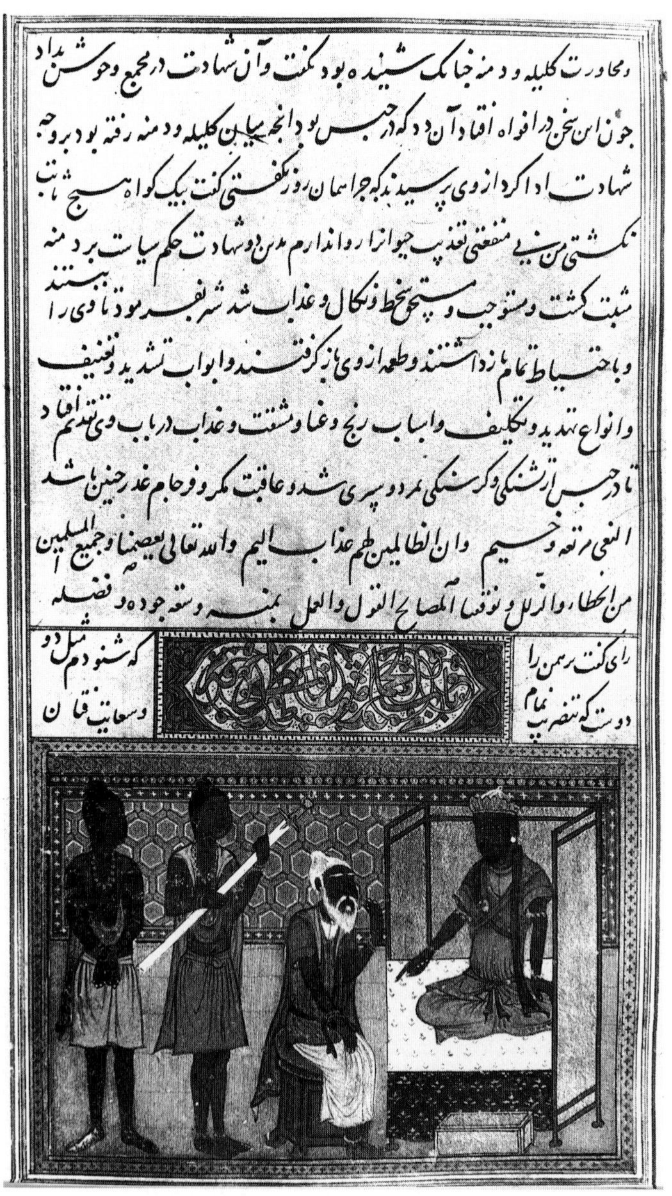

محاورت کلیله و دمنه چنانک شنیده بود بگفت و آن شهادت در مجمع وحوش بداد
چون این سخن در افواه افتاد آن دد که در حبس بود دانچه میان کلیله و دمنه رفته بود بر وجه
شهادت ادا کرد از وی پرسیدند که چرا تا امروز نگفتی گفت بیک گواه هیچ ثابت
نگشتی من بی منفعتی تعذیب حیوانرا روا ندارم بدین دو شهادت حکم سیاست بر دمنه
مثبت گشت و مستوجب و مستحق سخط و نکال و عذاب شد شیر بفرمود تا وی را ببستند
و باحتیاط تمام نگاه داشتند و طعمه از وی باز گرفتند و ابواب تشدید و تعنیف
و انواع تهدید و تکلیف و اسباب رنج و عنا و مشقت و عذاب در باب وی تقدیم افتاد
تا در حبس از تشنگی و گرسنگی بمرد و سپری شد و عاقبت مکر و فرجام غدر چنین باشد
البغی مرتعه وخیم و ان الظالمین لهم عذاب الیم والله تعالی یعصمنا و جمیع المسلمین
من الخطا و الزلل و یوفقنا لمصالح القول و العمل بمنه و سعة جوده و فضله

رای گفت برهمن را
دوست که بتضریب نمام

که شنودم مثل دو
وسعایت فتان

PLATE IV. A black king. From Topkapi Saray Müzesi MS H 362. See p. 958.
By courtesy of the Director, Topkapi Saray Müzesi

Elephants are very common; they ride on them and use them as beasts of burden. Everyone ties up his elephants at the gate. Everyone who has a shop ties up his elephant beside it, and rides it to go home and to carry goods. It is exactly the same with all the people of China and Khiṭā.[22] |

Account of the Sultan of Mul Jāwa. He is an infidel. I have seen 245
him outside his palace before a pavilion sitting on the ground
with no mat. The state officials were with him and the troops
paraded before him on foot. Nobody has horses there except
the Sultan. People ride elephants and they fight on them. The
Sultan learnt of me and summoned me. I came to him and
said: 'Greetings to whoever follows the true guidance.' They
understood only the word *salām*. The Sultan welcomed me
and ordered a cloth to be spread for me to sit on. I said to the
interpreter: 'How shall I sit on a cloth when the Sultan is
sitting on the ground?' He said: 'This is his custom. He sits on
the ground as a mark of humility. You are a guest and you have
come from a great Sultan. You must be treated with honour.' I
sat down | and he asked me about the Sultan (of India). His 245
questions were terse. He said to me: 'You will stay as our
guest for three days and then depart.'

Account of a wonderful thing I saw in his assembly. In this Sultan's
assembly I saw a man with a knife like a billhook. He laid it on
his neck and spoke at length what I did not understand. Then
he took the knife in both hands and cut his own throat. His
head fell to the ground because the knife was so sharp and his
grip of it so strong. I was astounded at what he had done. The
Sultan said: 'Does anyone do this among you?' I said: 'I have
never seen this anywhere.' He laughed and said: 'These are
our slaves and they kill themselves for love of us.' He ordered
the body to be carried away and burnt. The Sultan's deputies,
the state officials, the troops and the common people went out
to the cremation. | He granted ample pensions to his children, 247
wife and brothers, and they were highly honoured because of

[22] It is difficult to believe that I.B. would have written this is he had really been to China, but elephants were used extensively in the armies of the Mongol emperors and sometimes figured in the tribute they exacted from countries in SE Asia. Khiṭā, Cathay, refers to north China, not the part which remained under the rule of the Sung dynasty until Qubilai completed the Mongol conquest of the whole country.

what he had done. Someone who had been present at that assembly told me that what the man had said had been an affirmation of his love for the Sultan, and a declaration that he was killing himself for love of him, as his father had killed himself for love of the Sultan's father, and as his grandfather had done for love of the Sultan's grandfather.

When I had left the assembly the Sultan sent me three days' guest rations. We set sail and after thirty-four days reached the Sluggish or Tranquil Sea, which has a reddish colour; they claim that this is because of the earth of the land which bounds it.[23] It has no wind and no waves and no movement in spite of its extent. For this reason every Chinese junk is accompanied by three boats, as we have said. They are rowed
248 and tow it. Besides there are in every junk | about twenty very big oars like masts.[24] Some thirty men assemble by each oar and stand in two ranks facing each other. Two very big ropes like cables are attached to each oar. One party pulls the rope and then lets it go; then the other party pulls it. They sing with fine voices as they do this, and usually they sing *Laʿlā, laʿlā*.

We sailed on this sea for thirty-seven days. The sailors were surprised how easy was our voyage. They spend forty or fifty days on it and that is regarded as favourable. Then we reached the country of Ṭawālisī, where the king is called Ṭawālisī.[25] It is a spacious country and its king is like the king of China. He

[23] From the time of Khwārizmī (ninth century), who calls it the Dark Sea, Islamic geographers mention a sea with a more or less comparable name which affords an opening to the circumambient ocean. Unlike Ptolemy they did not regard Africa as joined to China by a continuous coastline. Mr Robert Nicholl informs me that the great rivers of Borneo 'discharge vast quantities of brownish-red laterite silt into the sea, and at this time, owing to the lack of defined currents, it spreads outwards like an immense oil slick'.

[24] Adopting Dozy's emendation *ṭawānīs* for *ṭawābīs* 'clubs', in the text.

[25] This country has been very variously, but not satisfactorily, identified. Candidates include Cambodia, Cochin China, Champa, Tongking, Celebes (Sulawesi), Tawal island in the Moluccas, Brunei and Sulu. Yule, who suggested the last, admitted to 'a faint suspicion that Tawalisi is really to be looked for in that part of the atlas which contains the Marine Surveys of the late Captain Gulliver' (*Cathay*, IV, p. 158). Professor Yamamoto would connect the name with the princely title *taval* in use in Champa ('Tawalisi described by Ibn Battuta', *Memoirs of the Research Department of the Toyo Bunko*. no. 8, 1936, pp. 93–133). Mr Robert Nicholl suggests that it represents the Brunei title *Dewa Lela Sura* or the shortened form *Dewa Sura*.

has numerous junks with which he fights the king of China |
until they sue for peace on conditions.[26] The people of this 249
country worship idols. They are of handsome appearance and
most resemble the Turks. Most of them have reddish colour-
ing. They are brave and intrepid. Their women ride horses,
understand archery, and fight just like the men. We anchored
in one of their ports in the city of Kailūkarī, one of their finest
and largest cities.[27] The king's son used to live there, but
when we anchored in the port soldiers came to us. The captain
disembarked to meet them and took a present for the king's
son. He enquired about him and the soldiers told him that his
father had made him governor of another place and had
appointed his daughter to that city. Her name is Urdujā.[28] |
Account of this princess. On the second day after our arrival at 250
the port of Kailūkarī the princess summoned the captain, the
karānī, who is the secretary,[29] the merchants, the pilots, the
tandīl, who is the officer of the foot soldiers,[30] and the *sipāh
ṣālār*, who is the commander of the crewmen,[31] to a banquet
she had prepared for them according to her custom. The
captain wanted me to attend with them, but I refused, for
they are infidels and it is not lawful to eat their food. When the
guests attended upon her she said: 'Is there any one of you who
has stayed behind and has not come?' The captain said to her:

[26] There are only two states in the region of which this could conceivably be claimed, Japan and Majapahit in Java, both of which had successfully repelled expeditions sent by Qubilai Khan in the second half of the previous century.

[27] No place name closely resembling this has been traced in south-east Asia, but it is the name of a small port in south-east India which Gibb thinks I.B. 'afterwards transported to somewhere in the China Sea' (*Selections*, p. 366, n. 3). Yamamoto sees it as an Arabic transcription of Klaung Garai (p. 117). Early in the century the king of Champa built a temple to Po Klaung Garai at Phanrang. The earliest Islamic monuments in SE Asia, dating from the eleventh century, occur in this region, which was part of Champa (S. Q. Fatimi, *Islam comes to Malaysia*, Singapore, 1963, pp. 42–60).

[28] This Turcophone Amazon princess cannot be comfortably accommodated anywhere in south-east Asia. I.B. has already given her name to one of the wives of Özbeg Khan. Mr Nicholl suggests that, 'since she was ruling as her father's viceroy, she probably had the traditional Brunei title of Urdana Raja'.

[29] The origin of Anglo-Indian *cranny*, used of clerks in public offices.

[30] The Anglo-Indian *tindal*. The French editors interpret I.B.'s explanation as meaning an infantry general, Dulaurier, Yule and Ferrand as referring to someone in charge of the sailors, which makes better sense and agrees with its modern use as equivalent to 'boatswain'.

[31] Persian for the commander-in-chief of the army.

'Only one man has stayed behind and he is the *bakshī*, which means qāḍī in their language,[32] 'and he does not eat your food.' She said: 'Summon him.' Her bodyguards and the captain's companions came and said: 'Obey the princess.' I
251 went to her. She was receiving in full state. Before her | were women in whose hands were the registers which they displayed to her. Around her were women past child-bearing who were her Wazīrs. They sat below the throne on sandal-wood chairs. The men were before her. Her seat was covered in silk and had silk curtains. It was of sandal-wood inlaid with many gold plaques. In the assembly hall were benches of carved wood on which were many gold vessels, both large and small, such as amphoras, jugs and goblets. The captain told me they were filled with a drink made from sugar mixed with aromatics, which they drink after eating, that it smells pleasantly, has a sweet taste, induces cheerfulness, sweetens the breath, helps digestion, and enhances sexual intercourse.

When I greeted the princess she said to me in Turkish: 'Hasan misan, yakshī misan', meaning 'How are you? Are you
252 well?'[33] She seated me near her. | She wrote Arabic well and said to one of her attendants: 'Dāwa wa batak kātūr', meaning '(Bring) an inkwell and paper.'[34] They were brought and she wrote: 'In the name of God the merciful, the compassionate'. She said: 'What is this?' I said: 'Tanḍarī nām',[35] meaning 'That is God's name.' She said: 'Khushun',[36] meaning 'Good'. Then she asked me from which country I came. I said: 'From India.' She said: 'The pepper country?' I said: 'Yes.' She asked me about that country and events there and I answered her. She said: 'I must invade it and take possession of it. Its wealth and its soldiers please me.' I said to her: 'Do so.' She ordered that I should be given robes, two elephant loads of rice, two buffalo cows, ten sheep, four pounds of julep, and

[32] The French editors have qāḍī, which is an emendation. Another MS., followed by Dulaurier, reads *faqīh* 'jurist', which seems preferable. The word *bakshi* has had a strange history (see *Hobson-Jobson*, s.v. 'buxee'). At this time it was used for a Buddhist priest.

[33] These phrases had been used by Sultan Tarmashīrīn in greeting him at his camp in Transoxiana, see III, p. 557.

[34] *Davet ve bitik getir*, 'Bring an inkstand and writing paper'.

[35] *Tanri nām*.

[36] *Hoş*.

four *marṭabāns*, which are | big vessels,[37] filled with ginger, 253
pepper, citrus fruit and mangoes, all salted with what is used in preparing for sea voyages.

The ship-owner told me that this princess had in her army women, serving women and slaves, who fought like men, and that she goes out among her troops of men and women, invades the territory of her enemies, is present at the fighting, and engages the champions. He told me there was a fierce battle between her and one of her enemies in which many of her soldiers were killed and her army was on the point of fleeing; she forced her way forwards and broke through the armies till she reached the king against whom she was fighting, pierced him with a lance thrust which caused his death, whereupon his troops fled, and she brought his head on
a spear, which his family recovered from her | for much 254
treasure. When she returned to her father he made her ruler of that city which was under her brother. He told me that the kings' sons used to ask for her in marriage, and she used to say: 'I shall marry only a man who fights against me and defeats me.' They avoided doing this being afraid of the disgrace if she were to defeat them.

[37] Big vessels of glazed pottery.

CHAPTER XXII

China

We left the country of Ṭawālisī and after seventeen days of sailing very rapidly and comfortably with a favourable wind we reached the country of China. The Chinese clime[1] is extensive and is rich in resources, fruits, cereals, gold and silver; no other clime in the world compares with it in this respect. A river known as *Āb-i ḥayāt*, meaning 'the water of life', divides it, and is also known as the Sabr, like the name of the Indian river. It rises in the mountains near the city of Khān Bāliq known as Kūh-i būznah, |
255 meaning 'the mountain of monkeys'.[2] It flows through China for a distance of six months' travel to finish at Ṣīn al-Ṣīn.[3] It is encompassed by villages, cultivated fields, orchards and bazaars, like the Nile in Egypt, but here there is more settlement. There are many waterwheels. There is much sugar in China, equal to Egyptian sugar or even better. There are grapes and plums. I used to think that the *ʿOthmānī* plum of

[1] *iqlīm*. The word is used here, not as by Idrīsī to denote a latitudinal division of the world, but as the Persian *keshwar*, one of seven regions among which Iran was in the centre.

[2] There is, of course, no such river; the great rivers of China flow roughly from west to east. Peking was linked to Hang-chou by a canal, and much, though not all, of the way from there to Canton could have been traversed by water. The alternative name of the river appears in the text as Sabr, which the editors emended to Sarū, that being the name I.B. gives to the Indian river (see II, p. 274, III, pp. 726, 762) which he says has the same name. They understand this to mean the Yellow River, the Huang-ho, *sari* being the Turkish for 'yellow'. In another MS it is called the *nahr al-Ṣīn*, 'the river of China'. Āb-i-ḥayāt and Kūh-i-būznah are Persian words, correctly translated by I.B. Professor Herbert Franke, to whom I am greatly indebted for his comments on several passages in this chapter, tells me that he knows of no river name in mediaeval China remotely like Water of Life. He also notes that a Mountain of Apes anywhere near Peking is highly improbable as no apes or monkeys are, or were, found there.

[3] Canton.

Damascus was unequalled till I saw the Chinese plum. There are wonderful melons resembling those of Khwārizm and Iṣfahān. All the fruits we have in our country are there as good or better. Corn is very plentiful and I have seen none better. It is the same with lentils and chickpeas. |

Account of Chinese pottery. Chinese pottery is made only in the 256
city of Zaitūn and in Ṣīn Kalān.[4] It is made from an earth from mountains there which burns like charcoal, as we shall explain. They add to it a stone which is found there and burn it for three days. Then they pour water on it and it becomes powdery again. Then they ferment it. The best is that which has fermented for a whole month, but no more. What has fermented for ten days is inferior. The price is that of pottery in our country, or less. It is exported to India and other parts of the world till it reaches our country in the Maghrib. It is the most superb kind of pottery.

Account of the Chinese fowls. The hens and cocks of China are
very fat, | fatter than our geese.[5] Their hens' eggs are bigger 257
than the eggs of geese among us. Their geese are not fat. We bought a hen which we wanted to cook but it would not fit into one pot; we used two. The cock in China is the size of an ostrich. Sometimes its feathers fall out and a mass of red flesh is left. The first time I saw the Chinese cock was in the city of Kawlam. I thought it was an ostrich and was astonished. Its owner said to me: 'In China there are bigger ones than this.' When I arrived in China I saw the proof of what he had told me.

Account of some particulars of the Chinese. The Chinese are infidels. They worship idols and burn their dead as the Indians
do.[6] The king | is a Tatar of the lineage of Tankīz Khān.[7] 258

[4] Ch'üàn-chou (Quanzhou) and Canton. Zaitūn has also been identified with Chang-chou (Zhangzhou) near Amoy; this was exhaustively discussed by Pelliot (*Notes on Marco Polo*, I, 1959, under 'Çaiton'). The manufacture of pottery, including porcelain, was far more widespread than I.B. supposed. Ṣīn Kalān is the same as Sīn al-Ṣīn.

[5] This is nonsense, but I.B.'s contemporary Odoric of Pordenone remarks on the size of Chinese poultry, including geese (Yule, *Cathay*, II, pp. 181–2).

[6] At this time cremation, though not universal, as I.B. implies, was common in China, especially in some of the coastal provinces (A. C. Moule, *Quinsai*, 1957, p. 50).

[7] The ruling emperor was Toghon Temür (1333–70), the last of the Mongol (Yüan) dynasty; he was eighth in descent from Chingiz Khan and was driven out of China in 1368.

In every city of China is a quarter where the Muslims live separately and have mosques for their Friday prayers and other assemblies. They are highly regarded and treated with respect. The Chinese infidels eat the meat of pigs and dogs and sell it in the bazaars. They live comfortably and in affluence but take little care about their food and clothing.[8] You will see an important merchant whose wealth is beyond reckoning wearing a tunic of coarse cotton. All the Chinese pay attention only to gold and silver vessels. Every one of them has a walking stick on which to lean when walking and they call it the third leg.

Silk is extremely plentiful for the worms attach themselves to
259 fruit, eat it and need little care. | This is why it is plentiful and
the poor and the destitute dress in it. If it were not for the merchants [trading in it] it would have no value. Among them a single robe of cotton is sold for the price of many of silk. It is the custom that a merchant melts the gold and silver he has to make ingots, each of them weighing a qintar, more or less. He places it over the door of his house. Anyone who has five ingots makes a seal-ring for his finger; anyone who has ten makes two rings; anyone who has fifteen is called *sati*,[9] which means the same as *kārimī* in Egypt.[10] They call a single ingot *barkāla*.[11]

Account of the paper dirham with which they buy and sell. The
people of China do not do business for dinars and dirhams. In
260 their country all the gold and silver they acquire | they melt
down into ingots, as we have said. They buy and sell with pieces of paper the size of the palm of the hand which are stamped with the Sultan's stamp. Twenty-five such pieces are called *balisht*, which is the same as dinar among us.[12] If these

[8] This cannot be taken seriously. Chinese cuisine was elaborate and very varied, though for religious reasons Muslims would have abstained from many of the dishes. Clothing was of social significance, could be sumptuous and was officially regulated in minute detail (Jacques Gernet, *La Vie quotidienne en Chine à la veille de l'invasion mongole*, 1959, pp. 138–52).

[9] Anglo-India 'chetty', denoting a member of any of the trading castes of south India. *Hobson-Jobson* (under 'chetty') cites this as one of I.B.'s 'questionable statements' about China.

[10] A reference to the Kārimī guild of merchants which dominated much of the commerce of the Red Sea and Indian Ocean.

[11] Persian *pargāla*, a piece or fragment.

[12] A Persian word, originally meaning 'cushion', later used for a gold or silver ingot.

pieces of paper become tattered from handling they take them
to a house which is like our mint and receive new ones
instead.[13] The new pieces are not given against payment of
any kind, for those in charge of this work receive regular
salaries from the Sultan. The amir in charge of that house is
one of the most important. If anyone goes to the bazaar with a
silver dirham or a dinar intending to buy something with it, it
is not accepted and he is disregarded until he pays with a
balisht and buys what he wants.[14] |

Account of the earth which they burn instead of charcoal. All the 261
people of China and Khitā[15] use for charcoal an earth which
has the consistency and colour of clay. Loads of it are brought
by elephants and it is cut into pieces the size of pieces of
charcoal with us. They set it alight and it burns like charcoal,
but it gives off more intense heat. When it is reduced to ash
they knead it with water, dry it, and cook with it a second
time; they go on doing this till it is used up. From this earth
they make vessels of Chinese pottery, adding another stone to
it as we have related.[16]

Account of the crafts in which the Chinese have special skill. The
Chinese are of all peoples the most skilful in crafts and attain
the greatest perfection in them. This | is well known and 262
people have described it and spoken at length about it. No
one, whether Greek or any other, rivals them in mastery of
painting. They have prodigious facility in it. One of the remarkable things I saw in this connection is that if I visited one
of their cities, and then came back to it, I always saw portraits
of me and my companions painted on the walls and on paper
in the bazaars. I went to the Sultan's city, passed through the
painters' bazaar, and went to the Sultan's palace with my
companions. We were dressed as Iraqis. When I returned from

[13] According to Marco Polo 3% of the value was charged.

[14] 'According to Yüan regulations, foreign merchants were required to convert their precious metals into paper currency as soon as they set foot in China' (Morris Rossabi, 'The Muslims in the Early Yüan Dynasty' in Langlois, J. D. (ed.) *China under Mongol Rule*', 1981, p. 282).

[15] Cathay, i.e. northern China, so-called after the Khitai, a semi-nomadic people related to the Mongols, who ruled over northern China from the ninth to the twelfth century as the Liao dynasty.

[16] I.B. appears to have confused three substances, coal, kaolin and a mixture of powdered coal and clay used as a cheaper substitute for coal.

the palace in the evening I passed through the said bazaar. I saw my and my companions' portraits painted on paper and hung on the walls. We each one of us looked at the portrait |
263 of his companion; the resemblance was correct in all respects. I was told the Sultan had ordered them to do this, and that they had come to the palace while we were there and had begun observing and painting us without our being aware of it. It is their custom to paint everyone who comes among them. They go so far in this that if a foreigner does something that obliges him to flee from them, they circulate his portrait throughout the country and a search is made for him. When someone resembling the portrait is found, he is arrested.

Ibn Juzayy said: 'This is like what historians relate about the case of Sābūr Dhu'l-Aktāf King of Persia when he went to Rūm in disguise and was present at a banquet given by the king. There was a portrait of him on one of the vessels. One of the attendants of Qayṣar noticed it and that Sābūr's portrait
264 was impressed on it. He said to the king: "This portrait | tells us that Kisrā is among us in this assembly." It was as he said and what ensued is written in books.'[17]

Account of their practice of recording whatever is in ships. It is the custom of the Chinese that when a junk wishes to set sail, the admiral and his secretaries come aboard and record the archers, servants and sailors who will sail; the junk is then free to leave. When it returns they come aboard again and compare what they recorded with the persons [on the junk]. If one of those recorded is missing they question the owner of the junk about him, asking for proof that he is dead, or has escaped, or whatever else it may be has happened to him. If he cannot provide this he is arrested.

265 When | they have done that they order the ship's master to dictate to them a manifest of all the merchandise in it, whether small or great [in value]. Then every one disembarks and the customs officials sit to inspect what they have with them. If they come upon any article that has been concealed

[17] The story, of which there are differing versions, is related of the Sasanian king Shapur II (309/10–379), but sometimes of other Persian rulers. He was called 'of the shoulder-blades' (*aktāf*) because he is alleged to have had the shoulder-blades of prisoners-of-war dislocated or pierced so as to prevent them from using weapons again.

from them the junk and whatever is in it is forfeit to the treasury. This is a kind of extortion I have seen in no country, whether infidel or Muslim, except China. However there used to be something like it in India, in that anyone detected with an article which had evaded financial dues should be fined eleven times the amount. Then the Sultan suppressed it when he suppressed the dues.

Account of their way of preventing depravity among the merchants.
When a Muslim merchant | arrives in a Chinese town he 266
chooses whether to stay with one of the Muslim merchants designated among those domiciled there, or in the *funduq*. If he prefers to stay with the merchant his money is impounded, the merchant with whom he is to reside takes charge of it, and spends from it on his behalf honestly. When he wishes to leave his money is examined and if any of it is missing the merchant with whom he has stayed and to whom it was entrusted makes it good.

If he wishes to stay in the *funduq* his money is entrusted to the master of the *funduq* who is put in charge of it; he buys for the merchant what he wants on his account. If he wants to take a concubine, he buys a slave-girl for him. He puts him in a room of which the door opens inside the *funduq* and he meets the expenses of them both. Slave-girls are cheap in price, but
all the Chinese sell their sons | and daughters, and it is not 267
thought shameful among them. They do not all the same compel them to travel with their purchasers, nor do they prevent them if they wish to do so. So if the foreign merchant wants to marry, he gets married, but there is no way he can spend his money on debauchery. They say: 'We do not want it said in the Muslim countries that they lose their money in our country, and that it is the land of debauchery and fleeting pleasure.'

Account of the protection they afford to travellers on their roads.
China is the safest and best country for the traveller. A man travels for nine months alone with great wealth and has nothing to fear. What is responsible for this is that in every post station in their country is a *funduq* which has a director living
there | with a company of horse and foot. After sunset or 268
nightfall the director comes to the *funduq* with his secretary and writes down the names of all the travellers who will pass

the night there, seals it and locks the door of the *funduq*. In the morning he and his secretary come and call everybody by name and write down a record. He sends someone with the travellers to conduct them to the next post station and he brings back a certificate from the director of that *funduq* confirming that they have all arrived. If he does not do this he is answerable for them. This is the procedure in every post station in their country from Ṣīn al-Ṣīn to Khān Bāliq. In them is everything the traveller needs by way of provisions, especially hens and geese. Sheep are rare among them.

Let us return to our journey. When we had crossed the sea
269 the first city to which we came was | Zaitūn.[18] There are no olives in it, or in the whole of China and India, but it has been given this name.[19] It is a huge and important city in which are manufactured the fabrics of velvet, damask and satin which are known by its name and which are superior to those of Khansā and Khān Bāliq. Its harbour is among the biggest in the world, or rather is the biggest; I have seen about a hundred big junks there and innumerable little ones. It is a great gulf of the sea which runs inland till it mingles with the great river. In this city, as in all cities in China, men have orchards and fields and their houses are in the middle, as they are in Sijilmāsa in our country.[20] This is why their towns are so big.
270 The Muslims live in a separate city. On the day I arrived | I saw there the amir who had been sent to India as ambassador with the present, had been in our company and had been in the junk which sank. He greeted me and informed the head of the customs about me,[21] and he installed me in handsome lodgings. I received visits from the qāḍī of the Muslims, Tāj al-Dīn of Ardabīl, a distinguished and generous man, from the Shaikh al-Islām Kamāl al-Dīn ʿAbdallāh of Iṣfahān, a pious

[18] Chü'an-chou.

[19] It is the Arabic word for 'olive'.

[20] This can have been true only of the more luxurious houses. Gernet quotes the recommendation that only a sixth of the area of a given property should be occupied by the dwelling, one half by water, and one third by plants (Gernet, 127).

[21] *dīwān*, 'the institution commonly known by that name in North Africa and Egypt in all ports open to foreign commerce . . . at one and the same time customhouse, warehouse, lodging house and bourse for foreign merchants . . . its controller was one of the principal officers of the realm' (Gibb, *Selections*, p. 370, n. 11).

man, and from the important merchants, among them Sharaf
al-Dīn of Tabrīz, one of the merchants from whom I borrowed
money when I arrived in India, and the one whose dealings
were best. He knows the Qur'ān by heart and recites it very
often. As these merchants live in infidel country they are
delighted when a Muslim arrives among them. They say: 'He
has come from the land of Islam', and give him the legal
alms[22] due on their property so that he becomes as rich | as one 271
of them. Among the pious shaikhs there was Burhān al-Dīn of
Kāzarūn who had a hospice outside the town[23] and to whom
the merchants make the oblations made to Shaikh Abū Isḥāq
of Kāzarūn.[24] When the head of the customs learnt about me
he wrote to the Qān, who is their Great King,[25] telling him I
had arrived on behalf of the king of India. I asked the head of
the customs to send with me someone to conduct me to the
province of Ṣīn which they call Ṣīn Kalān which is in his
jurisdiction, so that I could see it for myself while awaiting
what reply the Qān would give. He consented and sent one of
his companions to escort me. I sailed on the river in a boat like
the galleys in our country, except that the oarsmen row standing up in the middle of the ship.[26] The passengers are in the
prow and the stern. To shade themselves they spread over the
ship pieces of cloth made | from a plant of the country like 272
flax, but it is not that and it is thinner than hemp.

We sailed on this river for twenty-seven days. Every day about noon we cast anchor in a village where we bought whatever we needed and prayed the midday prayer. In the evening we stopped at another village. It was like this till we reached the city of Ṣīn Kalān, which is the city of Ṣīn al-Ṣīn.[27]

[22] 'According to the Qur'ān the legal alms are to be given to 'parents, kindred, orphans, and the wayfarer'. The . . . community at Zaytún was so wealthy that the only one of these five classes to which the alms were of any value was the last' (Gibb, *Selections*, p. 370, n. 12).

[23] The devotee Burhān al-Dīn the Lame, with whom I.B. stayed in Alexandria, had prophesied that he would meet his namesake in China (I, p. 24).

[24] See II, p. 319.

[25] Qān, from Khāqān, designating the supreme ruler of the whole Mongol empire; it is to be distinguished from Khān, a title of very much wider application.

[26] The text is defective; a word seems to have been omitted.

[27] Not all of the journey from Ch'üan-chou to Canton could have been made by water.

Pottery is made there and in Zaitūn. Here the Āb-i Ḥayāt river enters the sea; it is called the Meeting of the Two Seas. It is one of the biggest cities and the finest in respect of its bazaars. Among the largest bazaars is that of the potters, whose wares are exported to other provinces of China and to India and al-Yaman.

In the middle of the city is a huge temple with nine doors
273 inside each of which is a portico with stone benches | on which those living in the temple sit. Between the second and third gates is a place where there are rooms in which blind people and chronic invalids live. They are all maintained and clothed from the endowments of the temple. There are similar arrangements between all the other gates; there is a hospital for the sick, a kitchen for cooking food, and there are physicians and attendants in the temple. I was told that old men no longer strong enough to earn their living are maintained and clothed in this temple. It is the same with orphans and widowed people without means. The temple was built by one of their kings who made this city and the villages and orchards depending on it into an endowment for its benefit. The portrait of that king is in the aforesaid temple and people worship it.[28]

In one part of this city is the town of the Muslims who have there the congregational mosque, the hospice and the bazaar.
274 They have a qāḍī | and a shaikh and in every town in China there is a Shaikh al-Islām to whom all the affairs of the Muslims are referred. There is also a qāḍī who gives judgments among them. I lodged with Auḥad al-Dīn of Sinjār, a distinguished, important and very wealthy man. I stayed with him for fourteen days. Gifts to me from the qāḍī and the other Muslims came continuously. Every day there was a fresh banquet to which people came in splendid skiffs[29] with singers. There is no city, either of infidels or of Muslims, beyond this city. Between it and the rampart of Yājūj and Mājūj is sixty days' travel, as I have been told.[30] Wandering infidels live

[28] 'Canton has undergone many changes, and no temple now appears to correspond precisely with that described' (Yule, *Cathay*, IV, p. 122, n. 1).

[29] *'ushāriyyūn*, long, narrow boats like those used on the Nile.

[30] The Rampart of Gog and Magog, allegedly built by Alexander the Great to protect the civilized world from northern savages, was usually located near Derbend on the western shore of the Caspian, but was sometimes confused with the Great Wall of China.

there who eat the sons of Adam if they overcome them.[31] That is why people do not pass through their country or travel to it. I did not meet in that country anyone who had seen the rampart, or had seen anyone who had seen it. |
A marvellous anecdote. When I was in Ṣīn Kalān I heard that 275
there was there a venerable shaikh over two hundred years old who neither ate nor drank nor excreted nor had intercourse with women, though his powers were intact, and that he lived in a cave outside the city, giving himself to devotion. I went to the cave and saw him at the entrance. He was thin, very ruddy, showed the traces of his devotional practices, and had no beard. I greeted him; he took my hand, sniffed it, and said to the interpreter: 'This man is from one end of the world and we are from the other.' Then he said to me: 'You have seen a miracle. Do you remember the day you arrived at an island where there was a temple and a man sitting among the idols who gave you ten gold dinars?' I said: 'Yes.' He said: 'I am that man.' I kissed his hand. He thought for a while and then entered the cave and did not | come out to us again. It was as 276
though he regretted what he had said. We burst into the cave after him but did not find him. We did find one of his companions who had a bundle of paper *balishts* and said to us: 'This is your guest money.[32] Take your departure.' We said to him: 'We are waiting for the great man.' He said: 'If you were to wait for ten years you would not see him. It is his practice that he does not see again anyone to whom one of his secrets has been made known. Do not suppose he has gone away from you. On the contrary he is present with you.'

I was amazed at this and went away. I told the qāḍī and the Shaikh of Islam and Auḥad al-Dīn of Sinjār about what had happened. They said: 'This is how he behaves with strangers who come to see him. No one knows what religion he follows. The one you supposed to be one of his companions was the

[31] Marco Polo states that the people of 'the kingdom of Fuju' (Fukien) eat the flesh of men who have not died a natural death. It has often been assumed that this refers to aboriginal mountain tribes, but there have been allegations of cannibalism among Chinese, Mongols and Tibetans (*Marco Polo*, I, pp. 311–14, n. 9, II, p. 225). The range of the Chinese cuisine, which included many items repulsive to European taste and prohibited to Muslims by their dietary laws, made it natural to ascribe anthropophagy to them.

[32] See above, p. 895.

shaikh himself.' They told me that he had been away from
277 this country for about fifty | years and had come back a year
ago. Sultans, amirs and important people used to come and
visit him and he gave them presents according to their rank.
Faqirs came to him every day and he gave something suitable
to each one, though there was nothing to be seen in the cave
in which he lived. They said too that he told of things in past
years and spoke of the Prophet, God bless and give him
peace, and used to say: 'If I had been with him I would have
helped him.' He used to speak with the greatest respect of the
two Caliphs ʿOmar b. al-Khaṭṭāb and ʿAlī b. Abī Ṭālib and
praise them both, and used to curse Yazīd b. Muʿāwiya and
abuse Muʿāwiya.[33] They told me many things about him.

Auḥad al-Dīn of Sinjār said: 'I visited him in the cave. He
took my hand and I imagined I was in a vast palace and that he
278 was sitting | on a throne with a crown on his head. On either
side of him were beautiful maidservants and fruits were drop-
ping into rivers which were there. I imagined I took an apple
to eat and suddenly I was in the cave, in front of him, and he
was laughing at me. A severe illness afflicted me and stayed
with me for months. I did not go to him again.

The people of that country believe he is a Muslim, but nobody has seen him pray. As for fasting, he fasts perpetually. The qāḍī said to me: 'One day I spoke to him about prayer and he said to me "Do you know what I do? My prayer is certainly not the same as your prayer."' Everything one is told about this man is strange.

On the second day after meeting him I set out to return to
Zaitūn. Some days after arriving there an order came from the
279 Qān for me to go to | his capital in security and honour, either
by river or by land as I wished. I chose to travel by river. A
handsome boat, one of those used by the amirs, was prepared
for me. The amir sent his companions with me. He and the
qāḍī and the Muslim merchants sent us ample provisions. We

[33] These particulars indicate the shaikh's stance with reference to the schism between Shīʿīs and Sunnīs. The former would not speak with respect of the Caliph ʿOmar, whom they regard as having usurped the caliphate which rightly belonged to ʿAlī. Sunnīs, while accepting ʿOmar, repudiate Muʿāwiya, founder of the Umayyad dynasty, for his opposition to ʿAlī and execrate Yazīd his son and successor, holding him responsible for the death of ʿAlī's son Ḥusain (see I, p. 46, n. 140).

travelled as official guests, having our morning meal in one village and our evening meal in another. After travelling for ten days we reached the city of Qanjanfū, which is a big and handsome city in an extensive plain.[34] Orchards surround it as if it were the Ghūṭa of Damascus.[35]

When we arrived the qāḍī, the shaikh of Islam and the merchants came to meet us with flags, drums, trumpets and bugles and musicians. | They brought us horses which we 280
mounted. Except for the qāḍī and the shaikh they walked in front of us and did not ride with us. The amir of the town and his attendants came out to meet us for the Sultan's guest is treated by them with the utmost respect. We entered the city, which has four walls. Between the first and second walls live the Sultan's slaves, both the city guards and the night watchmen. The latter are called *baṣwānān*.[36] Between the second and third walls are the cavalry and the amir who governs the town. The Muslims live within the third wall and there we alighted with their shaikh Ẓahīr al-Dīn al-Qurlānī. The Chinese live inside the fourth wall. It is the biggest of the four cities. The distance from each gate to the next | is three to four miles. As 281
we have said everyone has his orchard, his house and his field.

Anecdote. One day when I was in the house of Ẓahīr al-Dīn al-Qurlānī a big ship arrived belonging to one of the jurists most highly regarded by them. I was asked if I would receive him and they said: 'Maulānā Qiwām al-Dīn of Ceuta.' I was surprised at his name but when we conversed after our formal greetings it occurred to me that I knew him. I looked at him for a long time. He said: 'I see you looking at me as though you knew me.' I said: Which country are you from?' He said: 'From Ceuta.' I said: 'I am from Tangier.' He greeted me again and wept and I wept too. I said: 'Have you been to India?' He said: 'Yes, I have been to the capital Dihlī.' When he said that to me | I remembered him and said: 'Are you al- 282
Bushrī!' He said: 'Yes.' He had come to Dihlī with his maternal

[34] Gibb argues that, because of its size, the fact that it was evidently accessible to ships, and its position on the way to Hang-chou, Fu-chou is 'the most natural identification' (*Selections*, p. 371, n. 19). Other cities have been suggested because their names resemble Qanjanfū, but they are remote from any conceivable route.

[35] The fertile plain around Damascus. See I, p. 119.

[36] Persian *pāsbānān*, 'watchmen'.

uncle Abu'l Qāsim of Murcia. He was then young and beardless but one of the ablest students; he had memorized the *Muwaṭṭa'*.[37] I had told the Sultan of India about him and he had given him three thousand dinars and asked him to remain with him. He had refused and intended to go to China where he prospered and acquired considerable wealth. He told me he had about fifty male and as many female slaves. He gave me two of each and many presents. Later on I met his brother in the country of the Blacks.[38] How far apart they were!

I stayed in Qanjanfū for fifteen days and then left. China,
for all its magnificence, did not please me. I was deeply
depressed by the prevalence of infidelity and when I left my
283 lodging I saw | many offensive things which distressed me so
much that I stayed at home and went out only when it was necessary. When I saw Muslims it was as though I had met my family and my relatives. This jurist al-Bushrī with extreme kindness travelled with me for four days when I left Qanjanfū until I reached Baiwam Quṭlū, a small town populated by Chinese, both soldiers and common people.[39] There are no Muslims there except four households of agents of the said jurist. We stopped at the house of one of them and stayed with him for three days. Then I said good-bye to the jurist and departed.

We sailed on the river in the same way, taking our morning
meal in one village and our evening meal in another, until
284 after seventeen days we reached | the city of al-Khansā.[40] Its
name is almost that of the poetess Khansā,[41] but I do not know whether it is Arabic or just coincides with Arabic. It is the biggest city I have seen on the face of the earth. It takes three days to cross it, the traveller journeying on and stopping [for

[37] 'The well trodden path', the famous collection of the sayings of the Prophet Muḥammad compiled by Mālik b. Anas, after whom is named the Mālikī *madhhab*, to which I.B. himself adhered.

[38] See below, p. 946.

[39] 'It is quite possible that it was not a place-name at all, but the name of some Turko-Tatar commander (? Bayan Qutlugh = "Bayan the Lucky") which Ibn Battúta erroneously took to be the name of a town' (Gibb, *Selections*, p. 371, n. 21). Bayan was the name of one of the principal generals who conquered southern China for Qubilai. Another Bayan was an important minister of Toghon Temür, the reigning emperor at the time of I.B.'s visit.

[40] Hang-chou, Marco Polo's Kinsai.

[41] The most famous Arabic poetess, born in the late sixth century.

the night] in the city. It is laid out as we have described in the Chinese style of building, everyone having his own orchard and house.[42] It is divided into six cities which we shall describe.[43] When we arrived the qāḍī Afkhar al-Dīn,[44] the Shaikh al-Islām and the descendants of ʿOthmān b. ʿAffān the Egyptian, who are the most prominent of the Muslims there, came out to meet us with a white standard, drums, trumpets and bugles. The amir of the city also came out with his cavalcade.

We entered the city, which is really six cities each with its own walls, while the whole is surrounded by one wall.[45] In the first city live the city guards | and their commander. The qāḍī 285
and others told me there were twelve thousand of them on the military register. We spent the night after our entry into the city in the house of their commander. On the second day we entered the second city by the gate known as the Jews' Gate.[46] In it live Jews, Christians, and Turks who worship the sun and are very numerous. The commander of this city is Chinese. We spent the second night with him. On the third day we entered the third city which is inhabited by Muslims. It is a fine city and the bazaars are laid out as in Muslim countries. There are mosques and muezzins, whom we heard giving the call to the noon prayer as we entered. We alighted at the house of the descendants of ʿOthmān b. ʿAffān the Egyptian. He was one of the important merchants who became fond of

[42] This is contradicted by I.B.'s contemporary, Odoric of Pordenone, who states that 'there is not in it a span of ground which is not well peopled' (Yule, *Cathay*, II, p. 104).

[43] Medieval Chinese cities were usually divided into quarters separated by low walls. Hang-chou had more than six such quarters (Franke).

[44] Other MSS read Fakhr al-Dīn.

[45] It is impossible to reconcile I.B.'s description with the Chinese accounts analysed, and the maps reproduced, by Moule (*Quinsai and Other Notes on Marco Polo*, 1957). Yule remarked that there were 'several very questionable statements' in I.B.'s account (*Cathay*, IV, p. 130, n. 1). Ross Dunn calls it 'cursory, blurred, and defective' (p. 260). Moule estimated the greatest extent of the disused outer wall at perhaps fifteen miles; the Mongols had forbidden the building of city walls and those in existence were perhaps being quarried for building stones by the inhabitants (Moule, 13). It is strange that I.B. makes no mention of the famous lake.

[46] Though the term Jews' Gate is not known from Chinese sources, there was a Jewish community at Hang-chou, attested for 1335–40. The officials of the state sugar monopoly were mostly rich Jewish or Muslim merchants (Franke).

286 this city and settled here. | The city itself was named after
him. His posterity inherited the respect and dignity he had
enjoyed, while they had their ancestor's predilection for faqirs
and benevolence to the needy. They have a hospice called the
ʿOthmānīya, handsomely built and well endowed. There is a
band of Sufis there. The said ʿOthmān built the congregational
mosque in this city and bestowed on it and on the hospice vast
endowments. The number of Muslims here is great. We
stayed with them for fifteen days; every day and night we
attended a fresh banquet. They always paid much attention to
the food they offered. Every day they rode out with us on
pleasurable excursions in the quarters of the city. One day
they rode with me into the fourth city, which is where the
government house is and the house of the great amir Qurṭay.[47]

When we passed through the gate my companions left me
287 and I was received | by the Wazīr who went with me to the
palace of the great amir Qurṭay. I have already related how he
took from me the *farajīya* given me by the saint Jalāl al-Dīn of
Shīrāz.[48] This (fourth) city is reserved for the dwellings of the
Sultan's slaves and attendants. It is the finest of the six cities
and three streams run through it. One is a canal which runs
from the big river and on it small boats bring to the city
supplies of food and stones for burning. There are also pleasure
boats. The citadel is in the middle of the city and is very big.
The government office is in the middle of the citadel which
surrounds it on all sides.[49] In it are arcades where artisans
make precious robes and weapons. The amir Qurṭay told me
there were one thousand six hundred master craftsmen, each
288 one of whom | had three or four apprentices working under
him. They are all slaves of the Qān and have fetters on their
legs. They live outside the palace and are allowed to go to the
city bazaars, but not to go outside the gate. They are paraded
before the amir every day, a hundred at a time, and if one of
them is missing his foreman is responsible for him. The

[47] Professor Franke identifies him as Hu-la-t'ai (Mongolian Quratai) who was made vice-chancellor (*p'ing-chang cheng-shih*) of Chiang-che province in 1329, after having previously held a similar post in Hu-kuang. He was the eldest son of Yesüder (Ye-su-te-erh), a Mongol of the Uriyangqai clan.

[48] See pp. 871–2, where the donor is called Jalāl al-Dīn of Tabrīz.

[49] The governor's residence was not in the centre, but at the southern end of the city.

practice is that when one of them has served for ten years his fetters are taken off and he chooses whether to stay in service unfettered, or to go where he pleases in the Qān's territory, which he may not leave. If he attains the age of fifty he is freed from work and he is supported. So it is with anyone else who attains this age or thereabouts. Anyone who attains the age of sixty is considered as a minor and legal penalties are not applied to him. In China old men are treated with very great respect. One of them is called *ata*, meaning father.[50] |

Account of the great amir Qurṭay. He is the supreme commander 289
in China. He gave us hospitality in his house. He gave a reception which they call *tuwa*[51] at which the principal men of the city were present. He brought Muslim cooks to kill the animals and cook the meat. For all his high rank this amir brought us the food and carved the meat with his own hand. We stayed as his guests for three days. He sent his son with us onto the canal on which we sailed in a ship like a fire-ship. The amir's son sailed in another with musicians and singers who sang in Chinese, Arabic and Persian. The amir's son much admired the Persian songs. They sang a song which he made them repeat time and again so that I learnt it by heart. It has a wonderful tune. Here is is: |

Tā dil bamiḥnat dādīm 290
Dar baḥr-i fikr uftādīm
Chun dar namāz istādīm
Qawī bimiḥrāb andarīm[52]

A large number of ships assembled on that canal with coloured sails and silk awnings and the ships were painted with great skill. They attacked one another throwing oranges and lemons. In the evening we returned to the amir's house and spent the night there. The musicians came and sang all kinds of attractive songs.

Anecdote of the conjuror. That night a conjuror who | was one of 291

[50] Turkish *ata*, 'father'.

[51] See III, p. 561, n. 78.

[52] When we gave our hearts to sorrow
We sank in an ocean of care,
But we were stalwart when standing
Upright at the miḥrāb in prayer. (Persian) The verses are by Saʿclī (d. 1292).

the Qān's slaves was present. The amir said to him: 'Show us some of your tricks.' He took a wooden ball in which were holes through which were long cords. He threw it up and it rose till it disappeared from sight, for we were in the (courtyard) in the middle of the citadel, this being the last season of intense heat. When only a little of the cord was left in his hand he ordered an apprentice of his to cling to it and climb up till he disappeared. The conjuror called to him three times and he did not answer. Then he took a knife in his hand as if he were infuriated and climbed up the cord till he too disappeared. Then he threw down to the ground the youth's hand, then his foot, then his other hand, then his other foot, then his trunk, then his head. Then he came down, panting and his robe bloodstained. He kissed the ground in front of the amir and spoke to him in Chinese. The amir told him to do something
292 and he took the youth's limbs, | attached them to each other, kicked him with his foot, and he stood up intact.[53] I was amazed at this and suffered palpitation of the heart like what I had had with the king of India when I had seen the same kind of thing. They poured out a medicine for me which relieved me. The qāḍī Afkhar al-Dīn was at my side and said: 'By God there was no climbing up or down or cutting off of limbs. It is all conjuring.'

Next day we passed through the gate of the fifth city, which is the biggest and is inhabited by the common people. It has fine bazaars and skilful craftsmen. In it are made the fabrics called Khansāwīya. Among the wonderful things made there are dishes called *dast*. They are made from reeds, pieces of which are fitted together very skilfully.[54] They are given a
293 shining red tincture. Ten of these dishes | are fitted together, each one in the hollow of another so finely that they look as if they were one dish. They make a lid which covers them all. They make platters which have remarkable properties; they

[53] A very similar display in described and illustrated in *Eduward Meltons . . . Zeeen Land-Reizen*, Amsterdam, 1681, pp. 468–9. See frontispiece.

[54] *Dast* is Persian, not Chinese, and is the usual word for 'hand'. Professor Franke cites a reference to an imperial wine cup shaped like a bowl for vegetables and provided with a *shou pa-tzu*, *shou* meaning 'hand' and *pa-tzu* 'handle', and suggests that I.B.'s use of *dast* may be a reflection of the Chinese word. He remarks that 'already under the Sung Hang-chou had famous workshops for lacquer'.

can fall from a great height without breaking and hot food can be put in them without their colours changing or being spoiled. They are exported to India, Khurāsān and elsewhere.

After we had gone into this city we spent a night as guests of its governor. Next day we passed through the gate called *kashtīwānān* into the sixth city, in which live the sailors, fishermen, caulkers, carpenters, who are called *dūdkārān*, sipāhīs, who are the archers, and the *piyāda*, who are the infantry.[55] They are all the Sultan's slaves; no others live with them and they are very numerous. This city is on the bank of | the great 294
river. We spent the night there as the guests of the governor. Amir Qurṭay had prepared for us a boat with all needful provisions and other supplies and sent his companions with us to ensure that we received hospitality. We left this city, which is the last province of China, and entered the country of Khiṭā.[56]

Khiṭā is the finest country in the world in respect of cultivation, for there is no place in its whole extent which is uncultivated. The inhabitants or their neighbours are responsible for paying the land tax. Orchards, villages and cultivated fields are ranged on both sides of the river from the city of Khansā to the city of Khān Bāliq, which is sixty-four days' travel.[57] In it there are no Muslims except for casual passers-by who do not

[55] The foreign words are not Chinese but Persian, and are properly *kashtībānān*, *dorūdgarān*, *sepāhīyān*, and *peyādeh*. The translations are correct, except that a *sepāhī* is a soldier or a cavalryman, rather than an archer. However, mounted archers were the most important element in Mongol and Turkish armies. Concerning the Sailors' Gate Professor Franke writes: 'The gate cannot have been on the inland side of the city but must have been on the eastern side, facing the Ch'ien-t'ang River from where the merchant ships came. One of the eastern gates was called Hou-ch'ao men "Gate for awaiting the tide". This gate is frequently mentioned in 13th-century descriptions of Hang-chou . . . We learn . . . that there was a brothel near this gate . . . Close to the gate was also located a postal station where the foreign envoys were lodged . . . All this suggests that the "Gate for awaiting the tide" was in a part of Hang-chou frequented by foreign travellers, such as I.B.'s informants. My remarks are of course quite hypothetical because the name . . . is nowhere attested in Chinese sources but the identity is perhaps not improbable'.

[56] Cathay, northern China. Early in the tenth century China came to be divided between the south, ruled from Hang-chou by the Sung dynasty, and the north, ruled successively by the Liao and then Chin dynasties. The Mongols completed the conquest of the Chin in 1234, of the Sung in 1279. By 'China' (*Ṣīn*) I.B. sometimes means the whole empire, sometimes the south only.

[57] 'Khān's city', the Turkish name for Peking.

have a home there, for it is not suited to fixed residence [for
295 them]. There is no populated city, | only villages and open spaces with grain, fruit and sugar [growing].[58] I have not seen anything like it in the world except for the four days' travel from al-Anbār to ʿĀna.[59] Every night we stopped at a village and received hospitality until we reached the city of Khān Bāliq, also called Khāniqū.[60] It is the Qān's capital and the Qān is their supreme Sultan whose dominion is China and Khiṭā. When we were ten miles away we anchored, as is their custom. A written report on us was sent to the naval commanders who allowed us to enter the port, which we did. Afterwards we stopped in the city which is one of the largest in the world. It is not laid out as in China with orchards inside it, but
296 as in other | countries, with them outside. The Sultan's city is in the middle like a citadel, as we shall explain. I stayed with shaikh Burhān al-Dīn of Ṣāgharj. It is he to whom the king of India sent forty thousand dinars with an invitation, but he accepted the dinars, and discharged his debts, but refused to go to him.[61] He went to China, where the Qān made him head of all Muslims in the country and gave him the title Ṣadr al-Jahān.

Account of the Sultan of China and Khiṭā called the Qān. *Qān* is the designation of whoever governs the kingdom and rules its [different] regions, as whoever rules the lands of the Lūr it called *Atābak*.[62] His name is Pāshāy.[63] The infidels have no kingdom bigger than his on the face of the earth. |

297 *Account of his palace*. His palace is in the middle of the city designated for his residence. It is built mostly of carved wood. It is admirably planned and has seven gates. At the first gate sits the *kutwāl* who is in charge of the gatekeepers. To the right and left of the gate are raised benches on which sit the

[58] 'The alleged absence of cities on the banks of the canal is so contrary to fact, that one's doubts arise whether Ibn Batuta could have travelled beyond Hang-chau' (Yule, *Cathay*, IV, p. 137, n. 2).

[59] Towns on the Euphrates, about 120 miles apart.

[60] No name for Peking that resembles this has been traced. However, by omitting one dot it can be read as Khānfū, a name used by Arab writers for Canton and K'an-p'u, Marco Polo's Ganfu, which was then confused with Hang-chou.

[61] See III, p. 677.

[62] See II, p. 288, n. 60.

[63] Probably a corruption of the Persian title Pādshāh. The emperor's Mongol name was Toghon Temür.

mamluk *pardadārīya* who guard the palace gate. There are five hundred of them and I was told that in former times there used to be a thousand. At a second gate sit the ṣepāhīs, who are the archers and number five hundred. At the third gate sit the *nizedārīs*, who are the spearmen and number five hundred. At the fourth gate sit the *tighdārīs*, who are men with swords and shields. In the fifth gate is the office of the Wazīr with
many galleries. | The Wazīr sits in the biggest on an imposing 298
elevated seat which they call the place of the throne. In front of the Wazīr is a big gold inkstand. This faces the gallery of the confidential secretary. To the right of this is the gallery of the secretaries for correspondence. To the right of the Wazīr's gallery is that of the secretaries for finances. Opposite these are four other galleries. One of them is called the office of control, in which sits the Controller. The second is the office of the *mustakhraj*. Its director is one of the great amirs. It is concerned with what is payable by the officials and amirs in respect of their fiefs. The third is the office of appeals, in which sits one of the great amirs with jurists and secretaries. Anyone who has suffered an injustice appeals to them. The fourth is the office of the post, in which sits the controller of
the reporters of news. At the sixth gate of the palace sit | the 299
jandārīs and their supreme commander. At the seventh gate sit the eunuchs, who have three galleries, one for the Abyssinians, the second for the Indians, and the third for the Chinese. Each of these corps has a Chinese officer.[64]

Account of the Qān's expedition to fight the son of his paternal uncle and of how he was killed. When we arrived at the capital, Khān Bāliq, we found the Qān was away. He had gone to encounter the son of his paternal uncle, Fīrūz,[65] who had rebelled against

[64] The palace was burnt about the end of the century. Like so many oriental palaces it seems to have consisted of three concentric enclosures. I.B.'s description cannot be reconciled with those of Polo or Odoric or the Chinese records. 'In the whole of this description . . . it is pretty clear that Ibn Batuta is drawing either on his imagination, or (more probably) on his recollections of the Court of Delhi, and hence we have the strongest ground for suspecting that he never entered the palace of Peking, if indeed he ever saw that city at all' (Yule, *Cathay*, IV, p. 140, n. 1). For *mustakhraj*, see III, p. 698, n. 152. The other terms used are again not Chinese but Persian, the correct forms being *pardeh-dārī*, *nīzeh dārī*, *tīghdārī* and *jāndārī*. On *sepāhī* in the sense of 'archer', see above, p. 905 and n. 55.

[65] No emperor of the Yüan dynasty, and no Mongol Khān, was called Fīrūz, a Persian name.

him in the district of Qarāqurum and Bish Bāligh in Khitā.[66] From the capital to these places is three months' journey through populated country. The Ṣadr al-Jahān Burhān al-Dīn of Ṣāgharj told me that when the Qān had assembled his soldiers and mobilized his forces, a hundred squadrons of
300 cavalry, each one | of ten thousand troopers, rallied to him. Their commander is called amir of a *ṭūmān*.[67] In addition the Sultan's private guards and the people of his household were another fifty thousand. There were five hundred thousand infantry. When he set out most of the amirs revolted and agreed to depose him, because he had diverged from the precepts of the *yasaq*,[68] that is to say, the precepts of their ancestor Tankīz Khān, who laid waste the lands of Islam. They went over to the rebel son of his uncle and wrote to the Qān urging him to abdicate when the city of Khansā would be his fief. He refused, fought against them, was defeated, and was killed.[69]

The news of these events arrived some days after we had reached the capital. The city was decorated, drums were beaten, trumpets and bugles were played, and amusements and entertainments were organized for the space of a month. Then the bodies of the dead Qān and about a hundred of his uncle's sons, his relatives and his favourites were brought [to
301 the capital]. They dug for the Qān a big *nā'ūs*, which | is an underground chamber,[70] spread with the finest carpets. The Qān and his weapons were placed in it with the gold and silver vessels from his palace. Four slave-girls and six of his favourite mamluks with jars of drink were placed with them. The gateway to the house was built up and earth was piled over it all till it made a big hill. Then they brought four horses and made them run at the grave till they collapsed. They erected a wooden structure over the grave and fixed the horses to it

[66] See III, p. 566, n. 162.

[67] See II, p. 493, n. 293.

[68] See III, p. 560, n. 77.

[69] No Yūan emperor was killed in battle, though two were assassinated. The supposed rebellion of Fīrūz may be a confused reflection of one of many conflicts between Mongol princes and leaders in the concluding years of the dynasty.

[70] Greek *naos*, 'temple', also used in Arabic for a subterranean tomb.

after driving a wooden stake through each horse from the anus
to the mouth. The aforesaid relatives of the Qān were placed
in *nā'ūses* with their weapons and their household vessels.
Over the graves of the great men among them, of whom there
were ten, they impaled three horses for each grave. Over the
rest they impaled one horse for each.[71]

This day was a day | of solemn holiday. No one stayed 302
away, neither man nor woman, Muslim nor infidel. They all
wore mourning, which means white capes for the infidels and
white robes for the Muslims. The *khātūns* of the Qān and his
favourites stayed in tents at his grave for forty days, and some
of them for longer, up to a year. A bazaar was set up at his
grave where food and other necessaries were sold. I do not
recall that any other nation except this follows these practices
in our time. The Indian infidels and the people of China burn
their dead; other nations bury their dead but do not put in
anyone else with the corpse. However, I was told on good
authority in the country of the Blacks that the infidels there,
when their king dies, make a *nā'ūs* for him and put in with him
some of his favourites and attendants, and thirty | of the sons 303
and daughters of important people, first breaking their hands
and feet, and place with them jars of drink. A prominent man
of the Massūfa who lived among the Blacks in the country of
Kūbar [Gobir], and was greatly favoured by their Sultan, told
me that he had a son and that when their Sultan died they
wanted to put his son into the tomb along with those of their
own sons whom they were putting in it. He said: 'I said to
them, "How can you do this when he is not of your religion or
of your race?" and I redeemed him for a considerable sum of
money.'

When the Qān was killed as we have related, his uncle's son
Fīrūz took possession of the kingdom and chose as his capital
the city of Qarāqurum because it is near the country of the
sons of his paternal uncle, the kings | of Turkistan and 304

[71] This is a plausible account of a pagan Mongol funeral. That of Hülegü, Chingiz Khan's grandson and the first Ilkhan of Persia, (d. 1265) is 'the last occasion on which human victims are recorded as having been buried with a Chingizid prince' (Boyle, J. A. (ed.) *The Cambridge History of Iran*, V, p. 354). Toghon Temür, expelled from China in 1368, survived I.B., dying in Mongolia in 1370.

Transoxania. Then the amirs who had not been present when the Qān was killed rebelled against him; they cut communications and there was great disorder.[72]

[72] During the fourteenth century Central Asia between China and Persia was sometimes united under Khāns descended from Chaghatai, the second son of Chingiz Khan; sometimes it was divided among two or more princes, usually of that family. By Turkistan I.B. means what was often called Mogholistan, the basin of the Ili and upper Chu rivers. From 1347 to 1363 this was ruled by Tughluq Temür who claimed descent from Chaghatai and eventually conquered Transoxania. None of these princes was a nephew of Toghon Temür, the Mongol emperor of China, or could have been a cousin of Fīrūz.

CHAPTER XXIII

From China to Morocco

Account of my Return to China and then to India. When the
rebellion broke out and disorders flared up Shaikh
Burhān al-Dīn and others advised me to return to China
before disorder became prevalent. They presented themselves with me to the deputy of Sultan Fīrūz, who sent three
of his suite with me and wrote giving me the right to hospitality. We travelled down the river to Khansā, then to Qanjanfū,
and then to al-Zaitūn. When I arrived there I found the junks
about to sail for India. Among them was a junk belonging to
al-Malik al-Ẓāhir, the lord of al-Jāwa. Its crew were Muslims.
His agent recognized me and was delighted that I had come.
We encountered favourable winds for ten days, but when we
were near the country of | Ṭawālisī, the wind changed, the sky 305
became dark, and there was heavy rain. For ten days we did
not see the sun. Then we entered an unknown sea, the crew
of the junk were frightened, and they wanted to return to
China, but it was not possible. We spent forty-two days without knowing in which sea we were.

Account of the Rukhkh. At first light on the forty-third day a
mountain became visible in the sea about twenty miles away.
The wind was carrying us directly towards it. The sailors were
amazed and said: 'We are not near land and there is no
knowledge of a mountain in the sea. If the wind drives us on
to it we shall perish.' Everyone resorted to self-abasement, to
devotion, and to renewed repentance, supplicating God in
prayer. We sought Him through His prophet, on whom be the
Blessing and Peace of God. The merchants swore | to give 306
plentiful alms, which I recorded in my own writing. The wind
became somewhat calmer and at sunrise we saw that mountain
had risen into the air and there was light between it and the

sea. We were amazed at this and I saw the sailors weeping and saying good-bye to each other. I said: 'What is the matter?' They said: 'What we took for a mountain is the *rukhkh*. If it sees us we shall perish.' We were then less than ten miles from it. Then God Most High gave us the blessing of a favourable wind which took us directly away from it. We did not see it or know its true shape.[1]

Two months after that day we reached al-Jāwa and landed at Sumuṭra. We found the Sultan al-Malik al-Ẓāhir had arrived
307 after one of his expeditions and had brought | many prisoners. He sent me two girls and two boys and lodged me as usual. I was present at the wedding of his son with his brother's daughter.

Account of the wedding of the son of al-Malik al-Ẓāhir. I was present on the day of the unveiling of the bride. I saw they had erected in the middle of the audience hall a big tribune and spread it with pieces of silk. The bride came on foot from within the palace with her face visible. With her were about forty ladies, wives of the Sultan, his amirs and his Wazīrs, who held up her train. They were all unveiled. Everyone present, whether high or low, could look at them. This was not their practice except at weddings. The bride climbed onto the tribune. In front of her were musicians, men and women, playing and singing. Then the groom came on an elephant |
308 caparisoned, with a throne on its back with a canopy over it as over a palanquin. The said groom had a crown on his head. To his right and left were about a hundred sons of maliks and amirs, dressed in white, riding caparisoned horses, and with caps on their heads encrusted with precious stones. They were of the same age as the groom and were all beardless.

At his entry dinars and dirhams were strewn among the people. The Sultan sat on a raised place from which he saw it all. His son dismounted, kissed his foot, and climbed the tribune to his bride. She rose and kissed his hand. He sat beside her and the ladies fanned her. They brought areca nuts and betel, which he took in his hand and put into her mouth. Then the groom took a betel leaf in his mouth and then put it
309 in hers, and this | was all done in the public eye. Then she did what he had done. Then she was veiled and the tribune with

[1] See Plate III, where the giant bird is called an *ʿanqā*'.

both of them on it was carried into the palace. The people ate and went away. Next day his father assembled the people and made his son heir apparent. The people swore allegiance to him and he gave them profuse gifts of robes and gold.

I stayed in this island for two months and then embarked in one of the junks. The Sultan gave me a great deal of aloes, camphor, cloves and sandalwood, and dismissed me. I left him and after forty days I reached Kaulam. I stayed there under the protection of al-Qazwīnī, the qāḍī of the Muslims. It was Ramaḍān and I was present at the *ʿīd* prayer in the congregational mosque. It is their custom to come to the mosque at night
and to continue calling upon God till first light and then to call
on Him till the time of | the *ʿīd* prayer. Then they recite this 310
prayer, the preacher delivers his sermon, and they depart.

We left Kaulam for Qāliqūṭ, where we stayed for some days. I wanted to return to Dihlī, but became afraid to do so. I took ship and after twenty-eight nights I reached Ẓafār. It was Muḥarram in the year forty-eight,[2] and I stayed at the house of the preacher ʿĪsā ibn Ṭa'ṭa'.

Account of the Sultan of Ẓafār. This time I found the Sultan to be al-Malik al-Nāṣir son of al-Malik al-Mughīth, who had been king when I arrived there previously.[3] His deputy was Saif al-Dīn ʿOmar, the *amīr jandar*,[4] Turkish by race. This Sultan accommodated me and treated me with honour. Then
I took ship and reached Masqiṭ, a small town where there is
plenty of the fish called | *qulb almās*.[5] Then we travelled to the 311
port of Quraiyāt, then to the port of Shabba, then to the port of Kalba, which is pronounced like the feminine of ***kalb*** (dog), and then to Qalhāt, of which we have spoken before.[6] All

[2] 1 Muḥarram 748 = 13 April 1347.

[3] See vol. II, p. 390 and n. 86. Professor G. Rex Smith informs me that Gibb's note confuses al-Malik al-Fā'iz Aḥmad, brother of al-Malik al-Muẓaffar Yūsuf, the second Rasūlid Sultan, with al-Malik al-Fā'iz, the father of al-Mughīth and grandson of al-Muẓaffar. See G. Rex Smith and Venetia Porter, 'The Rasulids in Dhofar in the VIIth–VIIIth/XIIIth–XIVth Centuries', *JRAS*, 1988, I.

[4] The guard commander.

[5] Already described in his account of the Maldives. See above, p. 823.

[6] The order in which these places are mentioned is puzzling. If he was sailing along the coast from Ẓafār he would have come successively to Qalhāt, Quraiyāt, Masqaṭ and Kalbā, now written Ghallā. Shabba might be Al-Shābb, a village near Tīwī, between Qalhāt and Quraiyāt. It is presumably the place called Shabā in II, p. 399.

these places are administered from Hurmuz, though they are reckoned to be part of ʿOmān. We then travelled to Hurmuz and stayed there for three days. Then we went by land to Kaurastān,[7] then to Lār,[8] and Khunju Pāl,[9] all of which we have mentioned before. Then we went to Kārzī,[10] where we spent three days, then to Jamakān, then to Maiman,[11] then to Bassā,[12] and then to the city of Shīrāz. We found its Sultan
312 Abū Isḥāq still reigning, but he | was away.[13] I met there our pious and learned shaikh Majd al-Dın the Grand Qāḍī who had gone blind.[14] May God profit him and us through him!

Then I went to Māyin,[15] then Yazdukhāṣ,[16] then Kalīl,[17] then Kushkizar,[18] then Iṣfahān,[19] then Tustar,[20] then Ḥuwaizā,[21] and then al-Baṣra. All these places have been mentioned before.[22] In al-Baṣra I visited the noble sepulchres which are there of al-Zubair b. al-ʿAwwām, of Ṭalḥa b. ʿUbaidallāh, of Ḥalīma al-Saʿdīya, of Abū Bakra, of Ānas b. Mālik, of al-Ḥasan of Baṣra, of Thābit al-Bunānī, of Muḥammad b. Sīrīn, of Mālik b. Dīnār, of Muḥammad b. Wāsiʿ, of Ḥabīb the Persian, and of Sahl b. ʿAbdallāh of Tustar.[23] May God be pleased with them all! Then we went from al-Baṣra to the shrine of ʿAlī b. Abī Ṭālib.[24] May God be pleased with him,

[7] Previously mentioned as Kaurastān (II, p. 405) and there identified as Kūristān in n. 132.

[8] See II, p. 405, n. 133.

[9] See II, p. 406, n. 136.

[10] Or Kārzīn, on the right bank of the Sakkān or Mand river.

[11] See II, p. 304, n. 114. Maiman is Mīmand, east of Fīrūzābād.

[12] Fasā.

[13] See II, pp. 306–11 and n. 118.

[14] See II, pp. 300–306 and n. 99, pp. 308, 314, 316; III, p. 677.

[15] See II, p. 299, where it is written Māyīn, and n. 94.

[16] Yazdikhwāst. See II, p. 298 and n. 91.

[17] See II, p. 298 and nn. 89, 90.

[18] Kushk i-zar, 'the Gold Castle', has been mentioned (III, p. 715), but is in India. The place meant here is Kushk-i-zard, 'the Yellow Castle'. This name appears on maps, but is listed as Kushk-e-Zar in the *Gazetteer of Iran* published by the Defense Mapping Agency, Washington DC, 1984.

[19] See II, pp. 294–8.

[20] See II, pp. 284–7.

[21] Properly al-Ḥuwaizā'. See II, pp. 321–2.

[22] See II, pp. 275–80.

[23] For all of these except Thābit of Bunāna, see II, pp. 278–9 and nn. 29–34. Thābit b. Aslam was a traditionalist of the first half of the eighth century; Bunāna was a quarter of al-Baṣra.

[24] See II, pp. 277–8, for a description of his previous visit to this mosque.

and visited it. Then we went to al-Kūfa and visited | its 313
blessed mosque, then to Ḥilla, where is the Sanctuary of the Master of the Age.[25]

It happened about that time that an amir was governor of the town and prohibited its people from going to the mosque of the Master of the Age, as was their custom, and waiting for him there. He forbade them the use of the mounts which they used to take from the amir every night. An illness struck this governor and he soon died. This served to increase the recalcitrance of the heretics. They said: 'He was afflicted like that only because he refused the use of the mounts.' Afterwards it was not refused.

Then I travelled to Ṣarṣar,[26] then to the city of Baghdād where I arrived in Shawwāl of the year forty-eight.[27] I met there with someone from the Maghrib, who informed me of the disaster of Ṭarīfa and the capture of Al-Khaḍrā [Algeciras] by the Christians.[28] May God repair this breach in Islam. |
Account of the Sultan of Baghdād. The Sultan of Baghdād and 314
Iraq when I arrived there on the said date was Shaikh Ḥasan, the son of the paternal aunt of Sultan Abū Saʿīd.[29] May God have mercy upon him! When Abū Saʿīd died Shaikh Ḥasan took control of Iraq and married his wife Dilshād, the daughter of Dimashq Khwāja, son of the Amir Chūbān, as Sultan Abū Saʿīd had done when he married the wife of Shaikh Ḥasan. Sultan Ḥasan was away from Baghdād at this time; he had gone to fight the Sultan Ātābak Afrāsiyāb, lord of the country of the Lūrs.[30]

Then I left Baghdād and came to the city of al-Anbār, then to Hīt, then to al-Ḥadītha, and then to ʿĀna. These places are among the most beautiful and most fertile in the world. The road between them is thickly populated and it is as though
someone travelling through it were in a bazaar. | We have said 315

[25] For the mosque at al-Kūfa, see II, pp. 322–4; for the mosque at al-Ḥilla, see II, pp. 324–5.

[26] The name of two villages, Upper and Lower Ṣarṣar on the ʿĪsā canal.

[27] January 1348.

[28] The defeat of Abu'l Ḥasan the Marīnid Sultan of Morocco by Alfonso XI of Castile at the Rio Salado near Tarifa in 1340, and the Christian capture of Algeciras in 1342.

[29] See II, pp. 338–41 and n. 231.

[30] See II, p. 288 and n. 59.

before that we have not seen anything like the country by the Chinese river except this country.[31] Then I reached the city of al-Raḥba which is the one given the name of Mālik b. Ṭauq.[32] The city of al-Raḥba is the most beautiful place in Iraq and is also the beginning of Syria. Then we travelled to al-Sakhna, a fine town, most of whose inhabitants are Christian infidels. It is called Sakhna because of the heat of the water there.[33] It has rooms for men and for women in which they bathe. They draw water and at night put it on the flat roofs to cool. Then we went to Tadmur, the city of the Prophet of God Sulaimān, Peace be upon him, which the jinns built for him, as Nābigha said:

> They built Tadmur with flagstones and columns.[34]

Then they went to the city of Damascus of Syria, from which I had been absent fully twenty years. I had left there a
316 pregnant wife.[35] While I was in | India I learnt that she had given birth to a male child. I had then sent forty Indian gold dinars for his mother to his grandfather, who was from Miknāsa [Meknes] in the Maghrib. When I came to Damascus this time I had no other concern than to ask after my son. I went into the mosque and luckily found Nūr al-Dīn al-Sakhāwī, the Imam of the Mālikīs and their leader.[36] I greeted him but he did not recognize me. I let him know who I was and asked him about my son. He said: 'He died twelve years ago', and told me that a jurist from Tangier lived in the Ẓāhirīya madrasa.[37] I went there to ask him about my father and my family. I found him to be a venerable shaikh. I greeted him and told him about my family. He told me my father had died fifteen years ago, and that my mother was still living.

[31] See above, p. 905.

[32] So-called after Mālik b, Ṭauq b. ʿAttāb al-Taghlibī, who restored it early in the eighth century, to distinguish it from several other towns with the same name.

[33] Arabic *sakhna, sukhna* 'feverish heat'. The name of the town is now usually written Sukhna.

[34] Yāqūt relates that the jinns built Palmyra for Solomon and quotes this hemistich by the famous pre-Islamic poet Nābigha al-Dhubyānī.

[35] He had visited Damascus in August 1326. See I, pp. 118–57. He does not refer to his marriage in describing his stay.

[36] See I, pp. 150–51. Ibn Baṭṭūṭa had stayed with him.

[37] See I, p. 137 and n. 257.

I stayed in Damascus of Syria for the rest of the year.[38] | Prices 317
were very high; bread rose to be seven okes for a silver dirham. Their oke is equal to four Maghribī okes. The Grand Qāḍī of the Mālikīs was then Jamāl al-Dīn al-Maslātī.[39] He was a companion of Shaikh ʿAlā' al-Dīn of Konya[40] and had come to Damascus with him. He became known there and was made a qāḍī. The Grand Qāḍī of the Shāfiʿīs was Taqī al-Dīn b. al-Subkī. The amir of Damascus was the malik of the amirs Arghūn Shāh.[41] *Anecdote.* At that time one of the important people of Damascus died and bequeathed his property to the poor. The trustee of his bequest used to buy bread and distribute it daily to the poor after the afternoon prayer. One night they assembled in great numbers and seized the bread that was to be distributed to them and laid hands on the bakers' bread. When news of this reached the amir Arghūn Shāh he sent out his myrmidons.
Whenever they | met with one of the poor they said to him: 318
'Come and get bread.' A considerable number of them gathered and they imprisoned them for the night. Next day he rode out, made them come to the castle, and ordered their hands and feet to be cut off, though most of them were innocent. He drove out the crowd of *ḥarāfīsh* from Damascus: they dispersed to Ḥimṣ, Hamā and Aleppo. I was told he lived only a short time after this, and that he was killed. I left Damascus for Ḥimṣ, Ḥamā, Maʿarra, Sarmīn and then Aleppo.[42] The amir of Aleppo at this time was the Ḥājj Rughṭay.[43]

[38] Recounting his previous visit to Damascus in 1326 I.B. gives a long list of scholars who gave him licence to teach (I, pp. 154–7). Gibb noted that it was difficult to see how he could have obtained them all in a stay of less than a month (I, p. 157, n. 338). It seems likely that, though he states explicitly that they were given him in that year, some of them were acquired during this much longer residence.

[39] Muhammad b. ʿAbd al-Raḥīm b. ʿAlī b. ʿAbd al-Malik al-Salamī al-Maslātī, Mālikī judge in Damascus for over twenty years, d. 1370. (*Durar*, IV, p. 11, no. 25.)

[40] See I, p. 134 and n. 245.

[41] Saif al-Dīn Arghūn al-Kāmilī al-Ṣaghīr (the Little), in succession governor (*nā'ib*) of Aleppo, Damascus and again Aleppo, d. 1357. In their index the French editors confuse him with Arghūn Shāh the Dawādār (I, p. 54 and n. 166), who died in 1330. For his biography see *Manhal*, II, pp. 319–25, no. 375.

[42] For I.B.'s previous visit to these towns see I, pp. 90–103.

[43] Ibn Taghrībirdī calls him al-Ḥājj Saif al-Dīn Urqatay b. ʿAbdallāh al-Qafjaq. The correct form of his name is probably Urughtay. He was successively governor of Ṣafad, Tripoli and Aleppo, then viceroy (*nā'ib salṭana*) of Egypt, then again governor of Aleppo. He died in 1357 on his way to Damascus to which he had been transferred. For his biography, see *Manhal*, II, p. 328, no. 378.

Anecdote. It happened at this time that a faqir known as the
319 shaikh of shaikhs was | living on a mountain outside the city of ʿAintāb. People used to seek him out and solicit his blessing. He had a pupil always with him, but he was solitary and celibate, having no wife. In one of his discourses he said: 'The Prophet, May God bless him and give him peace, did not do without women, but I do without them.' There was a witness of this and it was proved before the qāḍī. The case was referred to those amirs and he and his pupil, who had agreed with what he had said, were arraigned. The four qāḍīs, who were Shihāb al-Dīn the Mālikī, Nāṣir al-Dīn the Destitute, the Ḥanafī, Taqi al-Dīn son of the goldsmith, the Ṣhāfiʿī, and ʿIzz al-Dīn of Damascus, the Ḥanbalī, authorized the death penalty for them both, and they were executed.

In the first days of the month of Rabīʿ I in the year forty-nine news reached us in Aleppo that plague had broken out in
320 Ghazza and that the number of dead there exceeded | a thousand a day.[44] I went to Ḥimṣ and found that the plague had already struck there; about three hundred persons died on the day of my arrival. I went to Damascus and arrived on a Thursday; the people had been fasting for three days. On Friday they went to the Mosque of the Footprints, as we have related in the first book.[45] God alleviated their plague. The number of deaths among them had risen to two thousand four hundred a day. Then I went to ʿAjlūn, and then to Bait al-Muqaddas [Jerusalem], where I found the plague had ceased. I met the preacher ʿIzz al-Dīn, son of Jamāʿa, son of the paternal uncle of ʿIzz al-Dīn the Grand Qāḍī of Cairo.[46] He is a pious and generous man. His salary as preacher is a thousand dirhams a month.

Anecdote. The preacher ʿIzz al-Dīn gave a banquet one day and
321 invited me among | his guests. I asked him the reason for it. He told me that during the plague he had sworn he would give a banquet if the plague were to cease and a day were to pass during which he did not pray over a corpse. Then he said: 'Yesterday I did not pray over a corpse so I arranged the banquet as I had promised.'

[44] May/June 1348. The Black Death.
[45] See I, pp. 142–4.
[46] See I, p. 55 and n. 173.

I found that some of the shaikhs I had met in al-Quds [Jerusalem] had departed to be with God Most High. May He have mercy on them! Only a few of them were left like the learned traditionist the imam Ṣalāḥ al-Dīn Khalīl, the son of Kaikaldī al-ʿAlā'ī, and like the pious Sharaf al-Dīn al-Khushshī, the shaikh of the hospice of the mosque of al-Aqṣā. I met Shaikh Sulaimān of Shīrāz. He gave me hospitality. I met no one else in Syria and Egypt who had visited the Foot of Adam. Peace be upon him!

I left Jerusalem accompanied by the preacher and | tradi- 322
tionist Sharaf al-Dīn Sulaimān of Milyāna and the shaikh of the Maghribīs there, the admirable Sufi Ṭalḥa al-ʿAbd al Wādī. We reached the city of al-Khalīl [Hebron], Peace be upon it, and we visited his tomb and those of the prophets there, Peace be upon them. Then we went to Ghazza and found most of it deserted because of the numbers that had died during the plague. The qāḍī told me that only a quarter of the eighty notaries there were left and that the number of deaths had risen to eleven hundred a day. We then went by land to Dimyāṭ. where I met Quṭb al-Dīn of Naqshuwān who fasts incessantly.[47] He accompanied me to Fāras Kūr and Samannūd and then to Abū Ṣīr where we stayed in the hospice of one of the Egyptians.[48]

Anecdote. While we were in that hospice | a faqir entered and 323
greeted us. We offered him food, but he refused it and said: 'I came only to visit you.' He spent the whole night in prostration and bowing in prayer. We prayed the dawn prayer and gave ourselves over to the praise of God, while the faqir stayed in a corner of the hospice. The shaikh came with food and called him, but he did not answer. He went over to him and found him dead. We prayed over him and buried him. May God have mercy upon him!

Then I travelled to al-Maḥalla al-Kabīra, then to Naḥrārīya, then to Abyār, then to Damanhūr,[49] and then to Alexandria.[50]

[47] For his previous visits to Hebron, see I, pp. 73–7, to Gaza, I, p. 73, and to Damietta, I, pp. 36–9.

[48] For Fāraskūr (usually Fāriskūr) and Samannūd, see I, p. 40. Abū Ṣīr has not been mentioned previously; it is a small town near Tanta.

[49] See I, p. 34 and n. 91; I, p. 32 and n. 85; I, pp. 32–3 and n. 87, and I, p. 30.

[50] For I.B.'s description of Alexandria, see I, pp. 18–28.

I found the plague had abated after the number of deaths had risen to a thousand and eighty a day. Then I went to Cairo and was told that during the plague the number of deaths there had risen to twenty-one thousand a day. I found that all the shaikhs I had known were dead. May God Most High have mercy upon them! |

324 *Account of the Sultan of Cairo*. The king of Egypt at that time was al-Malik al-Nāṣir Ḥasan, son of al-Malik al-Nāṣir Muḥammad, son of al-Malik al-Manṣūr Qalāwun.[51] He was afterwards deposed and his brother al-Malik al-Ṣaliḥ became ruler. When I arrived in Cairo I found that the Grand Qāḍī ʿIzz al-Dīn, son of the Grand Qāḍī Badr al-Dīn, son of Jamāʿa,[52] had set out for Mecca in a huge caravan called Rajabī, because it leaves in the month of Rajab. I was told that the plague was among them until they reached the pass of Aila[53] where it ceased. I then went from Cairo to the Ṣaʿīd, which has already been spoken of, to ʿAidhāb,[54] whence I sailed to Judda,[55] and then went to Mecca, May God Most High ennoble and honour her! I arrived on the twenty-second of Shaʿbān of the year forty-nine.[56] I put myself under the protection of the Mālikī Imam,
325 the pious, the devout, | the excellent Abū ʿAbdallāh Muḥammad, son of ʿAbd al-Raḥmān called Khalīl.[57] I fasted through the month of Ramaḍān in Mecca. Every day I visited the holy places according to the Shāfiʿī *madhhab*. Among the shaikhs of Mecca I knew I met Shihāb al-Dīn al-Ḥanafī,[58] Shihāb al-Dīn al-Ṭabarī,[59] Abū Muḥammad al-Yāfiʿī,[60] Najm al-Dīn al-Uṣfūnī,[61] and al-Ḥarāzī.[62]

[51] Al-Malik al-Nāṣir Ḥasan, 1347–51, son of al-Malik al-Nāsir Muḥammad 1293–4, 1298–1308 and 1309–40, son of al-Malik al-Manṣūr Qalā'ūn, 1279–90. He was followed by his brother al-Malik al-Ṣāliḥ Ṣāliḥ, 1351–4.

[52] See I, p. 55 and n. 173.

[53] See I, p. 159 and n. 14.

[54] For his previous journey through the Saʿīd to ʿAidhāb, see I, pp. 59–69.

[55] For his previous visit to Judda, see II, pp. 360–61.

[56] 16 November 1348.

[57] See I, p. 203 and n. 69.

[58] See I, p. 219 and n. 127.

[59] See I, p. 216 and n. 119.

[60] ʿAbdallāh Asʿad b. ʿAlī b. Sulaimān b. Fallāh al-Yāfiʿī al-Yamanī al-Shāfiʿī, ʿAfīf al-Dīn. See also I, p. 221, where he is not identified. He spent much of his life in Mecca where he died in 1367. He had studied with Shihāb al-Dīn al-Ṭabarī, *Durar*, II, pp. 247–9; Subkī, *Ṭabaqāt al-Shāfiʿīya*, VI, p. 103.

[61] See I, p. 221 and II, p. 356.

[62] Either Aḥmad b. Qāsim b. ʿAbd al-Rahmān b. Abī Bakr al-Qurashī al-ʿAmrī, from Ḥarāz in al-Yaman, 1276/7–1354, *Durar*, I, pp. 235–6, or his son Muḥammad, 1306/7–1363–4, *Durar*, III, p. 348.

I made the pilgrimage in that year and then left with the Syrian caravan for Ṭaiba, the city of the Prophet of God. May God bless and give him peace. I visited his noble and perfumed tomb, may God increase it in perfume and honour. I prayed in the noble mosque, may God purify it and enhance its magnificence. I visited the Companions of the Prophet. God bless him and give him peace, who are in Al-Baqīʿ,[63] God be pleased with them. Among the shaikhs I met Abū Muḥammad, son of Farḥūn.[64]

We left Madīna the noble for alʿUlā and Tabūk, | then Bait 326
al-Muqaddas [Jerusalem], then the city of al-Khalīl, God bless him and give him peace, then to Ghazza,[65] then the desert stations, all of which have been described before, and then Cairo. There we learnt that Our Master the Commander of the Faithful, the Protector of True Religion, who places his trust in the lord of the worlds, Abū ʿInān, may God Most High assist him, had under God brought together the scattered pieces of the Marīnid dominion and by his blessing had healed the countries of the Maghrib after their being near to death, had poured forth benefits on high and low, and had enwrapped all the people in a profusion of favours.[66] They longed to stand at his gate in the hope of kissing his stirrup. Thereupon I sought to make my way to his exalted capital. The memory of my homeland moved me, affection for my people and friends, and love for my country which for me is better than all others. |

A land where charms were hung upon me 327
Whose earth my skin first touched

I sailed in a small *qurqura* belonging to a Tunisian. This was in Ṣafar of the year fifty.[67] I landed in Jarba but the boat went

[63] The cemetery of al-Madīna. See I, pp. 179–80.

[64] See I, p. 174 and n. 72.

[65] For his previous visits to, and descriptions of, these places, see I, p. 73 (Gaza), pp. 73–7 (Hebron), pp. 77–80 (Jerusalem), p. 161 (Tabūk), and pp. 162–3 (ʿUlā).

[66] In 1347 the Marīnid Sultan of Morocco Abu'l Ḥasan conquered the dominions of the Ḥafsid ruler of Tunis, but in April 1348 he was defeated by Arab tribes and was widely supposed to have been killed. His son Abū ʿInān Fāris was proclaimed Sultan at Tilimsān in June 1348, but his father returned and fought unsuccessfully against him until his own death in 1351.

[67] April–May 1349.

on to Tunis and the enemy captured it. Then I went in a small boat to Qābis [Gabes], where I landed and was the guest of two excellent brothers, Abū Marwān and Abu'l-ʿAbbās, sons of Makkī, the amirs of Jarba and Qābis.[68] I spent with them the birthday of the Prophet, God bless him and give him peace. Then I took a boat to Safāqus [Sfax], then went by sea to Bulyāna.[69] and then by land with the Arabs, after a troublesome journey reaching the city of Tunis, which the Arabs were besieging.[70] |

328 *Account of the Sultan of Tunis.* Tunis was under the government of Our Master, the Commander of the Muslims, the Protector of True Religion, the warrior who fights on behalf of the Lord of the Worlds, paladin of paladins, incomparable among generous kings, lion of lions, most magnanimous of the magnanimous, the devout, who turns to God, the humble, the just Abu'l-Ḥasan, son of Our Master the Commander of the Muslims, the warrior who fights on behalf of the Lord of the Worlds, the Protector of the faith of Islam, whose virtue has become a proverb, whose acts of generosity and graciousness are disseminated throughout the regions of the world, author of virtuous, glorious, illustrious and beneficent deeds, the just and excellent king Abū Saʿīd,[71] son of Our Master the Commander of the Muslims, the Protector of True Religion, the warrior on behalf of the Lord of the Worlds, the conqueror and destroyer of infidels, who began and then repeated the exploits of the holy war, the protector of true belief, the zealous in what pertains to
329 | the Merciful, the devout, the ascetic who bows and prostrates himself in prayer, the humble, the pious Abū Yūsuf son of ʿAbd al-Ḥaqq,[72] God be pleased with them all and cause the kingdom to remain with their descendants till the day of Judgment.

[68] Abū Marwān Aḥmad b. Makkī was entrusted with the government of the island of Jerba after the expulsion of the Sicilian garrison in 1335; he later extended his authority over Sfax. His brother Abu'l ʿAbbās ʿAbdul Malik was the virtually independent ruler of Qābis. The brothers affected the status of jurists (Brunschvig, I, pp. 158–9, 174).

[69] Belliana or Balliyāna near Sfax, Brunschvig, I, pp. 310–11. This supersedes Gibb's tentative identification with Nabeul, *Selections*, p. 375, n. 14.

[70] After defeating Abu'l Ḥasan at Qairawān the Arab tribes besieged Tunis where the garrison remained loyal to him. He reached the city in July and stayed there till December 1349, when he sailed for Bijāya.

[71] Abū Saʿīd ʿOthmān II, 1310–31.

[72] Abū Yūsuf Yaʿqūb, 1258–86.

When I reached Tunis I sought out al-Ḥājj Abu'l-Ḥasan because of the ties of relationship and citizenship between us. He accommodated me in his house and went with me to the audience hall. I went into the noble hall and kissed the hand of Our Master Abu'l-Ḥasan, God be pleased with him. He ordered me to sit down, which I did. He asked me about the noble Ḥijāz and the Sultan of Egypt and I answered him. He asked me about Ibn Tīfarājīn.[73] I told him what the
Maghribīs had done about him to assist | Our Master Abu'l- 330
Ḥasan, God be pleased with him. Among the jurists present at his assembly were the imam Abū ʿAbdallāh al-Saṭṭī[74] and the imam Abū ʿAbdallāh Muḥammad b. al-Ṣabbāgh[75] and among the Tunisians their qāḍī Abū ʿAlī ʿOmar b. ʿAbd al-Rafīʿ[76] and Abū ʿAbdallāh b. Hārūn.[77]

I left the noble assembly but after the afternoon prayer Our Master Abu'l-Ḥasan summoned me. He was in a tower overlooking the field of battle. With him were the illustrious shaikhs Abū ʿOmar ʿOthmān b. ʿAbd al-Wāḥid al-Tanālaftī,[78] Abū Ḥassūn Ziyān, son of Amriyūn al-ʿAlawī, Abū Zakarīyā' Yaḥyā son of Sulaimān al-ʿAskarī, and al-Ḥajj Abu'l-Ḥasan al-Nāmīsī. He asked me about the king of India and I answered his questions. I went on going back and forth to the noble assembly so long as I stayed in Tunis, which was for thirty-six days. |

[73] ʿAbdallāh b. Tīfarājīn or Tafrāgīn, an Almohad shaikh who acquired great influence at the Ḥafsid court in Tunis and arranged the marriage of the Marīnid Sultan Abu'l Ḥasan to a Ḥafsid princess. In the course of succession disputes which ensued after the death of the Ḥafsid Sultan Abū Bakr in 1346 Ibn Tafrāgīn and Abu'l Ḥasan came to support rival claimants. When Abu'l Ḥasan occupied Tunis in 1348 Ibn Tafrāgīn fled to Egypt. He returned in 1350 and was the virtual ruler of Tunis till his death in 1364.

[74] Muḥammad b. Salmān al-Saṭṭī, a Mālikī jurist and favourite of Sultan Abu'l Ḥasan, whom he accompanied at the battle of Qairawān and during his subsequent stay in Tunis. He was drowned off the coast near Bijāya (Bougie) when the Sultan's fleet was wrecked there in the winter of 1349–50 (*Nail al-ibtihāj*).

[75] Muḥammad ibn al-Ṣabbāgh al-Khazrajī of Miknāsa (Meknes), another Mālikī jurist who accompanied Sultan Abu'l Ḥasan to Tunis and was drowned along with al-Saṭṭī (*Nail al-ibtihāj*).

[76] Qāḍī for marriages and then communal qāḍī at Tunis, d. 1364–5, Brunschvig, II, p. 115.

[77] Muḥammad b. Hārūn al-Kinānī of Tunis, a celebrated mufti and commentator on Mālikī law, who died of the plague in 1349–50 (*Nail al-ibtihāj*).

[78] The last name should perhaps be Tan al-Ruftī or Tan al-Zuftī, associating him with either the district known as Tanerrouft in Algeria, or with Wadī Tanezzuft in Libya.

331 In Tunis I met the shaikh, the imam, the seal and chief of the ʿ*ulamā*ʾ Abū ʿAbdallāh of Ābila.[79] He was on a sickbed and he enquired about many matters concerned with my travels. I travelled from Tunis by sea with the Catalans. We reached the island of Sardāniya [Sardinia], a Christian island. There is a wonderful harbour with huge pieces of wood around it and an entrance like a gate, which is opened only with their permission.[80] In the island are fortresses, one of which we entered. There were many bazaars inside it. I vowed to God Most High that if He delivered us from this island I would fast for two months, because we had learnt that its people had resolved to follow us and take us prisoners when we left. We departed from the island and after ten days reached the city of Tanas, then Māzūna, then Mustaghānim,[81] and then Tilim-
332 sān. I sought out al-ʿUbbād | and visited the shaikh Abū Madyan, God be pleased with him and grant favours through him.[82] Then I left by the Nadrūma road,[83] followed the Akhandaqān road and spent the night at the hospice of Shaikh Ibrāhīm.[84] Then we continued our journey and when we were near Azaghnaghān[85] we were attacked by fifty men on foot and two horsemen. I was with Al-Ḥājj Ibn Qarīʿāt of Tangier and his brother Muḥammad who afterwards died a martyr at sea.

[79] The French editors read al-Ubullī, i.e. from Ubulla, which is in Iraq. See II, p. 281, for Ibn Baṭṭūṭa's description of it as having become a mere village. The correct reading is probably al-Ābilī. Muḥammad b. Ibrāhīm b. Aḥmad alʿAbdarī of Tilimsān called al-Ābilī was a Mālikī jurist whose father had migrated from Spain to Tilimsān. He was one of the religious advisers of Abu'l Ḥasan and Abū ʿInān and died at Fez in 1356. He is the subject of a long notice in *Nail al-ibtihāj*, pp. 245–8.

[80] Evidently Cagliari, then an Aragonese possession.

[81] Tenes, Mazouna and Mostaganem.

[82] A village near Tilimsān, sometimes marked Eubbad on maps, but generally known as Sidi Bou Mediene. Abū Madyan Shuʿaib b. al-Ḥusain or al-Ḥasan was born near Seville and died at Tilimsān in 1197–8. He had immense influence on popular Islamic mysticism in NW Africa. His shrine was built by Abu'l Ḥasan in 1339 in a cemetery already containing the tombs of many celebrated for their piety. See Brunschvig, II, pp. 317–19. It is illustrated in G. Marçais *L'Architecture musulmane d'Occident*, 1954, p. 281.

[83] Nedroma.

[84] Near Ghazaouet (formerly Nemours). Akhandaqān and Azaghnaghān in the next sentence may represent one name.

[85] 'A Berber tribe settled near the coast between Melilla and the Muluya river', Gibb, *Selections*, p. 375, n. 17. The name is not vowelled in the text and may be Segangan, some 15 km south of Melilla.

We decided to fight them and raised a flag. They then made peace with us and we with them, praise be to God. I reached the city of Tāzā, where I learnt that my mother had died of the plague, God Most High have mercy upon her. I left Tāzā and on the last Friday of Shaʿbān the blessed in the year seven hundred and fifty[86] I reached the capital city of Fez.

I stood before our exalted master, the most generous imam, the Commander of the Faithful, | who puts his trust in the 333
Lord of the Worlds, Abū ʿInān,[87] God establish his grandeur and crush his enemies. His majesty caused me to forget the majesty of the Sultan of Iraq, his beauty to forget that of the king of India, his gracious manners those of the king of al-Yaman, his courage that of the king of the Turks, his clemency that of the king of the Greeks, his devotion that of the king of Turkistan, his theological learning that of the king of al-Jāwa. Before him was his excellent Wazīr, author of renowned noble deeds and exploits, Abū Zayyān b. Wadrār.[88] He asked me about Egypt, where he had been, and I answered his questions. Our master, God Most High support him, overwhelmed me with favours for which I am unable to thank him [adequately]. God is able to recompense him.

I laid down my travelling staff in his noble country after verifying with superabundant impartiality that it is the best of countries. Its fruits are plentiful, | water and provisions are 334
easy to get, and few regions of the world have all these together. The poet spoke well who said:

> The West is the best of lands as I can prove
> The full moon is near to it and the sun runs thither

The dirhams of the West are small but they have many advantages. If you consider prices in Egypt and Syria the truth of what I say is apparent, and the excellence of the Maghrib obvious. I say that mutton is sold in Egypt at the rate of eighteen okes for a silver dirham, which is six Maghribī dirhams; in the Maghrib when the price is very high eighteen

86 6 November 1349.

87 After being proclaimed Sultan at Tilimsān Abū ʿInān had gained possession of Fez.

88 Fāris b. Zaiyān b. Wadrār, appointed a junior vizier after the proclamation of Abu ʿInān at Tilimsān, Ibn Khaldūn, *Berbères*, IV, 273, Ibn al-Aḥmar, p. 81, n. 2.

okes are sold for two dirhams, that is a third of the Egyptian
335 dirham. As for butter it is not to be had in Egypt | most of the
time. What is eaten with bread by the Egyptians are things
despised in the Maghrib. Mostly they are lentils and chick-
peas, which they cook in heavy cauldrons and on which they
put sesame oil; *basilla*,[89] which is a kind of peas which they
cook and to which they add olive oil; gherkins which they
cook and mix with curdled milk; purslane, which they cook in
the same way; the buds on the young shoots of the almond
tree, which they cook and on which they put curdled milk;
colocasia, which they cook. All these are easy to get in the
Maghrib but God has made them superfluous by the abundance of meat, butter, both clarified and fresh, honey, and
other things. Green vegetables are very rare in Egypt; fruit is
mostly imported from Syria; grapes, when they are cheap, are
336 sold among them | at three of their pounds for a silver dirham,
their pound being twelve okes.

In Syria fruit is plentiful but it is cheaper in the Maghrib.
Grapes are sold there at a silver dirham for one of their
pounds, their pound being three Maghribī pounds. When the
price is low two pounds are sold for a silver dirham. Plums are
sold at ten okes for a silver dirham. Pomegranates and quinces
are sold for eight *fals* apiece, which amounts to a Maghribī
dirham. Vegetables sold for a silver dirham are less in quantity
than are sold for a small dirham in our country. Meat is sold
there at two and a half silver dirhams for one of their pounds.
If you consider all that it will be obvious that the countries of
337 the Maghrib are the cheapest | in prices, the most abundant in
resources, and the foremost in amenities and advantages.

God has increased the lands of the Maghrib in honour after honour and in excellence after excellence through the imamate of our master the Commander of the Faithful, who has extended the shade of security over its countries, has caused the sun of justice to rise over its expanse, has made the clouds to deluge the countryside and the towns with beneficence, has purified it of evildoers and has established in it the foundations of secular and of religious life. I shall recount examples I have witnessed and verified of his justice, his clemency, his

[89] Italian *piselli*.

courage, his addiction to religious learning and the study of the holy law, his constant almsgiving and his alleviation of oppression.

Account of some of the virtues of Our Master, God strengthen him.
His justice is more renowned than can be recorded in a book.
An instance is that he has sessions to hear complaints from his
subjects; | he devotes Fridays to the poor, dividing the day 338
between men and women, giving women priority because of
their weakness. Their petitions are read from after the Friday
prayer until the afternoon prayer. Each one whose turn has
come is summoned by name. She stands in his precious presence and he speaks to her without an intermediary. If she has
been the victim of oppression, it is quickly rectified; if she
requests a favour, relief is at hand. When the afternoon prayer
has been prayed, the men's petitions are read and are dealt
with in the same way. The jurists and qāḍīs are present at the
audience and decisions connected with the religious law are
referred to them. I have not seen any other king act so impec-
cably and display such justice. The king of India appointed
one | of his amirs to receive petitions from the people and to 339
summarize them for him, but the petitioners themselves were
not in his presence.

As for his clemency I have witnessed wonderful instances of it, for he, God strengthen him, has pardoned many of those who have fought against his troops and resisted his authority, and also great criminals whose crimes no one would pardon unless he trusts in his Lord and who knows with *certain knowledge*[90] the meaning of the words of the Most High *pardon the offences of the people.*[91]

Ibn Juzayy remarks: 'One of the wonderful instances of the
clemency of our master, God strengthen him, that I have
witnessed since I came to his noble gate in the last days of the
year fifty-three until now, that is to say, in the first days of the
year fifty-seven,[92] I have not seen him order anyone to be
executed unless it was someone whose execution | was de- 340
creed in the religious law as the penalty stipulated by God
Most High as retaliation or in war, and this is in spite of the

[90] Qur'ān, sūra cii, 5.
[91] Qur'ān, sūra iii, 134.
[92] The year 757 began on 5 January 1356.

extent of his kingdom, the spaciousness of his provinces and the diversity of peoples. Nothing like it has been heard of in times past or in distant countries.

As for his courage, it is known what constancy and audacity he showed on illustrious fields, as on the day he fought the Banū ʿAbd al-Wādī and others.[93] I have heard the story of that day told in the country of the Blacks. It was related to their Sultan and he said: 'Like that, or not at all.'

Ibn Juzayy remarks: 'The kings of ancient times were always vying with one another in killing lions and in routing their enemies, but our master, God strengthen him, killed a
341 lion more easily than a sheep | is killed by a lion. A lion attacked the troops in Wādi al-Najjārīn in the cultivated part of the district of Salā. The champion fighters, both horsemen and foot soldiers, hovered round him and fled from him. Our master, God strengthen him, came out against him and casually and fearlessly thrust his spear between his eyes so that he fell dead. On hands and mouth![94]

'As for putting enemies to flight, this happens to kings because of the steadiness of their troops and the élan of their cavalry. The part of kings is to stand firm and incite them to fight. But our master, God strengthen him, advanced against the enemy, alone in his noble person, knowing that the mass of troops had fled and assured that no one who would fight had stayed with him; thereupon fear overcame the hearts of the
342 enemy | who fled before him. It was wonderful to see nations fleeing before one man. *That is a grace which God bestows on whomsoever he wishes,*[95] *Success is with those who fear God.*[96] This is nothing but the fruit of the favours he obtains from God through his trust in Him and his total reliance upon Him.'

As for his concern for religious knowledge, look how he, God Most High strengthen him, convenes meetings of the

[93] In June 1352 Abū ʿInān reconquered Tilimsān from the ʿAbd al-Wādid dynasty. I.B. probably refers to the battle of Angad when Marīnid light horse deserted and the Sultan led a charge against the enemy (Ibn Khaldūn, *Berbères*, IV, p. 293).

[94] On hands and mouth. A saying used to express pleasure at someone's misfortune the meaning being 'May God make him fall on his hands and mouth'. (Freytag, *Arabum proverbia*, II, 1839, p. 475, no. 243).

[95] Qur'ān, sūra v, 57, lvii, 21, and lxii, 4.

[96] Qur'ān, sūra vii, 128, and xxviii, 83.

learned every day after the dawn prayer in the mosque of his noble palace, attended by the principal jurists and the most distinguished scholars. The commentary on the Holy Qur'ān is read before him, and the Traditions of the Chosen One, God give him blessing and peace, and the elaborations of the *madhhab* of Mālik, God be pleased with him, and the books of the Sufis. In all these subjects his is the highest attainment; he solves their difficulties with the light of his understanding and illuminating apothegms are projected | from his memory. This 343
was the procedure of the rightly guided Imams and the Orthodox Caliphs. I have not seen any of the kings of the world whose concern for religious knowledge attains this degree. I have seen before the king of India discussions held after the dawn prayer, particularly on matters of rational knowledge. I have seen before the king of al-Jāwa discussions after the Friday prayer particularly on the application of the teachings of the Shāfi'ī *madhhab*. I admired the assiduity of the king of Turkistan in attending the night and dawn prayers in the congregation till I saw the assiduity of our master, God strengthen him, in the quest for all religious knowledge in the congregation in the mosque and in the observances of Ramaḍān. *God bestows his mercy on whom he wishes*.[97]

Ibn Juzayy remarks: 'If there were a scholar | with nothing 344
to do but study day and night he would not reach the lowest degree of the knowledge possessed by our master, God strengthen him, though he gives his attention also to the affairs of the community, and to the administration of remote provinces, supervises the affairs of his dominions more closely than any other king, and examines personally the complaints of those who have been wronged. In spite of all this, if a difficulty arises in any branch of knowledge in his noble assembly, he clarifies its obscurity, discusses its subtleties, elucidates its enigmas, and enables the scholars in the assembly to comprehend abstruse points which had eluded them.

'He, God strengthen him, then rose to the exalted knowledge of the Sufis, understood the symbols they use, and assumed their manners. The consequence has become evident in his humility for all his exalted rank, in his solicitude

[97] Qur'an, sūra ii, 105, and iii, 74.

for his subjects, and his affability in everything. He has
345 devoted himself greatly | to *belles-lettres*, which he has practised and the standing of which he has heightened. From him came the noble epistle and the poem which he sent to the noble, holy, pure Garden, the Garden of the chief of the prophets, the intercessor for sinners, the Prophet of God, God give him blessing and peace. He wrote them with his own handwriting, which for beauty puts the Garden to shame. That is something no other king of this age ever undertook or even aspired to do. Anyone who considers the rescripts issued by him, God Most High strengthen him, and who has fully comprehended their contents, will realize the pre-eminent eloquence with which God has endowed our master in creating him and which, both natural and acquired, has been conjoined in him.'

As for the stream of alms he dispenses and the hospices he has ordered to be built throughout his dominions to provide food for all who come and go, that is something which no |
346 other king has done except the Sultan Atābak Aḥmad,[98] and our master, God strengthen him, is his superior in giving food to the poor every day and in giving grain to those hermits who hide themselves away.

Ibn Juzayy remarks: 'Our master, God strengthen him, has devised practices in benevolence and almsgiving of which no one had thought and which the Sultans had not attained. Among them are the constant distribution of alms to the poor in every place in his realms; the designation of abundant alms for prisoners in all his realms; the stipulation that those alms should be in the form of baked bread that is easy to use; clothing for the poor, the sick, old women, old men, and those serving in the mosques throughout his realms; the allocation of sacrificial animals for these classes of people for the Feast of
347 Sacrifice; | the giving in alms of the tolls exacted at the gates in his realms on the twenty-seventh day of Ramaḍān in honour of that noble day and in support of its sanctity; feeding the people of the whole country on the night of the noble birth[99] and assembling them for its ceremonies; the circumcision,

[98] See II, pp. 288–90.
[99] I.e. of the Prophet Muḥammad on 12 Rabīʿ I.

feeding and clothing of orphan boys on the day of ʿĀshūrā';[100] his help to the chronically sick and infirm in providing them with partners to work their land and so ease their burdens; his giving to the poor in his capital soft rugs and wraps of good quality for them to spread out and sleep on, an unparalleled kindness; building hospitals in every town of his realms, providing ample endowments for feeding the sick, and appointing doctors | to cure them and take charge of their treatment, 348
as well as other kinds of beneficence and varieties of memorable acts which he has been the first to do. May God repay the favours he has bestowed and recompense his benefactions.'

As for relieving the oppression of his subjects, he, God strengthen him, ordered the total abolition of the tolls levied on roads, disregarding the fact that it was an important tax. *What is with God is better and more lasting.*[101] As for restraining the hands of oppression, that is something well-known. I have heard him, God strengthen him, say to his governors: 'Do not oppress the people' and he used to reiterate this directive to them.

Ibn Juzayy remarks: 'If the only instance of the benevolence of our master, God strengthen him, towards his subjects had been his abolition of the right of hospitality exercised upon them by the collectors of *zakāt* and the provincial governors, that alone would be | a manifest sign of his justice and 349
a shining light of beneficence. What can be said? He has removed grievances and dispensed benefits that are beyond computation. While this is being written a noble order has been issued by him relieving prisoners of the heavy duties exacted from them. How appropriate a kindness to them! How typical of his clemency! This order embraced all the provinces. In the same way he decreed the condign punishment of qāḍīs and governors whose oppressive conduct was proven, so driving out oppression and repelling the aggressors.'

As for his actions in helping the people of al-Andalus in the holy war, and protecting their frontiers by assisting them with money, provisions and arms, destroying the preparations the

[100] 10 Muḥarram, commemorating the death of Ḥusain b. ʿAlī at the battle of al-Karbalā'.
[101] Qur'ān, sūra xxviii, 60, and xlii, 36.

350 enemy had made, and giving a display | of force, all that is well-known and has not been forgotten in the Maghrib or in the East, and no king has surpassed him.

Ibn Juzayy remarks: 'It is enough for anyone who wants to know what support our master, God strengthen him, gave to the Muslim countries and to defending them from the infidels, to know what he did for the deliverance of Ṭarābalus [Tripoli] in Ifrīqiya. When the enemy gained possession of it and extended over it the hand of tyranny, he, God strengthen him, saw that, because of the distance, it was not feasible to send troops to its assistance. He wrote to his subordinates in the countries of Ifrīqiya to ransom it with money, and this was done for fifty thousand gold dinars in specie. When he heard the news of this he said: 'Praise be to God Who has recovered it from the hands of the infidels with this insignificant trifle.' He at once ordered that sum to be sent to Ifrīqiya, and the city
351 returned | to Islam at his hands.[102] It did not occur to anyone that five qintars of gold were an insignificant trifle till our master, God strengthen him, acted with this surpassing generosity and superb efficacy. Comparable deeds have been rare among the kings and the story of what he had done impressed them.

'Among the most widely known achievements of our master, God strengthen him, in the holy war was to have built war galleys along all the coasts, to have made ample provision in naval matters, and to have done so in time of peace and a truce in readiness for burdensome days, resolutely forestalling the greed of the infidels. He reinforced this with the journey he, God strengthen him, made in person to the mountains of Jānāta[103] last year to supervise the cutting of wood for shipbuilding, to show the importance he attached to it and to
352 directing | personally what concerns the holy war, hoping for a reward from God Most High and being sure of a splendid recompense.'

Among the greatest of his charitable works, God strengthen

[102] Tripoli was seized and looted by the Genoese admiral Filippo Doria in April 1355; it was ransomed with the help of Abū ʿInān in the following August for 50,000 gold doubloons (Brunschvig, I, p. 173).

[103] Some MSS read Janāya. Not identified. It cannot be Djanet (Fort Charlet) in the Tassili n'Ajjer mountains in eastern Algeria.

him, were building the new mosque in the white city, the capital of his exalted kingdom, a mosque distinguished by its beauty, its sound construction, its radiance, and its wonderful arrangement; building the great *madrasa* in the place known as the *Qaṣr* near the citadel of Fās [Fez], a building without compare in the inhabited world for its extent, its beauty, its uniqueness, its plentiful supply of water, and the beauty of the site:[104] I have seen nothing like it among the *madrasas* of Syria, Egypt, Iraq and Khurāsān; building the great hospice by the Chickpea Pond outside the white city, which is unequalled for its marvellous site and superb workmanship. The most superb hospice | I saw in the East is the hospice of 353
Siryāquṣ, built by al-Malik al-Nāṣir,[105] but this is more splendid, more properly and more soundly constructed. May God, glory to Him, assist our master, God strengthen him, in his noble designs, recompense his pre-eminent virtues, prolong his days for the sake of Islam and the Muslims, and assist his victorious flags and standards.[106] Let us return to the narrative of our travels.

[104] The White, or Pure, City is New Fez, Fās al-Jadīd. The mosque is the Azhar, built in 1357. For the *madrasa* see I, p. 53 and n. 166; it is also illustrated in the article 'Fas' in EI^2, pl. xii and xvi, and in Derek Hill, *Islamic Architecture in North Africa*, pl. 311–23.

[105] See I, p. 53 and n. 165.

[106] There is nothing to indicate precisely where each of Ibn Juzayy's interpolations comes to an end. The whole of this encomium on Morocco and its ruler is characteristic of the writings of the secretarial class to which he belonged.

CHAPTER XXIV

Spain

When it had happened to me to see this noble residence and I had been overwhelmed by the favours of his universal benevolence, I sought to visit my mother's grave. I reached my native town of Tangier, visited it, and went to the city of Sabta [Ceuta], where I stayed for some months. I was ill for three months. Then God cured me and I wanted to take part in the holy war and the frontier fighting. I sailed from Ceuta in a *shaṭṭī*[1] belonging to the
354 people of Aṣīlā [Arzila] and reached al-Andalus, | God Most High guard her, where the reward of those who live there is abundant and where recompense is treasured up for those who stay or travel there. This was just after the death of the Christian tyrant Adfūnus.[2] He besieged the mountain for ten months and supposed he would get possession of all of al-Andalus that still belonged to the Muslims. God took him unprepared and he died of the plague, which he feared more than anyone else.

The first town I saw in the Andalusian country was the Mountain of Victory.[3] I met there the excellent preacher Abū Zakarīyā' Yaḥyā b. al-Sirāj of Runda [Ronda],[4] and the qāḍī ʿIsā al-Barbarī, with whom I stayed. With him I made the circuit of the mountain and saw the wonderful works constructed by our master Abu'l-Ḥasan, God be pleased with him, the preparations he had made and the military equipment, and what our master, God strengthen him, had added

[1] A small two-masted ship, from Latin *sagitta*, 'arrow'.
[2] Alfonso XI of Castile, who died on 20 March 1350 while besieging Gibraltar.
[3] Gibraltar.
[4] Yaḥyā b. Aḥmad Muḥammad al-Nafsī al-Ḥimyarī of Ronda.

further. I would have liked | to be one of those serving there 355
till the end of my life.

Ibn Juzayy remarks: 'The Mountain of Victory is the stronghold of Islam, a choking obstruction in the throats of the worshippers of idols. It is a benefaction of our master Abu'l-Ḥasan, God be pleased with him, with which his name is associated; it is the work of piety he has placed before him as a beacon, the arsenal of the holy war, and the abode of the lions of the armies,[5] it is the frontier which has smiled on the triumph of faith, and has made the people of al-Andalus taste the sweetness of security after the bitterness of fear; here the great conquest began; here Ṭāriq b. Ziyād, the freedman of Mūsā b. Nuṣair, landed after his crossing, and it was named after him. It was called Jabal Ṭāriq and Jabal Fatḥ, because the conquest began from here.[6] The remains of the wall that he and his companions built survives to this day and
is called the Arabs' Wall.[7] | I saw it when I was there during 356
the siege of Al-Jazīra [Algeciras],[8] God restore it [to the Muslims].

Our master Abu'l-Ḥasan, the favour of God be with him, conquered it and recovered it from the hands of the Christians after they had ruled it for twenty years and more.[9] He sent his son, the illustrious amir Abū Malik, to besiege it, and helped him with a great deal of money and numerous soldiers. It was taken after a siege of six months in the year seven hundred and thirty-three.[10] At that time it was not as it is now. Our master Abu'l-Ḥasan, God's mercy on him, built the huge Calahorra[11] at the top of the fortress; till then there had only been a small turret which was destroyed by stones from the

[5] Another MS reads: 'where the foundations of armies are laid'.

[6] Ṭāriq landed in the Gibraltar area in the spring of 711 and defeated Roderick, the Visigothic King, in the following summer.

[7] It is unlikely that any substantial building was erected at the time of the conquest. The 'Arabs' Wall' was almost certainly built in 1160.

[8] Alfonso XI successfully besieged Algeciras in 1342 after his victory over Abu'l Ḥasan at the Rio Salado.

[9] It had been taken for Ferdinand IV of Castile in 709/1309.

[10] 1333.

[11] The French editors read *al-ma'thara*, which they translate 'tour', but note that another MS reads *al-qāhira*, i.e. the Victorious. Lévi-Provençal (p. 205) corrects this to *q.lhurra*, i.e. Calahorra.

mangonels. He built the tower in its place.[12] He built there an arsenal, which had been lacking before then, and a big wall
357 surrounding the Red Mound, going from | the arsenal to the tileyard. Later on our master the Commander of the Faithful Abū ʿInān, God strengthen him, renewed the fortifications and their embellishments and built on to the wall at the end of [the Mount] of Victory, which is the most effective of the walls and the most generally useful. He sent ample munitions, foodstuffs, and general supplies, acting to God Most High with pious intent and sincere devotion.

In the last months of the year fifty-six[13] there happened at Mount of Victory something that showed sure signs and the fruits of our master's reliance on God in his affairs, God strengthen him; it was manifest proof of the sufficient blessedness gathered together for him. The treacherous governor of the Mount, may his end be degradation, ʿĪsā b. al-Ḥasan b. Abī Mandīl, withdrew his criminal hand from obedience, diverged from protecting the community (of the faithful), revealed his
358 hypocrisy, and rushed | into perfidy and dissension.[14] He aspired to what was beyond his reach, being blind to the beginning and end of his evil state. People imagined that this was the beginning of a civil war, which it would require precious treasure to extinguish and the raising of cavalry and foot-soldiers to prevent. However, the blessed fortune of our master, God strengthen him, decreed that these imaginings should be vain. His steadfast integrity prescribed a wholly unaccustomed end to this disturbance. After only a few days the people of the Mount changed their minds, revolted against the rebellious wretch, and became dutifully obedient. They seized him and his son, who had aided him in hypocrisy,

[12] The tower has survived and is still known as the Calahorra Tower, or the Tower of Homage. Construction of an arsenal had begun during the Castilian occupation. Most of the masonry in the wall 'from the arsenal to the tileyard' is later than 1333. (H. T. Norris, 'The Early Islamic Settlement in Gibraltar', *Journal of the Royal Anthropological Institute*, XCI, pt 2, pp. 39–51.)

[13] The last day of 756 was 14 December 1357.

[14] ʿĪsā b. al-Ḥasan b. ʿAlī b. Abī al-Ṭalāq was one of Abū ʿInān's most trusted counsellors. When the fortifications of Gibraltar had been built he was made governor of the Marīnid possessions in Spain and paymaster of the garrisons. For his revolt see Ibn Khaldūn, *Berbères*, IV, pp. 307–10. He was executed in December 1355.

and brought them, bound, to the exalted capital where the sentence of God upon warmongers was executed upon them
both. God gave deliverance | from their evil. 359

When the fire of civil war was extinguished, our master, God strengthen him, showed a concern for al-Andalus that its people had not expected. He sent to the Mount of Victory his son, the most fortunate, the blessed, the most rightly guided Abū Bakr, called by the royal epithet al-Saʿīd [the Fortunate], God Most High assist him. The Sultan sent with him the bravest horsemen, the leading men of the tribes, and the most capable footsoldiers. He gave them ample provisions, granted them fiefs, freed their lands from dues, and overwhelmed them with favours. His concern for the affairs of the Mount was such that he, God strengthen him, ordered the construction of a model of the said Mount. In it were simulated the walls, the turrets, the fortress, the gates, the arsenal, the mosques, the magazines for munitions of war, the granaries,
the shape of the Mount and | the Red Mound adjoining it. 360
This was made in the auspicious audience hall. It is a wonderful model, which the craftsmen made perfectly. Anyone who has seen the Mount and has seen this model will recognize its worth. This was only because of his eagerness, God strengthen him, to inquire into the state of affairs there and his concern to strengthen its fortifications and its readiness. God Most High bring about the victory of Islam in the western peninsula by his hands and realize his hope for the conquest of the lands of the infidels and the scattering of the assembled worshippers of the cross.

I recall in connection with this composition the words of the eloquent man of letters, the distinguished poet Abū ʿAbdallāh Muḥammad b. Ghālib, of Ruṣāfa, of Balansīya [Valencia],[15] God be merciful to him, when describing this blessed mountain in his famous poem in praise of ʿAbd al-Mu'min b. ʿAlī,[16] which begins:

[15] Born at Valencia, lived at Granada, then at Málaga, died 1177, *Iḥāṭa*, II, p. 505.

[16] The first Almohad caliph and founder of the dynasty (r. 1130–63). By the time he died he ruled over North Africa from Tripolitania to the Atlantic, as well as Muslim Spain. He fortified Gibraltar in 1160 and named it Jabal Fatḥ, 'Mountains of Victory'.

361 | [17]'Had you come to the fire of true guidance from the side of al-Ṭūr [i.e. Sinai]
You would have learnt all you wished of knowledge and illumination'

Describing the Mount in the poem with unprecedented elegance he says, after describing the ships and the sea crossing:

Till the ships reached the mountain of the two victories, a mountain exalted in rank, famed among mountains,
Looming, its aspect shrouded by a hood with an open collar of clouds,
In the evening stars crown its parting,[18] hovering like dinars[19] in the air,
At times they stroke it with their superabundant locks, drawing them across its temples, |
362 A mountain that has lost its front teeth, which past ages have worn away with biting on wood,[20]
Made wise by experience, which has sucked the teats of the ages, driving them before it as the chanting camelman drives his caravan,
Hobbled, yet ever revolving in thought the wonders of the past and of what is now to be seen,
It fell silent, gazing down, meditating, showing its inner peace, its features covered in dust,
As if saddened because enslaved by fear of the two threats of crushing and removal,[21]

[17] The verses that follow are from a poem quoted in full by ʿAbd al-Wāḥid al-Marrākushī in his history of the Almohads entitled *al-Muʿjib fi talkhīṣ akhbār al-Maghrib*. This was edited by Dozy and translated into French by E. Fagnan as *Histoire des Almohades*, Alger, 1895. Fagnan's version of the poem will be found on pp. 186–8. I.B.'s text differs significantly from those published by Dozy (Leyden, 1817 and again, 1881) and by M. S. al-ʿAryān and M. al-ʿArabī (Cairo, 1949). I am very much indebted to Professor J. D. Latham for his help in correcting and explaining the text. Dozy remarked that the poet himself would have had difficulty in explaining some of his lines. He was less than twenty years old when he recited it before ʿAbd al-Mu'min soon after the latter first came to Spain. The preceding verses are concerned with his crossing of the strait from Ceuta.

[18] A reference to the cleft in the peak, seen by the poet as a head of hair.

[19] That is, gold coins.

[20] Professor Latham notes that wood for arrows and other uses was tested by biting on it to reveal flaws and other defects. The poet means that the rock has tested men and events throughout history and has worn down its teeth testing them.

[21] An allusion to mountains being crushed (Qur'ān, sūra lxix, 14) and moved (Qur'ān, sūra lxxxi, 3) on the Day of Judgment.

When other mountains tremble tomorrow may it be safe from every peril.

After that in his poem he goes on to praise ʿAbd al-Mu'min b. ʿAlī.' Ibn | Juzayy remarks: 'Let us return to the words of the 363
shaikh Abū ʿAbdallāh.'

I left the Mount of Victory for the city of Runda [Ronda], which is one of the strongest[22] and best sited Muslim strongholds. Its *qā'id* was then Shaikh Abu 'l-Rabīʿ Sulaimān b. Dā'ūd al-ʿAskarī;[23] its qāḍī was the son of my paternal uncle, the jurist Abu 'l-Qāsim Muḥammad b. Yaḥyā b. Baṭṭūṭa. I met there the jurist, the qāḍī, the man of letters Abu 'l-Ḥajjāj Yūsuf b. Mūsā of Montéjicar,[24] who lodged me in his house. I also met there the preacher, the pious al-Ḥājj, the excellent Abū Isḥāq Ibrāhīm, known as al-Shandarukh, who afterwards died in the city of Salā in the Maghrib. I met there a group of pious men, among them ʿAbdallāh al-Ṣaffār and others. I stayed there for five days and then went to the city of Marbala
[Marbella]. | The road between these two cities is difficult and 364
very rough. Marbella is a pretty little town with abundant supplies of food. I found there a cavalry troop goint to Mālaqa [Mālaga], and I wished to travel in their company. God Most High in His grace preserved me. They left before me and were taken prisoner on the road, as we shall relate. I left in their wake, and when I had gone beyond the limits of Marbella and entered those of Suhail I passed a dead horse in a ditch. Then I passed a basket of fish abandoned on the ground. This alarmed me. The guardian's watchtower was in front of me, and I said to myself: 'If the enemy had appeared here the warden of the tower would have given warning.' I went forward to a house and found in front of it a horse that had been killed. While I was there I heard cries from behind me. I had gone ahead of my companions, but I turned back
towards them. | I found the *qā'id* of the Suhail fort with 365

[22] Another MS reads: most spacious.

[23] Abu Al-Rabīʿ Sulaimān b. Dā'ūd al-ʿAskarī, a vizier of Abū ʿInān, who fought against the Ḥafsids in 1358 (Ibn Khaldūn, *Berbères*, III, pp. 61–2, 159; Ibn al-Aḥmar, p. 82, n. 3).

[24] Abu'l Ḥajjāj Yūsuf b. Mūsā al-Muntashāqarī, i.e. of Montéjicar, a poet, also called al-Judhāmī and al-Rundī, i.e. of Ronda (*Durar*, IV, 479; *Iḥāṭa*, IV, pp. 377–90).

them.[25] He informed me that four enemy war galleys had appeared there, some of those manning them had landed, the warden had not been in the tower, and horsemen coming from Marbella, twelve in number, had passed by them. The Christians had killed one of them, one had fled, and ten had been taken prisoner. A fisherman had been killed with them; it was he whose basket I had found lying on the ground.

The *qā'id* advised me to stay the night in his station so that he could conduct me to Málaga. I spent the night with him in the fort of the frontier post named after Suhail, the aforesaid war galleys being moored nearby. Next day the *qā'id* accompanied me on horseback and we reached the city of Málaga, one of the capitals of al-Andalus and one of its finest cities,
366 combining | as it does the amenities of land and sea; it has ample resources and fruits. I saw grapes sold in the bazaars at eight pounds for a small dirham; its Murcian ruby-red pomegranates have no equal in the world; its figs and almonds are exported from Málaga and its neighbourhood to the East and the West.

Ibn Juzayy remarks: 'This is what the preacher Abū Muḥammad ʿAbd al-Wahhāb b. ʿAlī of Málaga was referring to when he wrote, in a witty play on words:[26]

> Mālaqa, how many figs (*tīnahā*) you produce. Because of you ships load (*ya'tīnahā*) them.
>
> My doctor forbade (*nahā*) you to me when I was ill, but he does not have the equal (*nahā*) of my life.

The communal qāḍī Abū ʿAbdallāh b. ʿAbd al-Malik wrote a postscript to this, using word-play: |
367 'Ḥimṣ! You will not forget its figs (*tīnahā*). Remember its olives (*zayātīnahā*) as well.'

At Málaga is made the wonderful gilded pottery that is exported to the remotest countries. The mosque is very big in extent, and is famous for its sanctity. The courtyard is of

[25] The Arabic name for the constellation Canopus. According to Yāqūt it was not visible in Andalus except from a hill near Málaga, which was therefore so named. It is in fact an arabization of an older name. The fort was at Fuengirola.

[26] These verses are quoted by the historian al-Maqqarī with variants which include a reference to Seville. He explains that it was known as Ḥimṣ because so many of its inhabitants had originally come from there.

unparalleled beauty with very tall bitter orange trees. When I came to Málaga I found its qāḍi the excellent preacher Abū ʿAbdallāh, of Tangier,[27] sitting in the Great Mosque. With him were jurists and prominent citizens who were collecting money for the ransom of the captives who have been mentioned. I said to him: 'Praise be to God Who protected me and did not make me one of them.' I told him what had happened to me after they had gone. He was astonished at it and offered
me hospitality, God be merciful to him. | The preacher Abū 368
ʿAbdallāh al-Sāḥilī, known as al-Muʿammam (the Turban Man)[28] also offered me hospitality. I then travelled to the city of Ballash [Velez], twenty-four miles away. It is a fine city with a wonderful mosque. It has grapes, fruits and figs like Málaga. I then went to al-Ḥamma [Alhama],[29] a little town with a beautifully situated and wonderfully constructed mosque. There is a hot spring about a mile from the town on the river bank; there is a bath house for men and another for women. From there I went to the city of Gharnāṭa [Granada], the capital of al-Andalus and the bride of its cities. Its surroundings are unequalled in any country of the world. They extend for forty miles and are divided by the famous Shannīl [Jenil] river and many others.[30] It is surrounded on all sides by
orchards, gardens, meadows, palaces and vineyards. | One of 369
the wonderful places there is ʿAin al-Damaʿ (the Fountain of Tears), which is a mountain with meadows and orchards;[31] there is nowhere like it.

Ibn Juzayy remarks: 'If I were not afraid of being charged with excessive local patriotism I would try to describe Granada, since I have the opportunity. However, such is its fame that there is no sense in speaking at length about it. What a

[27] Abū Jaʿfar Aḥmad b. ʿAbdallāh b. Aḥmad al-Tanjālī, preacher and imam of the Málaga mosque, d. 1363 (*Durar*, I, p. 463, no. 192).

[28] Abu ʿAbdallāh Muḥammad b. Muḥammad b. ʿAbd al-Raḥmān b. Ibrāhīm al-Anṣārī al-Sāḥilī, born 1278/9, an eminent writer on religious questions, followed his father as preacher at the principal mosque in Mālaga, where he died in 1353 (*Iḥāṭa*, III, pp. 191–3). Some MSS of Ibn Baṭṭūṭa call him al-Muʿammar for al-Muʿammam; according to the *Iḥāṭa* al-Muʿammam was how he was known in Málaga.

[29] The name means 'hot spring'.

[30] Other MSS read: 'other big rivers'.

[31] It is marked on the map of Nasrid Granada, fig. 3, in Rachel Arié, *L'Espagne musulmane au temps des Nasrides*, Paris, 1973.

splendid poet is our shaikh Abū Bakr Muḥammad b. Aḥmad b. Shīrīn of Bust,[32] resident in Granada, when he says:

> God guard Granada, place of repose, which rejoices the sad and protects the exile
> My friend is disgusted with it when he sees its meadows frosted with snow |
> 370 It is the frontier (*thaghr*) and God protects those who settle there; it is not the best mouth (*thaghr*) that is not cool.'

Account of the Sultan of Granada. The king of Granada at the time I arrived was Sultan Abu 'l-Ḥajjāj Yūsuf,[33] son of the Sultan Abu 'l-Walīd Ismāʿīl, b. Faraj, b. Ismăʿīl, b. Yūsuf, b. Naṣr. I did not meet him because of an illness he had, but his nobly born, pious and excellent mother sent me some gold dinars, of which I made good use.

In Granada I met a number of its eminent men, among them the communal qāḍī, the noble and eloquent Abu 'l-Qāsim Muḥammad b. Aḥmad. b. Muḥammad al-Ḥusainī of Ceuta;[34] the jurist, the professor, the learned preacher Abū ʿAbdallāh Muḥammad b. Ibrāhīm of Bayyān [Baena];[35] the learned
371 Qur'ān reader, the preacher, Abū | Saʿīd Faraj b. Qāsim, famous as Ibn Lubb;[36] the communal qāḍī, the rarity of the age and masterpiece of the times, Abu 'l-Barakāt Muḥammad b. Muḥammad b. Ibrāhīm al-Salamī, al-Balaʿbaʿī.[37] He had

[32] Another MS reads Muḥammad b. Bashīr b. al-Sibtī, i.e. of Ceuta. Bust is in Afghanistan.

[33] Reigned 1333–54. The genealogy is correct.

[34] Abu'l Qāsim Muḥammad b. Aḥmad al-Ḥusainī of Ceuta, died as qāḍī in Granada in 1358–9 (*Dībāj*, II, pp. 267–8).

[35] Abū ʿAbdallāh Muḥammad b. Ibrāhīm of Baena, died in 1353 as a professor (*mudarris*) in the Madrasa Naṣrīya and preacher in the Manṣūra mosque in Granada (*Durar*, III, p. 295; *Dībāj*, pp. 276–7).

[36] Abu Saʿīd Faraj b. Qāsim b. Lubb (i.e. Lope) al-Thaʿlabī, also famous as a poet; d. 1381–2. At this time he was a professor at the Madrasa Naṣrīya in Granada (*Iḥāta*, IV, p. 253, where he is called al-Taghlibī instead of al-Thaʿlabī; *Dībāj*, II, pp. 139–42; *Nail al-ibtihāj*, p. 219.

[37] Abu'l Barakāt Muḥammad b. Muḥammad b. Ibrāhīm al-Salamī al-Balfīqī, i.e. of Velefique, a small town in Almeria province. The French editors read al-Bala'baʿī, of which there are variants in other MSS. Born in 1264–5, d. 1370. He was successively qāḍī of Málaga, of Almeria, of Granada and again of Almeria. (*Durar*, IV, pp. 155–7; *Iḥāṭa*, II, p. 101; *Dībāj*, II, pp. 269–74; *Nail al-ibtihāj*, pp. 254–5). He was evidently the source of some of the information about Ibn Baṭṭūṭa quoted in the *Durar* from Lisān al-Dīn ibn al-Khaṭīb, see I, ix. The garden was in the village of Nabla near Granada.

come from Almarīya [Almeria] recently. I encountered him in the garden of the jurist Abu 'l-Qāsim Muḥammad, son of the jurist and eminent secretary Abū ʿAbdallāh b. ʿĀṣim.[38] We stayed there for two days and a night.

Ibn Juzayy remarks: 'I was with them in that garden. Shaikh Abū ʿAbdallāh delighted us with the story of his travels. I took down from him the names of famous people he had met, and we profited greatly from him. A group of the notable people of Granada were with us, among them the gifted poet, the remarkable Abū Jaʿfar Aḥmad b. Riḍwān b. ʿAbd al-ʿAẓīm al-Judhāmī.[39] | The story of this young man is astonishing. He 372
grew up in the countryside, did not study or frequent the learned, yet he came to write excellent poetry of a quality rare among masters of eloquence and eminent men of letters, for example:

> You who have made my heart your home, its door is the eye that glances at it
> My insomnia opened the door after you left. Send your spectre who will lock it.'[40]

I also met in Granada the shaikh of the shaikhs and of the Sufis, the jurist Abū ʿAlī ʿOmar, son of the pious shaikh, the saint Abū ʿAbdallāh Muḥammad, b. al-Maḥrūq (the Burnt). I stayed for some days in his hospice outside Granada; he treated me with the utmost respect. I went with him to visit the hospice of renowned sanctity known as the Station of the Eagle. The Eagle is a hill overlooking the environs of Granada, | about 373
eighty miles away. It is close to the ruined city of Ibīra [Elvira].[41] I also met his nephew the jurist Abu 'l-Ḥasan ʿAlī b. Aḥmad b. al-Maḥrūq in his hospice known as The

[38] Muḥammad b. Muḥammad b. ʿĀṣim b. Muḥammad b. Abī ʿĀsim al-Anṣārī, Abū ʿAbdallāh, known as Ibn ʿĀsim, 1297–1342 (*Durar*, IV, p. 180).

[39] See *Durar*, I, p. 141.

[40] Ibn Ḥajar al-ʿAsqalānī quotes these lines with the difference of one word and gives a longer genealogy ((*Durar*, I, pp. 131–2); he says that al-Judhāmī was a peasant (*fallāḥ*).

[41] The hospice was to the west of Granada. The French editors read al-Tīra, but another MS has al-Bīra which is obviously correct. Elvira, about 10 km NW of Granada, at the foot of the Sierra de Elvira, had been the principal city of the district but declined in the 11th century, when the Zirid dynasty made Granada their capital. Gibb remarked that no place called Tira 'seems to be mentioned in any Spanish Arabic work' (*Selection*), p. 376, n. 6).

Bridle, which is at the top of the suburb of Najd outside Granada and adjoining Mount Sabīka (the Ingot). He is the shaikh of the petty traders among the faqirs. In Granada is a group of foreign faqirs who have settled there because it is like their own country; among them are al-Ḥājj Abū ʿAbdallāh of Samarqand, al-Ḥājj Aḥmad of Tabrīz, al-Ḥājj Ibrāhīm of Quniya [Konya], al-Ḥājj Ḥusain of Khurāsān, and the two Ḥājjīs ʿAlī and Rashīd, the Indians, and others. I went from Granada to Ḥamma, then to Velez, then to Málaga, and then to the fortress of Dhakwān, which is a beautiful place,
374 abounding in water, | trees and fruit.[42] I then went to Runda, then to the village of the Banū Riyāḥ, where I stayed with its shaikh Abu 'l-Ḥasan ʿAlī b. Sulaimān al-Riyāḥī. He is one of the most generous men and most excellent of the notables; he provides food for all comers and he offered me splendid hospitality. Then I went to the Mount of Victory and embarked in the galley in which I had previously made the crossing, and which belonged to the people of Arzila. I arrived at Ceuta; its *qā'id* at that time was Shaikh Abū Mahdī ʿĪsā b. Sulaimān b. Manṣūr; its qāḍī was the jurist Abū Muḥammad al-Zajandarī. Then I went to Arzila, where I stayed some months, then to the city of Salā. From Salā I travelled to the city of Marrākush.

It is one of the most beautiful cities, spacious and extending over a very wide area, and has ample resources. It has magnificent mosques, like the principal mosque, which is known as
375 the Kutubīyīn Mosque (Mosque of the Booksellers). | It has a wonderful awe-inspiring minaret, which I climbed and from which the whole town can be seen. However, ruin has overtaken it and I can compare it only with Baghdad, except that the bazaars of Baghdad are better. In Marrākush is the wonderful *madrasa* distinguished by the beauty of its site and the excellence of its construction, which was built by our master the Commander of the Faithful Abu 'l-Ḥasan, God be pleased with him.

Ibn Juzayy remarks: 'The qāḍī of Marrākush, the imam and historian Abu l-Ausī ʿAbdallāh Muḥammad b. ʿAbd al-Malik,[43] said of it:

[42] Coin, some 40 km west of Málaga. See Lévi-Provençal, p. 222, n. 1.

God's be the illustrious town of Marrākush
How splendid are the noble sayyids who live there!
If a stranger from afar arrives there
It consoles him with its friendliness for his people and home |
What one hears and sees of it 376
Give rise to envy between the eye and the ear.'

[43] Abū ʿAbdallāh Muḥammad b. Muḥammad b. ʿAbd al-Malik b. Saʿīd al-Ansārī al-Ausī, Qāḍī of Marrākush, born 1237 (*Dībāj*, II, p. 325).

CHAPTER XXV

The Country of the Blacks

I left Marrākush in the company of the exalted cortège, that of our master, God strengthen him, and we reached the city of Salā [Sallee], then the city of Miknāsa [Meknes], the wonderful, the green, the brilliant, with orchards and gardens and with plantations of olives surrounding it on all sides. Then we arrived at the capital, Fa's [Fez], God Most High guard it. There I said farewell to our master, God strengthen him, and set out on a journey to the country of the Blacks. I reached the city of Sijilmāsa, a very beautiful city.[1] It has abundant dates of good quality. The city of al-Baṣra is like it in the abundance of dates, but those of Sijilmāsa are superior. The *irar* kind is unequalled anywhere.[2] Here I
377 stayed with the jurist Abū Muḥammad al-Bushrī, | whose brother I had met at Qanjanfū in China.[3] How far apart they are! He treated me with the greatest generosity. Here I bought camels and four months' fodder for them.

On the first day of God's month of Muḥarram in the year fifty-three[4] I travelled in a caravan whose leader was Abū Muḥammad Yandakān al-Massūfī, God be merciful to him. There were a number of merchants from Sijilmāsa and other places in the caravan. After twenty-five days we reached Taghāzā. It is a village with no attractions. A strange thing

[1] It was destroyed in the next century. The ruins are west of Rissani in Tafilelt, on the left bank of the Ziz. The route is circuitous. It has been suggested that, if I.B.'s journey had political significance, he may have needed to take instructions from the Sultan, or that disturbances caused by the Banū Ma'qil made it impossible to travel through the western Atlas and the Sous valley (R. Mauny, *Textes et documents*, p. 54, n. 6).

[2] Dr James Bynon informs me that this is a Berber word meaning dates that ripen early.

[3] See p. 900.

[4] 14 February 1352.

about it is that its houses and mosque are built of blocks of salt and roofed with camel skins.[5] There are no trees, only sand in which is a salt mine. They dig the ground and thick slabs are found in it, lying on each other as if they had been cut | and 378
stacked under the ground. A camel carries two slabs. The only people living there are the slaves of the Massūfa, who dig for the salt and live on dates brought to them from Darʿa[6] and Sijilmāsa, camel meat, and *anlī*,[7] which is imported from the country of the Blacks. The Blacks come from their country to Taghāzā and take away the salt. A load of it is sold at Īwālātan [Walata][8] for eight to ten mithqals, and in the city of Māllī for twenty to thirty, sometimes forty. The Blacks trade with salt as others trade with gold and silver; they cut it in pieces and buy and sell with these. For all its squalor qintars of qintars of gold dust are traded there.

We spent ten days there, under strain, | for the water is 379
brackish and it is the place with most flies. Here water is taken in for the journey into the desert which lies beyond. It is ten days' travel with no water, or only rarely. We, however, did find plentiful water in pools left by the rain. One day we found a pool between two hills of rock which was sweet; we quenched our thirst and washed our clothes. Truffles[9] are plentiful in that desert, and so are lice, so much so that people wear round their necks string necklaces containing mercury, which kills them.[10]

In those days we used to go in front of the caravan and when we found a suitable place we pastured the animals there. We went on doing this till a man called Ibn Zīrī was lost in the

[5] The salt workings were abandoned in the sixteenth century, but the ruins of these structures are still visible. Houses built of salt on the borders of the Sahara are mentioned by Herodotus and Pliny; there was not enough rain to cause them to disintegrate.

[6] I.e. the Wādī Darʿa (Oued Dara) which drains the southern slopes of the Anti-Atlas.

[7] *Pennisetum typhoideum*, a millet.

[8] Īwālātan is 'a berberization of the Malinke name' and Walata 'an arabization of the Malinke word *wala* – "shady spot"' (Hunwick, *Sharīʿa in Songhay*, p. 14, n. 5).

[9] The desert truffle, *tirfās*, Terfozia. This is one of the most arid parts of the Sahara.

[10] Arab physicians used mercury in the treatment of skin diseases, and ointments containing mercury can be effective against cutaneous parasites.

380 desert. After that I did not go ahead | or fall behind the caravan. There had been a quarrel between Ibn Zīrī and the son of his paternal uncle called Ibn ʿAdī and they had exchanged insults, so Ibn Zīrī had fallen behind the caravan and lost his way. When the caravan halted there was no news of him. I advised his cousin to hire one of the Massūfa to follow his tracks and perhaps find him, but he refused. Next day a man of the Massūfa offered to look for him, without payment. He found his tracks; sometimes they followed the route and sometimes they did not, but he came upon no news of him. We met a caravan on the way. They told us that some men had become separated from them; they had found one of them dead under one of the bushes that grow in the sand. He had his clothes on him and a whip in his hand. There was water about a mile away. |

381 We then came to Tāsarahlā, where there is underground water.[11] Caravans stop there for three days. They rest, repair and fill their waterskins, and sew onto them coarse bags to protect them from the wind. The *takshīf* is sent forward from here.

Account of the takshīf. Takshīf is the name given to any man of the Massūfa whom the people of the caravan hire to go ahead of them to Īwālātan with letters from them to their friends there asking them to let houses to them and come four days' journey to meet them with water. Anyone who has no friend in Īwālātan writes to a merchant there known for his benevolent character who then enters into the same relationship with
382 him. Sometimes | the *takshīf* perishes in this desert and the people of Īwālātan know nothing of the caravan, and its people or most of them perish too. There are many demons in that desert. If the *takshīf* is alone they play tricks on him and delude him till he loses his way and perishes. There is no road to be seen in the desert and no track, only sand blown about by the wind. You see mountains of sand in one place, then you see they have moved to another.

A guide there is someone who has frequented it repeatedly and has keen intelligence. A strange thing I saw is that our

[11] The only well on the route from Taghaza to Walata is Bir al-Kusaib, 250 km from the former and 480 km from the latter (Mauny, *Textes et documents*, p. 38, n. 4).

guide was blind in one eye and diseased in the other, but he knew the route better than anybody else.[12] The *takshīf* we hired for this journey cost a hundred mithqals of gold. He was one of the Massūfa. On the night of the seventh day we saw the lights of those | who had come to meet us, and we were 383
extremely pleased.

This desert is luminous, radiant, one's chest is dilated, one is in good spirits, and it is safe from robbers. There are many wild cattle.[13] A troop of them will approach so near that the people can hunt them with dogs and wooden arrows. However, eating their meat produces thirst and so many people avoid it. It is remarkable that if these cattle are killed water is found in their stomachs. I have seen the Massūfa squeezing the stomach and drinking the water in it. There are also many snakes in this desert.

Anecdote. There was in the caravan a merchant of Tilimsān known as al-Ḥājj Zaiyān. He had a habit of taking hold of these snakes and playing about with them. I had told him not to do this | but he did not stop. One day he put his hand into 384
a lizard's hole to pull it out and found a snake there instead. He grasped it in his hand and was going to mount his horse but it bit the index finger of his right hand, giving him severe pain. It was cauterized, but in the evening the pain grew worse. He cut the throat of a camel and put his hand in its stomach and left it there for the night. The flesh of his finger dropped off and he cut off his finger at the base. The Massūfa told me that the snake had drunk water before biting him; if not the bite would have killed him.[14]

When the people coming to meet us with water had reached us, our mounts were given drink. We entered an extremely hot desert, not like the one we had experienced. We used to set off after the afternoon prayer, travel all night and halt | in 385

[12] There are many references to blind guides in the desert in Arabic literature. 'The Arabs know by smelling the Earth where the Water lays and and are seldom known to mistake the Spot' (Denham in E. W. Bovill, *Missions to the Niger*, III, p. 546).

[13] *Addax nasomaculatus*.

[14] The snake was probably a horned viper, *Cerastes cornutus*, but other poisonous snakes occur in the Sahara. Similar treatment is practised in the Setif region of Algeria with the warm stomach of a chicken (Mauny, *Textes et documents*, p. 40, n. 5).

the morning. Men from the Massūfa and Bardāma[15] and other tribes used to bring us loads of water for sale. We reached the city of Īwālātan at the beginning of the month of Rabīʿ I[16] after a journey of two full months from Sijilmāsa. It is the first district of the country of the Blacks. The Sultan's deputy there was Farbā Ḥusain; *farbā* means 'deputy'.[17]

When we arrived the merchants deposited their goods in an open space and the Blacks took responsibility for them. The merchants went to the Farbā who was sitting on a rug under a shelter; his officials were in front of him with spears and bows in their hands. The Massūfa notables were behind him. The merchants stood in front of him and he spoke to them through an interpreter as a sign of his contempt for them, although they were close to him.[18] At this I was sorry I had come to their
386 country, because of their bad | manners and contempt for white people. I made for the house of the Ibn Baddā', a kind man of Salā to whom I had written asking him to let a house to me, which he did.

The inspector of Īwālātan, named Manshā Jū,[19] invited those who had come in the caravan to a reception, but I refused to be present. My companions urged me very strongly to accept, and I went with the rest. At the reception coarsely ground *anlī* was served mixed with a little honey and curdled milk. This was put in a half gourd which they had made like a large bowl. Those present drank and then left. I said to them: 'Is it for this that the Blacks invited us?' They said: 'Yes. For

[15] Bardam is the name given by the Fulani to the Tuareg in general and to the nobles especially (H. Lhote, 'Recherches sur Takedda', *Bulletin de l'Institut Fondamental de l'Afrique Noire*, t. xxxiv, no. 3, p. 429, n. 1). It may represent the tribal name Iberdianen (Rodd, *People of the Veil*, p. 428) or Iberdiyanan (H. T. Norris, *The Tuaregs*, p. 4).

[16] 17 April 1352.

[17] The Malinke and Bamana term for a slave of the king sent to supervise or replace a local headman (Monteil, *Les Empires du Mali*, pp. 23–4). It was also the title of the head of the king's slaves and chief of his household (Levtzion, *Ancient Ghana and Mali*, p. 112).

[18] Though *tarjumān* means 'interpreter, translator', the use of an interlocutor was normal in the Sudanic courts and did not signify contempt. Thus the envoy of the Sultan of Egypt to Mansā Mūsā of Mali records that he was received with the utmost courtesy, but that the king, who spoke Arabic perfectly, talked to him through an interlocutor (Monteil, *Les Empires du Mali*, pp. 107–8).

[19] *mansa dyon*, royal slave. The inspector (*mushrif*) was a representative of the Sultan with the provincial governor.

them it is the greatest hospitality.'[20] I then became convinced
that no good was to be hoped for from these people, and I
wanted to join | the pilgrims travelling from Īwālātan, but I 387
decided to go and see the capital of their king. I stayed in
Īwālātan about fifty days. Its people treated me with respect
and gave me hospitality. Among them were the qāḍī of the
town Muḥammad b. ʿAbdallāh b. Yanūmar, and his brother the
jurist and professor Yaḥyā. The town of Īwālātan is extremely
hot. There are a few small palms and they sow melons in their
shade. Water comes from underground sources. Mutton is
plentiful. Their clothes are of fine quality and Egyptian origin.
Most of the inhabitants belong to the Massūfa. The women are
of outstanding beauty and are more highly regarded than the
men.

Account of the Massūfa inhabitants of Īwālātan. Conditions
among these people | are remarkable and their life style is 388
strange. The men have no jealousy. No one takes his name
from his father, but from his maternal uncle. Sons do not
inherit, only sister's sons![21] This is something I have seen
nowhere in the world except among the infidel Indians of al-
Mulaibār. Nevertheless these people are Muslims. They are
strict in observing the prayers, studying the religious law, and
memorizing the Qur'ān. Their women have no shame before
men and do not veil themselves, yet they are punctilious
about their prayers. Anyone who wants to take a wife among
them does so, but they do not travel with their husbands, and
even if one of them wished to, her family would prevent her.
Women there have friends and companions among men outside the prohibited degrees for marriage, and in the same way
men | have women friends in the same category. A man goes 389

[20] The constituents of the meal signified that no black arts would be used against the guest and that he would behave loyally (Hamdun and King, *Ibn Battuta in Black Africa*, p. 70, n. 29).

[21] 'Matrilineal forms of succession, more particularly a man's inheritance by his sister's son, ... survived in the Air Sultanate until the sixteenth century, if not later' (Norris, *The Tuaregs*, pp. 198–9). 'A man's status in Air, as elsewhere among the Tuareg, is determined by the caste and allegiance of his mother. Survivals of a matriarchal state of society are numerous among the People of the Veil. They colour the whole life of the race' (Rodd, *People of the Veil*, p. 148). In I.B.'s time the Massūfa, akin to the Tuareg, had not yet been displaced in the western Sahara by the Banū Ḥassān Arabs.

into his house, finds his wife with her man friend, and does not disapprove.

Anecdote. One day I called upon the qāḍī at Īwālātan after he had given permission for me to enter. I found him with a young and exceptionally beautiful woman. When I saw her I hesitated and was going to go back, but she laughed at me and showed no embarrassment. The qāḍī said to me: 'Why are you turning back? She is my friend.' I was astonished at them, for he was a jurist and a Ḥājj. I learnt that he had asked the Sultan's permission to go on pilgrimage that year with his female companion. I do not know whether this was the one or not, but permission was not given. |

390 *Comparable anecdote.* One day I called on Abū Muḥammad Yandakān al-Massūfī, in whose company we had arrived, and found him sitting on a rug. In the middle of the room was a canopied couch and upon it was a woman with a man sitting and talking together. I said to him: 'Who is this woman?' He said: 'She is my wife.' I said: 'What about the man who is with her?' He said: 'He is her friend.' I said: 'Are you happy about this, you who have lived in our country and know the content of the religious law?' He said: 'The companionship of women and men among us is a good thing and an agreeable practice, which causes no suspicion; they are not like the women of your country.' I was astonished at his silliness. I left him and did not visit him again. Afterwards he invited me a number of times but I did not accept.

391 When I decided to travel | to Māllī, which is twenty-four days' journey from Īwālātan for one who hurries, I hired a Massūfa guide. There is no need to travel in a caravan for the road is safe. I set out with three of my companions. The road has many trees of great age and size; a caravan can shelter under a single one of them.[22] Some of them have no branches or leaves but the trunk gives enough shade to shelter men. Some of these trees have rotted inside and rainwater has collected there, as if it were a well. People drink this water. In some of these trees are bees and honey, which people collect. I passed by one of these trees and found a man inside

[22] The tree is the baobab, *Adansonia digitata*. The trunk can reach 25 ft in circumference and is often excavated, as the wood is soft.

weaving; he had set up his loom and was weaving. I was amazed at him.

Ibn Juzayy remarks: 'In Andalus there are two chestnut
trees | and in the hollow trunk of each of them is a weaver 392
making cloth; one of them is on the slope of Wādī Āsh [Guadix], the other in Bushshāra [Alpujarras] in Granada.'

In this jungle between Īwālātan and Māllī are trees whose fruits resemble plums, apples, peaches and apricots, but they are not exactly the same. There are trees whose fruits are like large cucumbers. When it ripens the fruit splits open uncovering something like meal, which they cook and eat and sell in the bazaars.[23] They take out of the ground grains like beans which they fry and eat; their flavour is like fried chickpeas.[24] Sometimes they grind them to make something like a fritter, which is fried with *gharti*,[25] which is fruit like a very sweet plum, but it is bad for white people if they eat it. They crush the kernels and extract from them an oil for which they have |
several uses, among which they cook with it, feed lamps with 393
it, fry their fritters with it, anoint themselves with it, and mix it with an earth they have and plaster their houses with it, in the way lime is used.[26] It is plentiful among them and is easy to get. It is carried from one town to another in big calabashes; one of these calabashes holds what a jar holds in our country.[27] In the country of the Blacks the calabashes are huge; from them they make bowls, cutting a calabash into two parts and making two bowls from it. They decorate them beautifully. If one of them goes on a journey he is followed by his slaves and slave-girls carrying his bedding and his vessels for eating and drinking, which are calabashes.

The traveller in these countries does not carry food or

[23] The fruit of the baobab. 'The white mealy part of the fruit is very pleasant to the taste, and forms, with water, an agreeable acidulous beverage; which the natives, whose libidinous propensities incline them to such remarks, allege to possess the virtue of relieving impotency' (Clapperton in Bovill, *Missions to the Niger*, IV, p. 617).

[24] *Voandzeia subterranea*, or voandzou.

[25] The *karite* or shea butter tree, *Butyrespermum Parkii*.

[26] 'When ripe, the outer pulpy part is eaten, and the kernels, previously well bruised, are boiled in water, when the fat rising to the surface is skimmed off. It is not used in food, but only to burn in lamps' (Clapperton in Bovill, *Missions to the Niger*, IV, p. 711).

[27] *qulla*, a very large jar with a pointed base.

394 condiments or dinars or dirhams, but only | pieces of salt, glass trinkets, which people call *naẓm*, and some articles of perfumery. Among these they prefer cloves, mastic and *tāsarghant*,[28] which is their incense. When he arrives at a village the black women come with *anlī*, curds, chickens, flour of *nabaq*, rice, *fūnī*, which is like mustard seed and from which they make *couscous*, *ʿaṣīda*, and *lūbiyāʾ* bean flour.[29] He buys what he wants of these, but eating the rice is bad for white people; *fūnī* is better.

After travelling for ten days from Īwālātan we reached the village of Zāgharī,[30] which is a big village inhabited by black merchants called *wanjarāta*.[31] Along with them live a number
395 of white people who belong to the | Ibāḍī sect of the Khārijī and are called Ṣaghanaghū.[32] The Sunnī Mālikis among the whites are called Tūrīs among them.[33] From this village *anlī* is imported to Īwālātan. We left Zāgharī and reached the great river, the Nile,[34] on which is the town of Kārsakhū.[35] The Nile descends from there to Kābara and then to Zāgha.[36] In Kābara and Zāgha are two Sultans who obey the king of Māllī. The people of Zāgha adopted Islam long ago; they are devout and eager for religious knowledge. From Zāgha the Nile

[28] The root of *Corrigiola telephifolia*. The name is Berber.

[29] *nabaq* is *zizyphys spina Christi*; *fūnī* is fonio, *digitaria exilis*, a cereal resembling semolina; couscous will be well known to anyone who has visited NW Africa; *ʿaṣīda* is a porridge of flour and herbs; *lūbiyāʾ* is the name of several kinds of bean, notably *Vigna sinensis*, similar to the haricot.

[30] The name represents Malinke Diaghara, Fula Diagari, western Massina. The village meant may be Diabali east of Sokolo, where there are old ruins (Mauny, *Textes et documents*, p. 46, n. 9).

[31] An alternative name for the *dyulas*, traders, usually itinerant and often associated with Islamic proselytizing.

[32] For the Ibāḍīs see II, p. 397, n. 102. The Saghanughu are a Malinke clan, at one time Ibāḍī, later Mālikī, closely associated with the propagation of Islam (M. Hiskett, *The Development of Islam in West Africa* p. 45).

[33] Ture, a word of Soninke origin meaning 'foreigner', and the name of another marabutic clan of the Malinke.

[34] The Niger was still identified with the Nile by John Barrow in the early nineteenth century.

[35] Perhaps Kara Sakho, 'Kara Market', on the Niger above Diafarabe.

[36] Evidently not the Kabara which is the river port of Timbuktu. It has been identified with Diafarabe (M. Delafosse, 'Le Gaza et le Mali et l'emplacement de leurs capitales', *Bulletin du Comité d'études historiques et scientifiques de l'A.O.F.*, 1924, p. 526). Zāgha is often said to be Dia or Diagha, a short distance below Diafarabe on the Niger, at the beginning of the Massina flood plain, but see n. 40 below.

descends to Tunbuktū [Timbuktu] and then to Kaukau [Gao], of both of which we shall speak later. Then it flows to the town of Mūlī[37] in the country of the Līmīs, which is the last district of Māllī, then to Yūfī,[38] which is one of the biggest towns | of the Blacks and whose Sultan is one of their most 396
powerful Sultans. No white man goes there because they kill him before he reaches it. Then it flows down to the country of the Nubians, who are Christians, then to Dunqula [Dongola], the biggest of their towns. Its Sultan is called Ibn Kanz al-Dīn; he became a Muslim in the time of al-Malik al-Nāṣir.[39] Then it flows down to the Cataracts, which is the frontier district of the Blacks and the first district of Aswān in the Saʿid of Egypt.

At this place on the Nile I saw a crocodile near the bank looking like a little boat. One day I went down to the Nile to satisfy a need and one of the Blacks came and stood in the space between me and the river; I was amazed at his appalling manners and lack of decency. I mentioned it to someone, who said: 'He did that only to protect you from the crocodile | by 397
putting himself between you and it.' We left Kārsakhū and came to the Ṣanṣara river which is about ten miles from Māllī.[40] It is the custom that no one enters the city without

[37] Gibb (*Selections*, p. 379, n. 14) accepts Cooley's identification of Muli with Muri on the Niger (*The Negroland of the Arabs*, p. 90), which is the Niamey district, but not all scholars agree (Mauny, *Textes et documents*, p. 48, n. 7).

[38] Yūfī is often identified with Nupe. However, I.B. (II, p. 380) has spoken of it as being a month's journey from Sufāla (Sofala in Mozambique) and a source of gold dust. This implies that Yūfī included Zimbabwe, where gold was mined, not collected as dust. The Līmīs are mentioned in the same passage as having tattooed faces like those coming from Janāwa, i.e. Guinea. The name is a variant of Lamlam, applied by Arab geographers to cannibal and allegedly cannibal tribes south of the Sudanic belt.

[39] As so often I.B.'s history is at fault. Kanz al-Daula (not al-Dīn) was the title of the chief of the Banū Kanz, a tribe occupying territory south of, and at times including, Aswān. He was, of course, a Muslim, but not a convert to Islam. He became the first Muslim king of Muqurra, the northern Muslim kingdom whose capital was Dongola, about 1319. The Christian kings who preceded him had for some time been vassals of the Mamlūk Sultans of Egypt (P. M. Holt, 'The Coronation Oaths of the Nubian Kings', *Sudanic Africa*, I, 1990, pp. 5–9). Kanz al-Daula became king during the third reign of al-Malik al-Nāṣir Muḥammad as Sultan of Egypt.

[40] There has been much controversy over the location of the capital of the empire of Mali. Many have argued for Niami and would identify the Sansara with the Sankarani, a right bank tributary of the Niger. C. Meillassoux, in a paper read to the International Conference on Manding Studies at the School of Oriental and African Studies, London, 1972, claimed that I.B. travelled south-west from

permission. I had written beforehand to a number of the white people and their chief Muḥammad, son of the jurist al-Juzūlī, and to Shams al-Dīn b. Naqwīsh,[41] the Egyptian, asking them to rent a house for me. When I reached the said river I crossed it by the ford, and no one prevented me. I arrived in the city of Māllī, the capital of the king of the Blacks, alighted at the cemetery, and proceeded to the quarter of the white people, where I sought out Muḥammad Ibn al-Faqīh. I found that he had rented a house for me opposite his own. I went there and his son-in-law, the jurist and Qur'ān reader ʿAbd al-Wāḥid
398 came with a candle and food. Then | next day Ibn al-Faqīh, Shams al-Dīn [b.] al-Naqwīsh, and ʿAlī al-Zūdī of Marrākush, who is a scholar, came to me. I met the qāḍī of Māllī, ʿAbd al-Raḥmān, who came to me; he is a Black, a Ḥājj, an excellent man with noble qualities; he sent me a cow as a welcoming gift. I met the dragoman Dūghā,[42] one of the most distinguished and important of the Blacks; he sent me a bull. The jurist ʿAbd al-Wāḥid sent me two bags of *fūnī* and a calabash of *ghartī*. Ibn al-Faqīh sent me rice and *fūnī*. Shams al-Dīn sent me a welcoming gift. They provided for me completely. God recompense their kindnesses. Ibn al-Faqīh was married to the daughter of the Sultan's paternal uncle and she concerned herself with our food and other needs.

399 Ten days after our arrival we ate | ʿ*aṣīda* made from something like taro called *qāfī*, which is the food they prefer to all others.[43] All six of us were taken ill and one of us died. I attended the dawn prayer and fainted while it was in progress. I asked one of the Egyptians for a laxative and he brought me something called *baidar*,[44] made from the roots of plants, mixed it with aniseed and sugar and stirred it in water. I drank

---

Walata, that Zaghari (n. 36 above) is Diara in Futa Kingui, and that the capital of Mali was on the Gambia. Hunwick has concluded, partly because of the time taken for the journey, that Zaghari was near Sokolo and that the site of Mali must be sought between Segu and Bamako ('The Mid-Fourteenth Century Capital of Mali', *Journal of African History*, XIV, ii, 1975, pp. 195–206). Further archeological examination of the whole region is needed.

[41] Other MSS read Naghrīs and Naqrīs.

[42] His name means 'vulture' in Bamana.

[43] The yam, *Dioscorea*, *kahe* in Fula. Taro needs to be carefully washed and cooked for a long time before being eaten.

[44] Not identified.

it and vomited what I had eaten together with much bile. God spared me from death but I was ill for two months.

Account of the Sultan of Māllī. He is the Sultan Mansā Sulaimān; *mansā* means *sulṭān*[45] and Sulaimān is his personal name.
He is a miserly king and a big gift is not to be expected from
him. It happened that | I spent all this time in Māllī without 400
seeing him because of my illness. Then he arranged a mourn-
ing meal for our master Abu'l-Ḥasan, God be pleased with him, to which he invited the amirs, jurists, qāḍīs, and the preacher, and I went with them. They brought the Qur'ān cases and the whole Qur'ān was read. They prayed for our master Abu'l-Ḥasan, God be merciful to him, and for Mansā Sulaimān. When this was over I advanced and greeted Mansā Sulaimān. The qāḍī, the preacher and Ibn al-Faqīh told him about me, and he replied in their language. They said to me: 'The Sultan says to you "Give thanks to God".' I said: 'Praise and thanks be to God in all circumstances.'

Account of their meagre hospitality and exaggerated opinion of it.
When I had left a gift of welcome was sent to me. It was sent
to the qāḍī's house; he sent it with | his men to Ibn al-Faqīh's 401
house. He came out hurrying and barefoot and came in to me. He said: 'Stand up! The Sultan's things and his gift have come for you.' I stood up, supposing them to be robes of honour and money, but there were three rounds of bread, a piece of beef fried in *ghartī*, and a calabash with curdled milk. When I saw it I laughed and was greatly surprised at their feeble intelligence and exaggerated opinion of something contemptible.

Account of what I said to the Sultan afterwards and of his kindness to me. After I had received this gift I spent two months during which nothing reached me from the Sultan. The month of
Ramaḍān began and in the meantime I had been going repeat-
edly to | the audience hall, greeting him, and sitting with the 402
qāḍī and the preacher. I talked to Dūghā the dragoman, who said: 'Speak in his presence. I shall explain on your behalf what is necessary.' He held an audience in the first days of Ramaḍān. I stood before him and said: 'I have travelled through the countries of the world and I have met their kings.

[45] *Mansa* is a Malinke and Bamana word which at this time designated the supreme ruler. Sulaimān, brother of the famous Mansā Mūsā, reigned for some twenty years or more and died in 1360.

I have been in your country for four months, but you have not treated me as a guest, and you have not given me anything. What am I to say about you before (other) Sultans?' He said: 'I have not seen you and I know nothing about you.' The qāḍī and Ibn al-Faqīh stood up and answered him, saying: 'He greeted you and you sent food to him.' Thereupon he ordered that a house should be provided for my lodging, and my current expenses. On the night of the twenty-seventh of Ramaḍān he distributed money to the qāḍī, the preacher and the jurists, which they call *zakāt*,[46] and he gave me at the same time thirty-three and a third *mithqals*. When I left he gave me a hundred *mithqals* of gold. |

403 *Account of his audience in his cupola*. He has a raised cupola the door of which is in his house and where he sits most of the time. On the side of the audience hall are three arches of wood covered with silver plates, below which are three more, covered with plates of gold, or silver gilt. They have curtains of blanket cloth. On a day when there is an audience in the cupola, the curtains are raised and it is known that there is a session. When he takes his seat a silk tassel is put through the grill of one of the arches, to which is tied a striped Egyptian handkerchief. When people see the handkerchief drums are beaten and trumpets sounded. Then some three hundred slaves come out from the door of the palace, some with bows in their hands and some with short spears and leather shields.
404 The spearmen stand on the right and left; the archers sit | in the same way. Then two saddled and bridled horses are brought and with them two rams. They say that they are useful against the evil eye. When he takes his seat three of his slaves run and call his deputy Qanjā Mūsā. The *fararīya*,[47] who are the amirs, come, and the preacher and the jurists who all sit in front of the armed men on the right and left of the audience hall. Dūghā the dragoman stands at the door of the audience hall, dressed in splendid clothes of *zardkhāna*[48] and other fabrics; on his head is a turban with borders, arranged

[46] I.B. implies that the word is used in an unusual sense; properly, it means the alms that are obligatory under the religious law. The eve of 27 Ramaḍān is known as the 'Night of Power' when the petitions of the truly pious are granted.

[47] Military commanders, an arabicized plural of Malinke *fari*, 'brave man'.

[48] A brocaded fabric with animal designs, made especially in Alexandria.

with exceptional artistry; he is girded with a sword with a gold scabbard; on his feet are boots and spurs. No one except him wears boots that day. In his hand he has two short spears, one of gold and the other silver, tipped with iron. The soldiers, the governors, the pages and the Massūfa and the rest | sit 405
outside the audience hall in a wide thoroughfare with trees. Each *farārī* has in front of him his men with spears, bows, drums, trumpets made from elephants' tusks, and musical instruments made from reeds and gourds, which are struck with sticks and make a pleasant sound. Each *farārī* has his quiver hung between his shoulders and his bow in his hand. He is on a horse; some of his men are on horseback, some on foot. A man stands in the audience hall under the arches. If anyone wishes to speak to the Sultan he speaks to Dūghā, who speaks to that man, and he speaks to the Sultan.

Account of the session in the audience hall. On some days he also sits in the audience hall. There is a bench under a tree, which has three steps and which is called *banbī*.[49] | It is covered with 406
silk and cushions are placed on it. A parasol, that is to say, something like a silken cupola, is raised over it. On top of it is a gold bird the size of a falcon. The Sultan comes out of a door in a corner of the palace with his bow in his hand, his quiver between his shoulders, a gold skull-cap on his head held in place by a gold headband with points like thin knives, longer than a span. He is mostly dressed in a hairy, red tunic of the European cloth called *muṭanfas*.[50] He comes out preceded by singers with gold and silver *qanbaras*.[51] He is followed by about three hundred armed slaves. He walks slowly and often pauses, and sometimes stands still. When he reaches the *banbī* he stops and looks at the people. Then he climbs up it slowly as the preacher climbs the pulpit. When | he takes his seat the 407
drums are beaten and the trumpets and bugles sounded. Three slaves come out running and summon the Sultan's deputy and the *farārīs*, who enter and sit down. Two horses and rams are brought. Dūghā stands at the gate and the rest of the people are in the street under the trees.

[49] Malinke *bembe*, platform, Banana *bambali*, platform of beaten earth.

[50] This fabric has not been precisely identified.

[51] A rudimentary lute, the *genbru* or *genbiri* of Moroccan popular music. For a detailed description see Mauny, *Textes et documents*, p. 55, n. 4.

Account of the humility of the Blacks before their king, how they pour dust on themselves, and other things about them. The Blacks are the most respectful of people to their king and abase themselves most before him. They swear by him, saying *Mansā Sulaimān kī.*[52] If he summons one of them at his session in the cupola we have mentioned, the man summoned removes his robe and puts on a shabby one, takes off his turban,
408 puts on a dirty skull-cap and goes in | with his robe and his trousers lifted half way to his knees. He comes forward humbly and abjectly, and strikes the ground hard with his elbows. He stands as if he were prostrating himself in prayer, and hears what the Sultan says like this. If one of them speaks to the Sultan and he answers him, he takes his robe off his back, and throws dust on his head and back like someone making his ablutions with water. I was astonished that they did not blind themselves.

When the Sultan makes a speech in his audience those present take off their turbans from their heads and listen in silence. Sometimes one of them stands before him, recounts what he has done for his service, and says: 'On such and such a day I did such and such, and I killed so and so on such and such a day.' Those who know vouch for the truth of that and he does it in this way. One of them draws the string of his bow, then lets it go as he would do if he were shooting. If the
409 Sultan says to him: 'You are right' | or thanks him, he takes off his robe and pours dust on himself. That is good manners among them.

Ibn Juzayy remarks: 'I was told by the keeper of the signet the jurist Abu'l-Qāsim b. Riḍwān,[53] God make him great, that when the Ḥājj Mūsā al-Wanjarātī came as a messenger from Mansā Sulaimān to our master Abu'l-Ḥasan, God be pleased with him, and he entered the noble assembly, one of the people with him carried a basin of dust, which he poured on himself whenever our master spoke graciously to him, as he used to do in his own country.'

[52] Malinke 'King Sulaimān has ordered'.

[53] Abu'l Qāsim ʿAbdallāh b. Yūsuf b. Riḍwān al-Bukhārī al-Khazrajī, also called al-Najjārī. A native of Málaga who served as secretary to several Marīnid Sultans and as *ṣāḥib al-ʿalāma*, writer of the decorative signature on documents, to Abū ʿInān (Ibn al-Aḥmar, p. 83).

Account of what he did about the prayer on the Feast and on the Feast days. I was in Māllī for the Feasts of Sacrifice and of Breaking the Fast. The people went out to the prayer ground which is near the palace | of the Sultan, wearing fine white clothes. 410
The Sultan is on horseback with the *ṭailasān* on his head.[54] The Blacks wear the *ṭailasān* only for the Feast Day, except that the qāḍī, the preacher and the jurists wear it on other days. On the Feast Day these go in front of the Sultan calling out: 'There is no God but God' and 'God is most great.' Before him are flags of red silk. A tent was erected in the prayer-ground; the Sultan went in and made himself ready. Then he came out onto the prayer-ground, the prayer was recited and the sermon delivered. Then the preacher came down, sat in front of the Sultan and spoke at length. A man was there with a spear in his hand explaining to the people what the preacher said in their own language. What he said comprised admonitions, warnings, praise of the Sultan, exhortations on the need to obey him, and to accord him his due. |
On the two Feasts the Sultan sits on the *banbī* after the 411
afternoon prayer. The armour bearers come with splendid weapons, quivers of gold and silver, swords ornamented in gold, as are the scabbards, spears of gold and silver, and maces of crystal.[55] Four amirs stand by his head driving off the flies; in their hands they have a silver ornament like a stirrup. The *farārīs*, the qāḍī, and the preacher are seated according to custom. Dūghā the dragoman comes in with his four wives and his concubines, who are about a hundred, in fine clothes; on their heads are gold and silver bands with gold and silver apples attached to them.

A chair is placed for Dūghā, where he sits playing an instrument made from reeds | with tiny calabashes underneath. He 412
sings poems praising the Sultan and recounting his campaigns and his exploits. His wives and concubines sing with him and play with the bows. With them are some thirty slave-boys dressed in tunics of red blanket-cloth with white skull-caps on their heads. Each one of them has his drum hung from his neck and beats it. Then come young companions of his who

[54] A light veil covering the head and shoulders.
[55] Perhaps beryl rather than crystal.

play and turn over in the air, as the Sindis do. In this they show remarkable grace and agility. They play with swords most elegantly. Dūghā plays with his sword with exceptional skill, the Sultan orders a gift to be given him, and a purse is brought containing two hundred mithqals of gold-dust. He is told what is in it in front of all the people. The *farārīs* stand up and bend their bows as a sign of thanks to the Sultan. Next
413 day each of them gives Dūghā a gift | according to his ability. Every Friday after the afternoon prayer Dūghā repeats the ceremony we have described.

Account of the comical way poetry is recited to the Sultan. On the Feast Day when Dūghā has finished his playing, the poets come in. They are called *julā*, each one being a *jālī*.[56] Each of them is inside a costume made of feathers resembling the *shaqshāq* on which is a wooden head with a red beak like the head of the *shaqshāq*.[57] They stand before the Sultan in this laughable get-up and recite their poems. I have been told that their poetry is a sort of admonition. They say to the Sultan: 'This *banbī*, formerly such and such a king sat on it and
414 performed noble actions, | and so and so did such and such; do you do noble acts which will be recounted after you.'

Then the chief poet climbs the steps of the *banbī* and puts his head in the Sultan's lap; then he climbs to the top of the *banbī* and puts his head on the Sultan's right shoulder, then on his left shoulder, talking all the time in their language. Then he comes down. I have been told that this custom has continued among them since ancient times before Islam, and that they have persisted in it.

Anecdote. One day when I was present at the Sultan's assembly a jurist came forward who had come from a distant province. He stood before the Sultan and spoke at length. The qāḍī stood and confirmed what he had said. Then the Sultan stated his agreement. Each of them took off his turban and covered
415 himself with dust before the Sultan. | A white man was by my side and he said: 'Do you know what they said?' I said: 'I do not.' He said: 'The jurist stated that locusts had attacked their

[56] Malinke *dyeli*, bard, griot.

[57] The green woodpecker, but the bird represented may have been the hornbill, *Bucerbus abyssinicus*.

province, and that one of the pious men had gone to the place where they were and had been dismayed at what he saw. He had said, "There are very many of these locusts." A locust had answered him, "God sends us to destroy the crops of a province where there is great injustice."' The qāḍī and the Sultan confirmed what he had said. The Sultan thereupon said to the amirs: 'I am innocent of injustice and I punish any of you who are guilty of it. Whoever knows of injustice and does not inform me of it is himself guilty of it and is answerable for that injustice. God will be his reckoner and will call him to account.' When he said this the *farārīs* took off their turbans and declared themselves innocent of injustice. |

Anecdote. I was present one Friday when a Massūfa merchant 416
and student of theology, named Abū Ḥafṣ, stood up and said: 'People of the mosque, I call you to witness that I call to account Mansā Sulaimān whom I summon before the Prophet of God, God's blessing and peace be upon him.' When he said this a group of men came out from the Sultan's enclosure and said to him: 'Who has wronged you? Who has taken something from you?' He said: 'Manshā Jū of Īwālātan (that is to say the inspector) took from me something worth six hundred mithqals and wanted to give me only one hundred mithqals in compensation.' The Sultan sent for him at once; he arrived after a few days and they were both referred to the qāḍī, who conceded his rights to the merchant, who received them, while the inspector was removed from his post. |

Anecdote. While I was staying in Māllī it happened that the 417
Sultan became angry with his senior wife, the daughter of his paternal uncle, who was entitled Qāsā, a word which means 'queen' among them.[58] In accordance with the custom of the Blacks she shares in the kingdom and her name is mentioned along with his in the pulpit.[59] She was confined in the house of one of the *farārīs*, and the Sultan replaced her with his other wife, Banjū, who was not a king's daughter. People talked much about this and disapproved of what he had done. His

[58] Malinke *kasa*, the chief wife of a ruler.

[59] 'We may be in this narrative witnessing the Sultan's attempt to replace the African type of queen by the consort-type of queen, a person who owed her position to her husband' (Said Hamdun and Noel King, *Ibn Battuta in Black Africa*, p. 78, n. 59).

uncle's daughters came to congratulate Banjū on becoming queen; they put ashes on their arms, but they did not put dust on their heads. Later, the Sultan released Qāsā from confinement and his uncle's daughters came to congratulate her on her release, pouring dust on themselves in the customary way.
418 Banjū complained to the Sultan about this | and he was angry with his cousins. They were afraid of him and sought refuge in the congregational mosque. However, he pardoned them and invited them to see him. It is their custom to take off their clothes and come naked into his presence, which they did. He was pleased with them, and for seven days they kept on coming to the Sultan's gate, morning and evening, for this is what people do whom he has pardoned.

Every day Qāsā rode out with her girl- and boy-slaves with dust on their heads. She used to stop by the audience hall, with her face veiled so that it could not be seen. The amirs talked much about her, and the Sultan assembled them in the audience hall and Dūghā said to them in their language: 'You have spoken much about Qāsā. She has committed a great crime.' One of her slave-girls was brought in, shackled with her hands chained to her neck. She was told to say what she
419 knew. She related | that Qāsā had sent her to Jāṭal,[60] the son of the Sultan's paternal uncle, who was a fugitive from him in Kanburnī,[61] to invite him to depose the Sultan. She had said to him: 'I and all the troops obey you.' When the amirs heard that they said: 'This is a great crime and she deserves to be killed.' Qāsā was frightened and took refuge in the preacher's house. Their custom is to take refuge in the mosque, and if that is not possible, in the preacher's house.

The Blacks disliked Mansā Sulaimān because of his avarice. Before him was Mansā Maghā, and before Mansā Maghā was Mansā Mūsā,[62] who was generous and virtuous. He loved the white people and did them favours. He it was who gave to

[60] Probably Malinke *dyata*, a lion. He may be the prince who later ruled as Mari Diata II (? 1360–74), who was the son of Mansā Maghā, Sulaimān's nephew and predecessor.

[61] Perhaps Konbere in the Bendugu region beyond the Bani river.

[62] The most famous of the rulers of Mali. During his reign (probably 1307–32 or 1312–37) he made a celebrated pilgrimage to Mecca. He was succeeded, first by his son Maghā, then by his brother Sulaimān.

Abū Isḥāq al-Sāḥilī[63] on one day four thousand mithqals. A trustworthy person told me that he gave Mudrik b. Faqqūs three thousand | mithqals in a single day; his grandfather 420
Saraq Jāṭa[64] had become a Muslim through the grandfather of this Mudrik.

Anecdote. This jurist Mudrik told me that one of the people of Tilimsān known as Ibn Shaikh al-Laban had made a present to the Sultan Mansā Mūsā in his youth of seven mithqals and a third. He was then only a stripling and of no consequence. Later, it happened that Ibn Shaikh al-Laban came to him in connection with a lawsuit. He was now the Sultan. He recognized him, called him, brought him near, and made him sit beside him on the *banbī*. Then he made him repeat what he had done to him, and said to the amirs: 'What reward should he have who has done the generous deed he has done?' They said: 'A benefit ten times as great. Give him seventy mithqals.'[65] Thereupon he gave seven hundred mithqals, a robe, slaves of both sexes, | and ordered him not to leave him. 421
I was told this story by the son of Ibn Shaikh al-Laban, who was one of the learned teaching the Qur'ān in Māllī.

Account of what I found good and what I found bad in the conduct of the Blacks. Among their good practices are their avoidance of injustice; there is no people more averse to it, and their Sultan does not allow anyone to practise it in any measure; the universal security in their country, for neither the traveller nor the resident there has to fear thieves or bandits: they do not interfere with the property of white men who die in their country, even if it amounts to vast sums; they just leave it in the hands of a trustworthy white man until whoever is entitled to it takes possession of it: | their punctiliousness in 422

[63] Abū Isḥāq Ibrāhīm b. Muḥammad al-Sāḥilī al-Anṣārī of Granada, poet, man of letters and jurist. He accompanied Mansā Mūsā on the pilgrimage, returned to Mali with him, was the architect of several buildings in the capital and in Timbuktu, where he settled. He died in 1346. He was known as al-Ṭuwaijin, 'the little cooking-pan', but it is not known why. (J. O. Hunwick, 'An Andalusian in Mali', *Paideuma*, XXXVI, 1990, pp. 59–66).

[64] Another MS reads Mār Jāta. I.B. refers to Mārī Jāta, better known as Sundiata, the legendary founder of the empire of Mali. The genealogy and chronology of the early rulers of the dynasty are very uncertain. Mansā Mūsā's father Abū Bakr was the brother, or possibly the uterine nephew, of Sundiata.

[65] 'Whoever brings a good deed shall receive ten like it', Qur'ān, sura vi, 160.

praying, their perseverance in joining the congregation, and in compelling their children to do so; if a man does not come early to the mosque he will not find a place to pray because of the dense crowd; it is customary for each man to send his servant with his prayer-mat to spread it out in a place reserved for him until he goes to the mosque himself; their prayer-mats are made of the leaves of a tree like the date-palm, but which has no fruit.[66] They dress in clean white clothes on Fridays; if one of them has only a threadbare shirt he washes it and cleans it and wears it for prayer on Friday. They pay great attention to memorizing the Holy Qur'ān. If their children appear to be backward in learning it they put shackles on them and do not remove them till they learn it. I called on the qāḍī on the
423 Feast Day. His children | were in shackles. I said to him: 'Are you not going to free them?' He said: 'Not till they learn the Qur'ān by heart.' One day I passed by a handsome youth, who was very well dressed, with a heavy shackle on his foot. I said to the person with me: 'What has he done? Has he killed someone?' The youth understood what I said and laughed. I was told: 'He has been shackled to make him memorize the Qur'ān.'

Among their bad practices are that the women servants, slave-girls and young daughters appear naked before people, exposing their genitals. I used to see many like this in Ramaḍān, for it is customary for the *farārīs* to break the fast in the Sultan's palace, where their food is brought to them by twenty
424 or more slave-girls, who are naked. | Women who come before the Sultan are naked and unveiled, and so are his daughters. On the night of the twenty-seventh of Ramaḍān I have seen about a hundred naked slave-girls come out of his palace with food; with them were two daughters of the Sultan with full breasts and they too had no veil. They put dust and ashes on their heads as a matter of good manners. There is the clowning we have described when poets recite their works. Many of them eat carrion, dogs and donkeys.[67]

Account of my departure from Māllī. I arrived there on the fourteenth of Jumādā the First in the year fifty-three and left

[66] The palmyra palm may be meant; it does not bear fruit.
[67] All forbidden food under the religious law.

on the twenty-second of Muḥarram in the year fifty-four.[68] I was accompanied by a merchant named Abū | Bakr b. Yaʿqūb. 425
We took the Mīma road.[69] I rode a camel, for horses are very dear, one costing a hundred mithqals.[70] We came to a big channel which runs from the Nile and can be crossed only in boats. That place abounds in mosquitoes and no one passes it except by night. We reached the channel in the first third of the night, which was moonlit.

Account of the horses there are in the Nile. When we reached the channel I saw on the bank sixteen beasts with huge bodies. I wondered at them and supposed they were elephants, which are numerous there. Then I saw they had gone into the river. I said to Abū Bakr b. Yaʿqūb: 'What are these beasts?' He said: 'They are hippopotamuses which have come out | to graze on land.' 426
They are bigger than horses, they have manes and tails, their heads are like horses' heads, and their feet are like elephants' feet. I saw them another time when I was sailing on the Nile from Tunbuktū to Kawkaw. They swim in the river and lift their heads and blow. The boatmen were afraid of them and drew near to land to avoid being drowned by them. They have an ingenious trick for hunting them. They have spears pierced with holes through which they put strong cords. They strike the hippopotamus with them and, if the blow strikes the foot or the neck it pierces right through and they pull on the rope till it comes to the bank when they kill the hippopotamus and eat the flesh.[71] There are many of the bones lying on the bank.

We stopped by the channel in a big village whose governor was a black Ḥājj, an excellent man named Farbā | Maghā. He 427
was one of those who had accompanied the Sultan Mansā Mūsā when he went on pilgrimage.

Anecdote. Farbā Maghā told me that when Mansā Mūsā reached this channel there was with him a white qāḍī surnamed Abu'l-ʿAbbās, known as al-Dukkālī.[72] The Sultan gave

[68] 29 June 1352 and 28 February 1353.

[69] Mema is the name given by the Soninke to a ruined site near Nampala in northern Massina.

[70] Perhaps because of the prevalence of the tsetse fly in this region.

[71] This method of hunting the hippopotamus was still employed at the beginning of the twentieth century.

[72] Probably Abū Saʿīd ʿOthmān al-Dukkālī, i.e. of the Dukkāla tribe of Morocco, who claimed to have lived in Mali for thirty-five years.

him four thousand mithqals for his expenses. When they reached Mīma he complained to the Sultan that the four thousand mithqals had been stolen from him in his house. The Sultan sent for the amir of Mīma and threatened him with death if he did not produce the thief. The amir sought for the thief and did not find him, for there are no thieves in that country. He went to the qāḍī's house and rigorously examined his servants, and threatened them. One of the slave-girls said
428 to him: 'Nothing is lost, but he buried it | with his own hand in that place.' She indicated the place and the amir dug them up, took them to the Sultan, and told him what had happened. The Sultan was angry with the qāḍī and banished him to the country of the infidels who eat the sons of Adam.[73] He spent four years there, then the Sultan brought him back to his own country. The infidels had not eaten him because he was white, for they say that eating a white man is harmful because he is unripe. They claim that a Black is ripe.

Anecdote. A group of these Blacks who eat the sons of Adam came to the Sultan Mansā Sulaimān with their amir. It is their custom to put in their ears big pendants, the opening of each pendant being half a span across. They wrap themselves in
429 silk and in their country is | a gold mine. The Sultan treated them with honour and gave them in hospitality a slave woman, whom they killed and ate. They smeared their faces and hands with her blood and came to the Sultan to thank him. I was told that this is their custom whenever they come on an embassy to him. It was reported of them that they used to say that the best parts of the flesh of human females were the palm of the hand and the breast.

We travelled from this village by the channel and reached the town of Qurī Mansā.[74] Here the camel I was riding died.

[73] 'The head-hunting and cannibal tribes are located in the central pagan belt extending from Yola to the confines of Zaria province' (C. K. Meek, *The Northern Tribes of Nigeria*, 1925, II, p. 48). Thirty-four cannibal tribes are listed, and the same author notes that among the non-cannibal peoples we find many traces of former cannibal customs. It is related by al-ʿOmarī that a merchant gave some salt to a pagan king of the Blacks and in return was sent two young women for him to eat.

[74] Not identified. Some translators have taken the first part of the name to mean 'villages' (*qurā*) and understand the phrase as 'the built-up area of the villages of Mansā'. However, I.B. spells out the vowelling as *qurī*; he would not have bothered to spell out the vowels of such a common word as *qurā*.

The driver told me this and I went out to look at it. I found that the Blacks had already eaten it in accordance with their practice of eating carrion.[75] I sent two young men whom I had hired for my service to buy a camel for me at Zāgharī, which is two days' journey away. Some of Abū Bakr b. Ya'qūb's companions stayed with me, while he went to await us | at Mīma. 430
I spent six days receiving the hospitality of Ḥājjis in this town, until the two young men arrived with the camel.

Anecdote. One night while I was staying in this town I saw in my sleep a person who said to me: 'Oh Muḥammad ibn Baṭṭūṭa, why do you not recite the sūra Yā Sīn[76] every night?' Since then I have not failed to recite it every day, whether I have been travelling or stationary.

Then I travelled to the town of Mīma. We alighted near some wells outside the town. Then we travelled to the city of Tunbuktu [Timbuktu] which is four miles from the Nile. Most of the inhabitants are Massūfa, the people of the *lithām*.[77] Their governor is named Farbā Mūsā. I was present one day when he promoted | one of the Massūfa to be amir of 431
a group. He gave him a robe, turban and trousers, all coloured, and seated him on a leather shield. The chiefs of the tribe lifted it up above their heads. In this town is the grave of the illustrious poet Abū Isḥāq al-Sāḥilī of Granada, known in his own country as al-Ṭuwaijin ('the little cooking pan'),[78] and also of Sirāj al-Dīn b. al-Kuwaik,[79] one of the great merchants among the people of Alexandria.

Anecdote. When the Sultan Mansā Mūsā went on pilgrimage he stopped at a garden that belonged to this Sirāj al-Dīn at Birkat al-Ḥabash ('the pool of the Abyssinians') outside Cairo,[80] which is where the Sultan alights. He was in need of money and borrowed it from Sirāj al-Dīn; the amirs also borrowed from him. Sirāj al-Dīn sent his agent with them to recover the

[75] See p. 966 above.

[76] Sūra xxxvi of the Qur'ān, traditionally recited over the dead or dying.

[77] The veil covering the face below the eyes, worn by Tuareg men.

[78] See n. 63 above.

[79] 'Abd al-Laṭīf b. Aḥmad b. Maḥmūd b. Abi'l Fatḥ b. Maḥmūd b. Abi'l Qāsim, Sirāj al-Dīn ibn al-Kuwaik (1260/1–1334), a wealthy merchant of Alexandria, originally from Takrīt (*Durar*, II, p. 415).

[80] The location of this pool is known; it was south of Fustat. Some MSS read Birkat al-Khashsh.

432 money but he stayed in Māllī. | Then Sirāj al-Dīn himself went with his son to recover the money. When he reached Tunbuktū he was given hospitality by Abū Isḥāq al-Sāḥilī. It was fated that he should die that night. People talked about it and suspected he had been poisoned. His son said to them: 'I was with him and ate exactly the same food that he ate. If it had been poisoned we should both have been killed, but his appointed time had come.' His son went to Māllī, recovered the money, and went back to Egypt.[81]

At Tunbuktū I embarked on the Nile in a little boat hollowed out from a single piece of wood. Every night we stopped at a village where we used to buy the food and butter we needed, paying with salt, aromatics and glass trinkets. We reached a town whose name I have forgotten; the amir was an excellent man, a Ḥājj, named Farbā Sulaimān, famous for his
433 courage and strength; nobody tries | to pluck his bow. I saw none of the Blacks taller or with a bigger body than he. In this town I needed a little millet so I went to him. That day was the birthday of the Prophet of God,[82] God's blessing and peace on him; I greeted him and he asked me about my visit. There was with him a jurist who acted as his secretary. I took a tablet that was in front of him and wrote on it: 'Jurist, tell this amir that we need a little millet for our provisions. Greetings.' I handed over the tablet to the jurist for him to read to himself and then recount to the amir in their language, but he read it aloud and the amir understood it. He took me by the hand and brought me into his audience hall, where there were many weapons, leather shields, bows, and spears. I found he
434 had the *Kitāb al-mudhish* of Ibn al-Jauzī[83] | and I began to read it. I was brought a drink which they call *daqnū*, which is water and pounded millet mixed with a little honey or curdled

[81] According to another version Sirāj al-Dīn lent Mūsā 30,000 dinars and sent two successive agents to Mali to recover them, but they both died there. He then sent his son Fakhr al-Dīn Abū Jaʿfar and a third agent, but Mūsā died and they recovered nothing (Monteil, *Les Empires du Mali*, p. 113).

[82] 12 Rabīʿ 1754/25 August 1353.

[83] *Kitāb al-mudhish fi'l-muḥāḍarāt*, 'The Book of Amazing Retorts', by Abu'l Faraj ʿAbd al-Raḥmān b. ʿAlī of Baghdad, known as Ibn al-Jauzī, a Ḥanbalī jurist who died in 1200/1201. It is a miscellany of Qur'ānic, legal and historical apothegms.

milk.[84] They drink this instead of water because, if they drink plain water, it is bad for them. If they cannot find millet they mix it with honey or curdled milk. Then they brought a water-melon and we ate some of it.

A five span high[85] slave-boy came in. The amir called him
and said to me: 'This is your welcoming gift. Guard him so
that he does not escape.' I accepted him and wanted to leave,
but he said: 'Stay till food is brought.' A slave-girl of his, a
Damascene Arab, came to us and spoke to me in Arabic.
While this was going on we heard crying inside his house. He
sent the girl to find out what was happening. She came back
and told him that one of his daughters had died. He said: 'I |
do not like lamentations. Come, let us go to the river', mean- 435
ing the Nile. He has houses on its banks. A horse was brought
and he said to me: 'Mount.' I said: 'I shall not ride when you
walk.' We walked together and came to his houses by the
Nile, where food was brought. We ate and I said farewell to
him, and left. I saw no one among the Blacks more generous
and more admirable than he. The boy he gave me is still with
me to this day.

I travelled to the city of Kaukau [Gao] on the Nile. It is one
of the finest and biggest cities of the Blacks, and best supplied
with provisions. It has plentiful rice, curds, chickens, fish and
has the 'tabby' cucumber, which is incomparable.[86] Its inhabitants transact business, buying and selling, with cowries, as do
the people of Māllī. I stayed there about a month and received
hospitality from | Muḥammad b. ʿOmar, one of the people of 436
Miknāsa, a witty, jocular and admirable man, who died there
after I had left; al-Ḥājj Muḥammad al-Wajdī of Tāzā, one of
those who visited al-Yaman, and the jurist Muḥammad al-
Filālī, imam of the mosque of the white people.

[84] As Cooley noted (*The Negroland of the Arabs*, London, 1841, p. 85, n. 38) this is Caillé's *dokhnou*, described as 'un mélange de farine de mil et de miel que l'on délaie pour ensuite le boire' (R. Caillé, *Un Voyage à Tombouctou*, Paris 1830, II, p. 236).

[85] A phrase used to indicate that he was not fully grown, when he would be six spans high.

[86] *faqqūṣ ʿinānī*. Gibb follows the French editors in translating *faqqūs* as 'cucumber' (*Selections*, p. 334). Mauny has 'melon' (*Textes et documents*, p. 72). All leave *ʿinānī* untranslated as the name of a variety. Dozy, *Supplément aux dictionnaires arabes*, II, p. 95, proposes to read *ʿattābī*, 'tabby', the name of a variegated fabric, and cites an instance of its being applied to a kind of melon.

I travelled from there overland in the direction of Takaddā[87] with a big caravan of people from Ghadāmas. Their guide and leader was al-Ḥājj Wujjīn, which means 'wolf' in the language of the Blacks.[88] I had a camel for riding and a she-camel to carry provisions. When we had covered the first stage the she-camel came to a stop. Al-Ḥājj Wujjīn took what she had been carrying and divided it among his companions who distributed it among themselves. There was in the caravan a Maghribī from the people of Tādalā[89] who refused to carry any of it as others had done. One day my slave-boy was thirsty and I
437 asked | this man for water, but he gave him none.

We then came to the country of the Bardāma, who are a Berber tribe.[90] Caravans travel only under their protection, and in this connection women are more important than men. They are nomads and do not stay in one place. Their tents are strange in form. They set up wooden poles and put matting on them. On top of these they put a network of poles, which they cover with skins or strips of cotton. Their women are the most perfectly beautiful of women and have the most elegant figures; they are pure white and very fat. I have not seen in the country any who are as fat. They feed on cows' milk and pounded millet, which they drink mixed with water, uncooked, night and morning. Anyone who wants to marry among them settles with them as near to their country as
438 possible | and does not go with them further than Kaukau and Īwālātan.

In this country I fell ill from the extreme heat and excess of bile. We hastened our march to reach the city of Takaddā. I lodged there near the shaikh of the Maghribīs, Saʿīd b. ʿAlī al-Juzūlī.[91] I received hospitality from the qāḍī Abū Ibrāhīm

[87] Tigidda is a common place name, or constituent of place names, in the Ayar (Air) region. There has been much controversy over the identification of I.B.'s Takadda, but it now seems fairly certain that it was Azelik. (Djibo M. Hamani, *Au Carrefour du Soudan et de la Berbérie: le sultanat Touareg de l'Ayar*, 1989, pp. 95–8).

[88] There are no wolves in Africa. Dr James Bynon informs me that the Arabic word *Dhi'b*, *dīb* in Moroccan Arabic, means 'jackal' throughout the whole region, the Berber equivalent being *ushshn*. He suggests that the initial *w* may have been added because I.B. did not hear the word in isolation.

[89] Tadla in Morocco.

[90] See n. 15 above.

[91] I.e. of the Jazūla, the Arabic name for a Berber tribe of the Sous valley.

Isḥāq of Jānāta [Djaneh], an excellent man. I also received hospitality from Jaʿfar b. Muḥammad al-Massūfī. The houses of Takaddā are built of red stone. Its water runs through copper mines, spoiling its colour and taste. There is no cultivation there except for a little wheat, which is eaten by the merchants and foreigners, which sells at twenty of their *mudds* for a mithqal of gold, their *mudd* being a third of the *mudd* of our country. Millet is sold among them at a gold mithqal for ninety *mudds*.[92]

There are many | scorpions, which kill young children who 439
have not reached puberty, but only rarely kill men. One day while I was there a scorpion stung a son of the shaikh Saʿīd b. ʿAlī in the morning. He died at once and I attended his funeral. The inhabitants of Takaddā have no occupation except trade. Every year they travel to Egypt and import some of all the fine fabrics and other such things there are in that country. These people live in ease and luxury, vying with one another in the number of their male and female slaves. It is the same with the people of Māllī and Īwālātan. They sell educated females only rarely and at a high price.

Anecdote. When I came to Takaddā I wanted to buy an educated slave woman, but could not find one. Later the qāḍī Abū
Ibrāhīm sent me one belonging to one of his friends. | I 440
bought her for twenty-five mithqals. Then her (former) owner regretted it and wanted to revoke the sale. I said: 'If you show me another like her I will revoke the deal.' He pointed out to me a slave woman belonging to ʿAlī Aghyūl,[93] the Maghribī of Tādalā who had refused to take any of my belongings when my she-camel collapsed, and had refused a drink of water to my slave-boy when he was thirsty. I bought her from him, and she was better than the first slave. I revoked the deal with the first owner. Later on the Maghribī regretted the sale of the slave and wanted to revoke it. He begged me to do so but I refused if only to repay him for his bad behaviour, and he

[92] Other MSS read twenty instead of ninety. The *mudd* was an extremely variable measure of capacity; surviving mediaeval standards from Morocco are 0.75 of a litre. Others were much greater.

[93] Dr Bynon informs me that *aghyul* is a Berber word and always means a donkey; 'it would be a perfectly likely Berber nickname for a man – and by no means necessarily pejorative or indicative of stupidity'.

nearly went mad or died of vexation. Afterwards I cancelled the deal.

Account of the copper mine. The copper mine is outside Takaddā.
441 They dig | it from the ground and bring it to the town where they smelt it in their houses. This is done by male and female slaves. When they have smelted the red copper they make it into rods a span and a half long, some thin and some thick. The thick rods are sold at four hundred for a gold mithqal, the thin ones at six or seven hundred the mithqal. These rods are used as currency. With the thin rods they buy meat and firewood, with the thick male and female slaves, millet, butter and wheat. The copper is carried to the city of Kūbar[94] in infidel country, to Zaghāy[95] and to the country of Barnū [Bornu], which is forty days' journey from Takaddā. Its people are Muslims. They have a king named Idrīs,[96] who does not appear before the people and speaks to them only from be-
442 hind a curtain. From this country come | beautiful slave-girls and boys and fabrics dyed in saffron. The copper from Takaddā is also taken to Jaujawa,[97] to the country of the Muwartabun[98] and elsewhere.

Account of the Sultan of Takaddā. While I was there the qāḍī Abū Ibrāhīm, the preacher Muḥammad, the professor Abū Ḥafṣ, and the shaikh Saʿīd b. ʿAlī went to the Sultan of Takaddā, who is a Berber named Izār,[99] who was one day's journey away. A dispute had arisen between him and the Takarkarī,[100] who is also one of the Berber Sultans. These

[94] Gobir.

[95] The identification of this place is uncertain. Other MSS read Zāghāy and Zāgh.rī. It has been assumed to be the Zagha already mentioned (p. 954) and so to be Diagha (but see n. 40 above), to be the same as Songhay or to be connected with the Zaghawa people of the central Sahara. Professor Hunwick, in a letter dated 29 April 1991, advances strong arguments for identifying it with central Hausaland; he remarks that Dr Murray Last has contended that Katsina was originally called Zaye or Za'i ('Before Kano, before Katsina' in B. M. Barkindo (ed.), *Kano and Some of her Neighbours*, 1989, pp. 129–30).

[96] Sultan of Kanem, 1329–53. At this time Bornu was part of the empire of Kanem. (Y. Urvoy, *Histoire de l'Empire de Bornou*, Paris, 1949, p. 55.)

[97] Perhaps Kukawa in Bornu.

[98] Or Murtibīn. Not identified.

[99] 'This was unlikely to have been his proper name. It suggests the Tamashegh word *Imūzar* 'chief' or the roots *izar/ezzer/yezzaren* signifying 'first', 'to come before' (Norris, *The Tuaregs*, p. 36).

[100] The Tagaraigarai, occupying the mountainous region of Air.

four went out to arrange a peace between the two Sultans. I wanted to meet him, so I hired a guide and set out towards him. The aforesaid persons told him of my coming and he rode to meet me on a horse without a saddle | which is their 443
practice. Instead of a saddle he had a superb red rug. He wore a cloak, trousers and a turban, all of them blue. His sister's sons were with him; it is they who will inherit his kingdom. We rose up when he came and shook hands with him. He asked about me and my coming, and was told my story. He lodged me in one of the tents of the Yanāṭibūn, who are like the *wuṣfān* among us.[101] He sent me a sheep roasted on a spit and a bowl of cow's milk. His mother's and sister's tent was near us and they came to visit and greet us. His mother used to send us milk after the night prayer; that is the time when they milk the cattle, and they drink then and in the early morning. They do not eat cereal food and know nothing of it. I stayed among them for six days and every day he used to send me two roasted rams, in the morning and in the evening. He gave me | a she-camel and ten gold mithqals. I parted from 444
him and returned to Takaddā.

Account of the august command I received. When I returned to Takaddā a young slave of al-Ḥājj Muḥammad b. Saʿīd of Sijilmāsa arrived with an order from our master the Commander of the Faithful, the defender of the faith, who puts his trust in the lord of the worlds, commanding me to come to his exalted capital. I kissed it and obeyed instantly. I bought two riding camels for thirty-seven and a third mithqals, meaning to travel to Tawāt [Tuat]. I took on provisions for seventy nights, for no grain is found between Takaddā and Tawāt. Only meat, curdled milk and butter are to be had; they are bought with cloth.

I left Takaddā on Thursday the eleventh of Shaʿbān in the year | fifty-four[102] with a big caravan in which was Jaʿfar of 445
Tawāt; he is an excellent man. With us was the jurist Muḥammad b. ʿAbdallāh, the qāḍī of Takaddā. There were some six hundred female slaves in the caravan. We reached Kāhir in the

[101] Dr Bynon informs me that *woṣfān* is the regular Moroccan Arabic plural of *ūṣēf* 'negro, slave'. It refers to the palace guards, slaves of the Sultan, who were the nucleus of a standing army, as opposed to the tribal levies.

[102] 12 September 1353.

country of the Sultan al-Karkarī.[103] It is land rich in pasture. People buy sheep from the Berbers there and cut their meat into strips, which they dry. The inhabitants of Tawāt take these to their country. From here we entered a plain where there was no cultivation and no water for three days' journey. Then for fifteen days we travelled over a plain without cultivation but there was water. We reached the place where the road to Ghāt, which leads to Egypt, divides from the road to Tawāt.[104] There are underground springs here. The water flows over iron; if white cloth is washed in it, it becomes black.

446 We travelled from there for ten | days and reached the country of the Hakkār [Hoggar], a Berber clan who wear the *lithām* and who are scoundrels. One of their chiefs met us and stopped the caravan till they were forced to give him cloth and other such things. We had arrived in their country in the month of Ramaḍān, during which they do not go on raids or intercept caravans; if their robbers find goods on the road in Ramaḍān they do not take them. It is so with all the Berbers along this road.

We travelled for a month in Hakkār country. It has little vegetation and is stony. The road is rough. On the Feast of Breaking the Fast we arrived in the country of Berbers who wear the *lithām*, like these (Hakkār). They gave us news of our own country. They informed us that the Aulād Kharāj and Ibn Yaghmūr[105] had revolted and were at Tasābīt in Tawāt.
447 This alarmed | the people of the caravan. Then we arrived at Būdā[106] which is one of the biggest villages of Tawāt. The soil is sand and salt flats. Dates are plentiful, though they are not good, but the inhabitants prefer them to the dates of Sijilmāsa. There is no cultivation, no butter, and no olive oil; these are imported from the Maghrib. The people eat dates and locusts; the latter are plentiful and they store them as they do dates

[103] Kāhir, in another MS Kāhirī, is Air (Ayar, Ahyar); al-Karkarī must be the Takarkarī recently mentioned (see n. 100).

[104] Azawa or Asiu, where the roads to Tuat and Djanet divide.

[105] The Aulād Kharāj, an Arab tribe whose summer quarters were between Tlemcen, Oujda and the sea, and who wintered in the desert around Tasābīt, an oasis 60 km north of Adrar. They rebelled against Sultan Abū 'Inān under Ya'qūb b. Yaghmūr and remained in the desert defying his authority.

[106] 20 km north-west of Adrar.

and feed on them. They go out to collect them before sunrise, as they do not fly then because of the cold.

We stayed in Būdā for some days, then left by caravan and reached Sijilmāsa in the middle of Dhu'l-Qaʿda. I left it on the
second of Dhu'l-Ḥijja.[107] It was a time of intense cold and | a 448
great deal of snow had settled on the road. I have seen difficult roads and much snow in Bukhārā, Samarqand, Khurāsān, and the country of the Turks, but I never saw one more difficult than the Umm Junaiba road.[108] On the night of the Feast of Sacrifice we reached Dār al-Ṭamaʿ.[109] I stayed there for the Day of Sacrifice, then left.

I arrived at the capital city of Fez, the residence of our master the Commander of the Faithful, God strengthen him. I kissed his noble hand and I had the happiness of seeing his blessed countenance. I have taken shelter in his benevolence after long travelling. May God Most High reward him for his profuse favours and abundant benefactions to me, prolong his days and cause the Muslims to rejoice by the long duration of his life.

Here ends the book of travels entitled *A Gift to those who contemplate the wonders of cities and the marvels of travelling.* Its composition was completed on the third day of Dhu'l-Ḥijja of
the year | seven hundred and fifty-six.[110] Praise be to God and 449
peace to those of his servants whom he has chosen.

Ibn Juzayy remarks: 'This completes the epitome I made of the composition of the shaikh Abū ʿAbdallāh Muḥammad b. Baṭṭūṭa, God ennoble him. It is obvious to anyone of intelligence that this shaikh is the traveller of the age. If anyone were to call him "the traveller of this (Muslim) community" he would not exaggerate. He travelled to the countries of the world and then chose the capital city of Fez in which to settle and make his home only because he was certain that our master, God strengthen him, is the greatest of kings, who has the most merit, bestows the most favours, has the most concern for those who visit him, and who bestows

[107] 29 December 1353.

[108] A defile in the Atlas 90 km south-east of Fez. Another MS reads Umm Ḥabība.

[109] Perhaps the pass of Tamelalt between Azrou and Sefrou.

[110] 13 December 1355.

the fullest protection on those intent on seeking knowledge.

'It is fitting that someone like me should praise God Most High for the good fortune he accorded me in my first years |
450 setting out to make my home in this capital which this shaikh chose after travelling for twenty-five years. It is an inestimable blessing for which sufficient thanks are not possible. May God Most High extend His help to us in the service of our master, the Commander of the Faithful, May He cause the shadow of his protection and his mercy to remain over us. May He recompense him on behalf of us who are strangers devoted to him with the best recompense of the beneficent.

'Oh God, since You have exalted him above the kings in the two merits of knowledge and the faith, and have distinguished him by forbearance and sound intellect, extend over his kingdom the ropes of strength and stability. Cause him to know the benefits of divine help and of sure victory. Preserve the kingdom in his descendants till the Day of Judgment. Oh most merciful of the merciful, make him delight in himself, his children, his kingdom and his subjects. |

451 'God grant His blessing and His peace to our lord, our master, our prophet Muḥammad, the seal of the prophets, the imam of His messengers. Praise be to God the lord of the worlds.'

The copying of this was completed in Ṣafar of the year seven hundred and fifty-seven.[111] God reward him who copied it.

[111] February 1356.

BIBLIOGRAPHY

This bibliography is in no way an attempt to provide a complete list of works concerned with Ibn Baṭṭūṭa or relevant to his narrative. It is intended merely to give fuller details of books and articles to which reference is made in the annotations.

Oriental texts and translations

AḤMAD BĀBĀ. *Nail al-ibtihāj fi taṭrīz al-dībāj*. Fez, 1317/1899.

BADAUNI, ʿABD AL-QĀDIR. *Muntakhab al-tawārīkh*, vol. I. Trans. J. S. Ranking. Calcutta, 1898.

IBN BAṬṬŪṬA. *Description de l'archipel d'Asie*. Trans. E. Dulaurier. *Journal asiatique*, série IV, t. xii, 1847.

IBN BAṬṬŪṬA. *Voyages d'Ibn Batoutah, texte arabe, accompagné d'une traduction*. Ed. and trans. C. Defrémery and B. R. Sanguinetti. Paris, 1874–9. 4 vols.

IBN BAṬṬŪṬA. *Die Reise des Arabers Ibn Batuta durch Indien und China*. Ed. Hans von Mžik. Hamburg, 1911.

IBN BAṬṬŪṬA. *Ibn Battuta, Travels in Asia and Africa, 1325–1354*. Trans. and selected by H. A. R. Gibb. London, 1929.

IBN BAṬṬŪṬA. *Textes et documents relatifs à l'histoire de l'Afrique. Extraits tirés des Voyages d'Ibn Baṭṭūṭa*. Trans. and notes by R. Mauny, V. Monteil, A. Djenidi, S. Robert, J. Devisse. Dakar, 1966.

IBN BAṬṬŪṬA. *Ibn Battuta in Black Africa*. Ed. Said Hamdun & Noel King. London, 1975.

IBN AL-AḤMAR. *Rauḍat al-nisrīn fī daula Banī Marīn*. Rabat, 1962.

IBN FARḤŪN. *AL-dībāj al-mudhdhahab*, Cairo, undated.

IBN ḤAJAR AL-ʿASQALĀNĪ. *Al-durar al-kāmina*. Hyderabad, 1929–31. 4 vols.

IBN AL-JAUZĪ. *Kitāb al-mudhish fi al-muḥādarāt*. (in MS).

IBN KHALDŪN. *Histoire des Berbères et des dynasties musulmanes de l'Afrique septentrionale*. Paris, 1925, 1927. 2 vols.

Ibn al-Khaṭīb. *Al-iḥāṭa fi akhbār Gharnāṭa*. Cairo, 1319. 2 vols.

Ibn Taghrībirdī. *Al-manhal al-safī*. Summarized translation in G. Wiet *Les Biographies du Manhal Safī*, Cairo, 1932.

Maqqarī. *The History of the Mohammedan Dynasties in Spain*, Trans. P. de Gayangos. London, 1840, 1843. 2 vols.

Marrākushī. *Al-muʿjib fi talkhīṣ akhbār al-Maghrib*. ed. R. Dozy. Leyden, 1817 and 1881.

—*Histoire des Almohades*. (Trans. E. Fagnan). Alger, 1893.

Subkī. *Ṭabaqāt al-Shāfiʿīya*. Cairo, undated. 6 vols.

Yāqūt. *Muʿjam al-buldān*. Leipzig, 1866–73. 6 vols.

Books and articles in Western languages

Arié, Rachel. *L'Espagne musulmane au temps des Nasrides*. Paris, 1973.

Barkindo, B. M. (ed.) *Kano and Some of her Neighbours*. Kano, 1989.

Bovill, E. W. *Missions to the Niger*. Hakluyt Society, Cambridge, 1964–6. 4 vols. (Including Clapperton's narrative in vol. IV and Denham's in vols II and III.)

Boyle, J. A. (ed.) *The Cambridge History of Iran*. Vol. V. Cambridge, 1968.

Brunschvig, R. *La Berbérie orientale sous les Hafsides*. Paris, 1946–7. 2 vols.

Caillé, R. *Un Voyage à Tomboctou*. Paris, 1850.

Clapperton, H. See Bovill, E. W.

Cooley, W. D. *The Negroland of the Arabs Examined and Explained*. London, 1841.

Couto, Diogo do *Asia*. Lisbon, 1778–88. 24 vols.

Crawfurd, J. *A Descriptive Dictionary of the Indian Islands*. London, 1856.

Delafosse, M. 'Le Gana et le Mali et l'emplacement de leurs capitales', *Bulletin du Comité d'études historiques et scientifiques de l'A.O.F.*, 1924.

Denham, D. See Bovill, E. W.

Dozy, R. *Supplément aux dictionnaires arabes*. Leiden, 1881. 2 vols.

Dunn, Ross E. *The Adventures of Ibn Battuta*. London & Sydney, 1986.

Encyclopedia of Islam. New edition. Leiden, 1954–.

Enthoven, R. E. *The Tribes and Castes of Bombay*. Bombay, 1920. 3 vols.

Fallon, S. W. *A New Hindustani–English Dictionary*. Banaras, 1879. 2 vols.

Fatimi, S. Q. *Islam comes to Malaysia*. Singapore, 1963.

Ferrand, G. *Relations de voyages et textes géographiques arabes, persans et turcs relatifs à l'Extrême-Orient*. Paris, 1913, 1914. 2 vols.

Forbes, A. 'The Mosque in the Maldive Islands: a Preliminary Historical Survey', *Archipel*, 26, 1983.

Freytag, G. W. *Arabum proverbia*. Bonn, 1838–43. 4 vols.

Gazetteer of Iran. US Board of Geographic Names. 2nd edn. Washington, 1984. 2 vols.

Gernet, J. *La Vie quotidienne en Chine à la veille de l'invasion mongole*. Paris, 1959.

Hamani, D. M. *Au Carrefour du Soudan et de la Berberie: le sultanat de l'Ayar*. 1989.

Hill, A. H. 'The Coming of Islam to North Sumatra', *Journal of Southeast Asian History*, 4, 1963.

Hill, D. *Islamic Architecture in North Africa*. London, 1976.

Hiskett, M. *The Development of Islam in West Africa*. London & New York, 1984.

Holt, P. M. 'The Coronation Oaths of the Nubian Kings', *Sudanic Africa*, I, 1990.

Hunwick, J. O. 'An Andalusian in Mali', *Paideuma*, XXXVI, 1990.

—'The Mid-Fourteenth Century Capital of Mali', *Journal of African History*, XIV, ii, 1975.

—*Sharīʿa in Songhay*. Oxford, 1985.

Knox, R. *An Historical Relation of the Island Ceylon, in the East-Indies*. London, 1681.

Krom, N. J. *Hindoe-Javaansche Geschiedenis*. 2nd ed., 's Gravenhage, 1931.

Langlois, J. D. (ed.) *China under Mongol Rule*. Princetown, 1981.

Last, M. 'Before Kano, before Katsina', in Barkindo *Kano and some of her Neighbours*.

LÉVI-PROVENÇAL, E. 'Le Voyage d'Ibn Battuta dans le royaume de Grenade', *Mélanges offerts à William Marçais*, Paris, 1950.

LEVTZION, N. *Ancient Ghana and Mali*. London, 1973.

LHOTE, H. 'Recherches sur Takedda', *Bulletin de l'Institut fondamental de l'Afrique Noire*, XXXIV, no. 3, 1972.

MAJUMDAR, R. C. (ed.) *The Delhi Sultanate*. Bombay, 1960.

MARÇAIS, G. *L'Architecture musulmane d'Occident*. Paris, 1954.

MAUNY, R. (et. al.) See IBN BAṬṬŪṬA.

MEEK, C. K. *The Northern Tribes of Nigeria*. London, 1925. 2 vols.

MELTON, E. *Zee- en Land Reizen*. Amsterdam, 1681.

MONTEIL, C. *Les Empires du Mali*. Paris, 1968.

MOULE, A. C. *Quinsai with other notes on Marco Polo*. Cambridge, 1957.

NORRIS, H. T. 'The Early Islamic Settlement in Gibraltar', *Journal of the Royal Anthropological Institute*, XCI, ii, 1961.

—*The Tuaregs*. Warminster, 1975.

PELLIOT, P. *Notes on Marco Polo*. I. Paris, 1950.

POLO, MARCO. *The Book of Ser Marco Polo*. Trans. Sir H. Yule. 3rd ed. revised by H. Cordier. London, 1921. 2 vols.

PYRARD DE LAVAL, F. *The Voyages of François Pyrard of Laval*. Trans. and ed. by Albert Gray with the assistance of H. C. P. Bell, London, 1887–90. 2 vols.

RODD, F. R. *People of the Veil*. London, 1926.

SEGAL, J. B. *A History of the Jews of Cochin*. London, 1993.

SIDDIQI, J. M. *Aligarh: Snippets from the Past*. Aligarh, 1975.

SKEEN, W. *Adam's Peak*. London, 1870.

SMITH, G. R. and PORTER, V. 'The Rasulids in Dhofar in the VIIth–VIIIth/XIIIth–XIVth Centuries', *JRAS*, 1988, I.

TIBBETTS, G. R. *A Study of the Arabic Texts containing Material on South-East Asia*. Leiden & London, 1979.

University of Ceylon History of Ceylon, Colombo, 1959–73. 3 vols.

URVOY, Y. *Histoire de l'empire de Bornou*. Paris, 1949.

VALENTIJN, F. *François Valentijn's Description of Ceylon*. Trans. and ed. S. Arasaratnam. Hakluyt Society, London, 1978.

WHEATLEY, P. *The Golden Khersonese*. Kuala Lumpur, 1961.

YAMAMOTO, T. 'On Tawalisi as described by Ibn Battuta', *Memoirs of the Research Department of the Toyo Bunko*, VIII, 1936.

YULE, H *Cathay and the Way Thither*. New edition by H. Cordier, Hakluyt Society, London, 1913–16. 4 vols.

—and BURNELL, A. C. *Hobson-Jobson*. New edition by W. Crooke. London, 1968.

162009